Seashore Life of Puget Sound, the Strait of Georgia, and the San Juan Archipelago

Seashore Life of Puget Sound, the Strait of Georgia, and the San Juan Archipelago

BY EUGENE N. KOZLOFF

J. J. DOUGLAS LTD.
VANCOUVER 1973

PHOTOGRAPHIC CREDITS
All photographs are by the author except for those listed below.

COLOR (numbers refer to plates)

Charles Birkeland: II, *Aglaophenia, Abietinaria, Ptilosarcus gurneyi*; III, *Epizoanthus scotinus*; V, *Balanophyllia elegans* and *Didemnum*; VIII, *Dendronotus frondosus*; IX, *Archidoris odhneri*; X, *Cadlina luteomarginata* and *Metandrocarpa taylori*

Lee Braithwaite: XIV, *Solaster stimpsoni*; XVIII, *Cucumaria miniata* (extended oral tentacles)

K. Cameron Campbell: VIII, *Hermissenda crassicornis*; XI, *Triopha carpenteri, Laila cockerelli*

Friday Harbor Laboratories: XII, *Melibe leonina* (photo by Anne Hurst); XIX, *Aplidium californicum* (photo by Hiroshi Watanabe)

Gordon Robilliard: II, *Metridium senile*; XII, *Octopus dofleini*; XIV, *Pycnopodia helianthoides*

BLACK-AND-WHITE (numbers refer to figures)

H. F. Dietrich: 14

State of Washington, Department of Fisheries (through Cedric Lindsay): 155, 177

PREFACE

THE need for a reasonably comprehensive, accurate, and well-illustrated guide to seashore life of Puget Sound and adjacent waters has been apparent for many years. As interest in the marine environment of our region has grown, through recreational and educational opportunities, the lack of such a book has become more vexatious. I sincerely hope that my effort to remedy the situation will provide amateurs, students, and professional biologists with a helpful reference.

Early in the course of my work on this book, I had to decide which geographic areas to cover, what animals and plants to include, and how to organize the text and pictures. First, it seemed best to restrict my attention primarily to Puget Sound, the San Juan Archipelago, and nearby regions of Washington and British Columbia. Thus the guide will be about as useful at Port Angeles, Bellingham, Vancouver, and Victoria as at Port Townsend, Seattle, and Tacoma. It will be less reliable on the outer coasts of Oregon, Washington, and Vancouver Island, where the fauna and flora of rocky shores are characterized in part by some species rarely or never found in protected situations. Sandy beaches exposed to heavy surf do not occur within the area covered by this guide, but they will be discussed briefly.

It was more of a problem to decide which organisms should be included. I have tried to make it easy for the user of this book to identify most of the more common and more conspicuous animals and plants likely to be found on or near floating docks or at the shore between low tide and high tide. A few small organisms, especially those involved in symbiotic associations with larger species, are dealt with. However, microscopic organisms are as a rule omitted, even though many of them have key positions in the web of life in the sea. Animals and plants found only in deeper water, and therefore not likely to be observed by the visitor to the shore, are also routinely excluded. This omission is unfortunate, I am quick to admit, because of the strong interest of many divers in what they encounter. However, many of the organisms discussed in this book are also found in the domain of divers, and may actually be more common in deeper water than between tide marks. In any case, it is impossible to make a regional guide of this sort even close to complete, so I decided to concentrate on intertidal invertebrates and seaweeds. Birds and mammals, being adequately treated in other guides, are not covered; only a few smaller fishes that are regularly found in tide pools and other strictly shore situations are considered.

There are two principal ways in which a book on seashore animals and plants of a particular area can be organized: the fauna and flora can be discussed in connection with the habitats they occupy or according to the groups to which they belong. Either approach is valid, but I have chosen the first. In dealing with the more common organisms in a particular type of situation, the user of this book will therefore have a relatively restricted list of species to consider. Moreover, he will from the beginning connect certain animals or plants with others upon which they may depend, or with which they at least are regularly associated. Although nearly every species discussed in the text is illustrated by a photograph or drawing, those that are not illustrated can probably be recognized by distinctive characteristics briefly noted.

The preparation of this little book has given me much pleasure. I especially enjoyed the many field trips. These were supposed to refresh my memory, but I soon found that not everything at the shore was quite the way I remembered it and that there are many irregularities in the fauna and flora of this region. The photographic work, both in nature and in the laboratory, helped me to appreciate some aspects of our marine animals and plants that I had previously overlooked.

Although many colleagues have aided me in one way or another, I am most deeply indebted to Alan Kohn of the Department of Zoology, University of Washington. He generously applied his knowledge of the marine invertebrates of our region to the task of reading almost all of the manuscript. He weeded out errors and made many helpful suggestions with respect to organization of the text and other matters. Dr. Robert Waaland, of the Department of

Botany, similarly criticized the portions of the manuscript dealing with marine plants.

Many others have aided me with specific problems of nomenclature and natural history, supplied specimens that I could use in preparing illustrations, or commented on portions of the manuscript. I am especially grateful to Stephen Bloom, Robert Fernald, Lemuel Fraser, Paul Illg, Gail Irvine, Joyce Lewin, Charles Moffett, Thomas Mumford, Bette Nicotri, Richard Norris, Carl Nyblade, Janet Osborn, and Cleave Vandersluys.

By expressing appreciation to all who have helped me with scientific aspects, I do not mean to imply that I am sure no errors or inconsistencies remain. I will welcome information that will improve any part of this book, and will carefully consider suggestions for additions.

For a number of fine color photographs, I am indebted to Charles Birkeland, Lee Braithwaite, K. Cameron Campbell, and Gordon Robilliard. Two others, taken by Anne Hurst and Hiroshi Watanabe, were borrowed from the Synoptic Collection at Friday Harbor Laboratories. Black-and-white photographs were supplied by the Department of Fisheries, State of Washington (through the courtesy of Cedric Lindsay), and by H. F. Dietrich, George Mackie, and Chaman Singla.

Many of the line drawings prepared for this book are the work of Catherine Eaton; a few were done by Margaret Siebert, who also assisted me in processing photographs. I thank Robert Scagel, University of British Columbia, and J. B. Foster, Director of the British Columbia Provincial Museum, for allowing me to use a number of figures drawn by Ernani G. Meñez for the *Guide to Common Seaweeds of British Columbia,* published by the Museum and printed by K. M. Macdonald, the Queen's Printer. Some of these illustrations of algae are reproduced without modification; others have been redrawn to adapt them to a format different from that of the original. C. Leo Hitchcock and Jeanne R. Janish very kindly permitted me to use three line drawings prepared by Mrs. Janish for *Vascular Plants of the Pacific Northwest.*

In addition to the illustrations whose sources are acknowledged here, I have used a number of figures published in various works that were not copyrighted or that are now in the public domain. Chief among these are *The Fishes of North and Middle America,* by D. S. Jordan and B. W. Evermann; *The Marine Decapod Crustacea of California,* by W. L. Schmitt; and *A Review of the Cephalopods of Western North America,* by S. S. Berry.

Finally, I wish to thank my daughter, Rae, for typing many sections of the manuscript, and my wife, Anne, for joining me in the labor of reading all of the proofs.

EUGENE N. KOZLOFF

Friday Harbor, Washington
1973

CONTENTS

Seashore Life of Puget Sound, the Strait of Georgia, and the San Juan Archipelago

1: INTRODUCTION

THE rich variety and abundance of seashore life in the Pacific Northwest are due in large measure to the diversity of habitats found in this region. There are rocky shores with reefs, tide pools, and boulders; sandy beaches exposed to heavy surf; quiet bays in which the substrate ranges from clean sand to smelly, blackish mud; and estuaries in which the salinity may fluctuate widely. The runoff of many rivers and the phenomenon of upwelling—the flow of cold water upward from the depths to replace surface water that moves offshore—replenish nutrients necessary for the photosynthetic activities of microscopic plants. As these plants flourish, small animals prosper at their expense and serve, in turn, as food for larger animals.

As most animals and plants have specific environmental requirements, each distinctly different habitat has a characteristic fauna and flora. In this book, discussions of seashore life within the area of Puget Sound and the San Juan Archipelago will be organized into three habitat-oriented chapters, covering floating docks and pilings, rocky shores, and sandy and muddy habitats.

PUGET SOUND, WASHINGTON SOUND, AND THE SAN JUAN ARCHIPELAGO

The basin of the Puget Sound area—that is, Puget Sound proper and the branches of the Strait of Juan de Fuca—is basically a trough between the Cascade and Olympic mountains. When this basin sank below sea level, its rivers and valleys were drowned. In the northern portion of the basin, between Vancouver Island and the Cascade Mountains, the islands of the San Juan Archipelago, numbering about four hundred fifty, represent the higher peaks of submerged mountains. The various reefs, banks, channels, and straits of the area reflect to a considerable extent the nature of the earlier land forms of this area.

3

Puget Sound proper is the body of water that can be entered from the north by way of the channel between Port Townsend and Whidbey Island, through Deception Pass (between Whidbey and Fidalgo islands), or through the Swinomish Slough (which separates Fidalgo Island from the mainland). The main body of the sound extends southward past Seattle, Bremerton, and Tacoma to Olympia. A westerly offshoot, consisting of Hood Canal and Dabob Bay, runs between the Olympic and Kitsap peninsulas, and at two points it closely approaches the principal portion of the sound.

The water mass between the southern portion of Vancouver Island and the mainland, from Anacortes to well north of Vancouver, and thus containing the American and Canadian islands of the San Juan Archipelago, is called Washington Sound. The principal channels of water circulation in this region are Haro Strait, Rosario Strait, and the Strait of Georgia. On the whole, Washington Sound has fewer subsidiary channels and blind inlets than Puget Sound, since its submergence was more nearly complete than that of Puget Sound.

From the somewhat arbitrary boundary between Puget Sound and Washington Sound, the Strait of Juan de Fuca runs almost directly westward between Vancouver Island and the Olympic Peninsula to the Pacific Ocean. Exchange of water between the open sea and the Puget Sound and San Juan area is brought about by swift tidal currents in the strait. However, there are many narrow passes between islands, and the entrances to Puget Sound proper are not especially large when one considers the size of this body of water. Hence, water conditions, in terms of salinity, temperature, organic nutrients, and other factors, are far from homogeneous. In some of the channels the tidal turbulence is violent, and mixing is rapid and complete; but in some of the bays removed from such channels, the interchange of water is relatively slight. Thus bays such as East Sound and West Sound, on the southern side of Orcas Island, are not immediately influenced by what goes on in San Juan Channel, just a few miles to the west.

The runoff of fresh water also contributes to the variety of water conditions. Puget Sound proper receives a number of small rivers draining the Cascade Mountains, and Hood Canal receives several rivers from the Olympic Mountains. Washington Sound likewise receives some moderately important rivers, as well as the great Fraser River of southern British Columbia. When the runoff of the Fraser River is at its peak—usually in June, when the snows in the mountains melt away rapidly—the influence of the runoff in reducing the salinity of surface waters may be felt over a wide area.

TIDES

A brief explanation of tides is called for because the student of seashore life is going to think of many animals and plants at least partially in terms of where they live in relation to low tide or high tide. Both the sun and the moon exert a gravitational force on the earth and on the water that covers most of its surface. The moon, though smaller than the sun, has the greater effect because it is so much closer to the earth. The gravitational force of the passing moon pulls the water nearest it away from the earth, and at the same time pulls the earth away from the water farthest from it. Thus, where the water is heaped up, there will be high tides; but somewhere else the tides will have to be low. When the moon is between the sun and the earth (new moon), the gravitational effect of the sun reinforces that of the moon. When the moon is on the side of the earth opposite the sun (full moon), the gravitational pull of the moon opposes that of the sun; however, because the gravitational effects of sun and moon are exerted on the earth itself as well as on the water mass, there will in this case also be a heaping up of water on opposite sides of the earth. When the sun and moon are at right angles with respect to the earth (first quarter moon, last quarter moon), the tides are less well marked.

The moon orbits around the earth once each 27 days and 8 hours, making 13 lunar cycles a year. Since the earth rotates as it orbits around the sun, a particular longitudinal meridian comes under the influence of the moon each 24 hours and 50 minutes. Thus the daily tidal cycle is a bit longer than 24 hours. The maximum tidal effect does not coincide with the moment the moon passes over a given meridian; instead, there is a lag of several hours, which is constant for each location. Even this lag, however, cannot be used to predict the exact times of tides, because tides in particular ocean basins depend in large part upon conformations of the sea coast and ocean floor, and also because there are interactions between tidal patterns in contiguous ocean basins.

In our area—as along the Pacific coast of North America in general—each daily cycle has typically two unequal high tides and two unequal low tides. On the open coast, the higher of the high tides is usually succeeded by the lower of the low tides, and then the lower of the high tides is succeeded by the higher of the low tides. The overall pattern therefore looks like the one shown below:

At certain times in the tidal cycle, however, and rather regularly in Puget Sound, the San Juan Archipelago, and adjacent areas, the lower of the low tides succeeds the lower of the high tides, resulting in the pattern shown below:

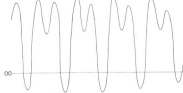

In tables of tides predicted for a given reference point—as Seattle or Port Townsend—the levels to which the water is expected to rise or drop are given in feet and tenths of feet. The average of the lower low tides (mean lower low water, or MLLW) of the annual cycle is expressed as 0.0 feet.[1] So-called minus tides (− 0.1 feet down to about − 3.0 feet) are therefore below the average of lower low tides. In some parts of Puget Sound proper, an exceptionally high tide may reach 12.0 or 13.0 feet, and an extremely low tide in the same daily cycle may bring the water level down to − 3.5; thus the tidal amplitude (the difference between high and low tide) is about 15 feet. Outside Puget Sound, however, the highest tides rarely exceed 9.0 feet, and the maximum amplitude is about 12 feet.

1. Tide tables for Canadian reference stations (Victoria and Vancouver, British Columbia) are not reckoned on the same system as tables for the United States. To make Canadian tables conform to the pattern in which 0.0 equals mean lower low water, subtract 2.5 feet from predictions for Victoria and 3.8 feet from those for Vancouver.

About every two weeks, there are periods of several days in which the daily amplitude is decidedly greater than in intervening periods. The tidal graph below illustrates the way in which the amplitude gradually diminishes and then increases again.

In the spring and summer, the best low tides for collecting or observing intertidal organisms come during the daytime in our area. In the fall and winter, the only really good tides are at night. In planning field work, remember that a tide of 0.0 feet is at the average of the lower low tides for the year and exposes much of the intertidal area. Tides of −1.0, −2.0, and −3.0 feet expose progressively more of the intertidal area, and they are of progressively less frequent occurrence. However, there is much to observe at tide levels between 0.0 and +3.0 feet. Even the higher reaches of the intertidal zone have some extremely interesting organisms, and certain of them show special adaptions to life on the fringes of the sea. A case in point is the big sow bug, *Ligia pallasii,* which, shunning water and yet requiring moisture, lives in crevices at levels normally reached only by spray.

Official tide tables for the West Coast are published by the United States Department of Commerce. These provide predictions, on standard time, for a number of principal stations (mostly port cities), with corrections for other localities near the reference stations. Gasoline companies and other firms reprint the information published in government tide tables and make it available free of charge to their patrons. The reprinted tables are usually corrected to daylight saving time, for more convenient use in the late spring, summer, and early autumn.

Sometimes actual tides do not fit what was predicted, generally as a result of atmospheric conditions. Low barometric pressure and offshore winds tend to raise the level of the water; high barometric pressure and inshore winds tend to lower it. Thus some tides that should be good for field work are not as suitable as predicted; others are slightly better than might be expected.

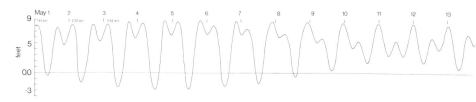

SCIENTIFIC NAMES

Many who are not biologists—and some biologists, too—may wonder about the wisdom of using scientific names in a book of this sort. However, although names like "bent-nosed clam" and "clingfish" are somewhat standardized by common usage, most of the animals and plants dealt with here just do not have dependable vernacular names. If you have no particular difficulty with *Geranium* and *Rhododendron,* you should be able to handle *Cadlina* and *Protothaca*—and probably even *Membranipora* and *Strongylocentrotus.* The Latin names also vary to some extent, as systematists revise their views on classification of certain organisms and re-examine the history of names applied to them. This is as it should be. Yet nothing could create more confusion for us than inventing a number of vernacular names or making use of names that have been indiscriminately applied to more than one kind of animal or plant. Perhaps someday we will be ready for what professional and amateur ornithologists almost take for granted: a set of common names that are standardized and just as precise as scientific names.

For our purposes a compromise can be worked out. Scientific names—at least the genus—will almost always be given. If the common name is generally accepted, it will be used more or less interchangeably with the scientific name. Scientific names usually consist of two parts: the first refers to the genus, the second to the species. There may be a third part, which refers to a subspecies, a variation—usually with a particular geographic distribution—of the species. A genus may consist of from one to many species, so in a sense the species name is like an adjective modifying a noun. For instance, in our area are found four species of clams of the genus *Macoma: M. nasuta, M. irus, M. secta,* and *M. inconspicua.* They are all rather closely related, hence they are all put into the same genus; but they differ at the species level, one having a bent shell, the others likewise having distinctive characteristics.

Scientific names of genera, species, and subspecies, as well as those applied to higher categories—classes, orders, families, and so on—are developed as Latin words. They do not have to be from the Latin language as spoken by the Romans, and just about anything goes, if it can be latinized—names of people *(lewisi, Smithora),* names of places *(pugettensis, oregonensis, sanjuanensis),* and even an allusion to a pleasant holiday on the links *(Golfingia).* However, most of the roots used in compounding scientific names are drawn from Latin or Greek; most Greek words have related Latin counterparts, anyway. If you enjoy words and language, you will probably find that understanding the roots of scientific names will help you to use them, at least in conversations with yourself.

THE METRIC SYSTEM

Unrelated to the problem of scientific names versus common names, but something else that begs for justification here, is the use of the metric system instead of the so-called English system. Most of us think we can cope more easily with 4 inches than with 10 centimeters, or even with 3⅝ inches instead of 9 centimeters; but this is just a matter of tradition. In reckoning with money, we all understand very early in life that a dollar is worth 100 cents. We can certainly adapt, after a little habituation, to dealing with meters, centimeters, and millimeters. Just about every nation but ours has converted to the metric system, but there are two other reasons for its use in this book: it is easier to use in giving precise measurements of small things, because it does not involve fractions; and other scientific works to which the reader may need to refer for further study will almost invariably use the metric system.

In the metric system, the meter (about 39⅓ inches in the English system) is divided into 100 centimeters, and each centimeter is divided into 10 units called millimeters (thousandths of a meter). If you must think in terms of inches and fractions of inches, you may find some comfort in the side-by-side comparison of metric and English scales given below. Note that 2.5 cm just about equals 1 inch, so 1 mm is $\frac{1}{25}$ of an inch.

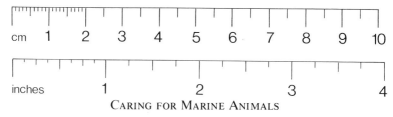

CARING FOR MARINE ANIMALS

Many who are excited by life at the shore may contemplate prospects for keeping a few animals alive in the living room. Unfortunately, the chances for their survival are slim, unless the aquarium into which they are placed is large and the water is kept cold and well aerated. Even in the summer, the temperature of sea water throughout most of our region is not likely to exceed 12° C (about 54° F). At this temperature, the water holds considerably more dissolved oxygen than it will at room temperature (20° C, or 68° F), so even those animals that can adjust to room temperature will not survive long unless they have a large volume of water in proportion to their size and number, or unless the water is aerated. In general, an aquarium for marine animals of temperate waters is not practical for most of us. If you insist on trying it, take care to select animals that are most likely to survive. Animals from sand or mud are hopelessly out of place, and those from the lower reaches of rocky intertidal habitats will require too much oxygen. Try a small crab or hermit crab from near the middle of the intertidal zone, and arrange some rocks so that it can hide among them, both above and below the surface. Small sea anemones from floating docks are sometimes quite hardy. It would be preferable to keep the aquarium on a shaded and cool porch rather than in the house. If the tank has a metal frame, the cement that holds the glass had better be of a type that effectively seals the metal from any contact with the sea water.

Remember that oxygen, temperature, and toxic metal ions are not the only problems these animals have to face in a container in which the sea water is not continually being renewed. Unless there is a large volume of water in proportion to the size and number of the animals, wastes will soon reach a toxic concentration. Overfeeding is another problem. A crab or sea anemone will relish a few bits of fish or clam; but if there are leftovers, the whole tank may soon turn putrid. To summarize, most animals one sees—even on floating docks, where there is pollution—will not survive in home aquariums. Even those that might are better left where one finds them. Few of our algae will live in water that is not cold and constantly moving; so if you think you can solve the problem of oxygen for the animals by putting in a little seaweed, after the fashion of a balanced, freshwater aquarium, you should be willing to accept defeat—and a stinking mess—graciously.

Even transport of a few animals or plants for study in the laboratory requires care. From the standpoint of the collector, plastic pails and plastic bags are safer than glass; metal should be avoided for the sake of the organisms. Most animals and plants travel better if they are kept just wet rather than submerged, unless the volume of the container is very large and the water can be kept cold or agitated. In a small pail of water, a number of animals may quickly consume the available oxygen, whereas if these same animals are kept wet, as under a cover of paper towels or seaweed (but do not use any species of *Desmarestia,* because the sap that exudes from them is very acid), in a plastic bag or in a shallow layer of sloshing water, their moist surfaces will constantly be in contact with atmospheric oxygen. Besides, they are liable to be physiologically less active in this state than if they are submerged. Some animals and seaweeds, however, are so soft or otherwise so delicate that they must be transported in cold water in order to prevent them from rupturing, collapsing, or trapping air bubbles. Sponges, hydroids, and jellyfishes are among the more vulnerable animals, and most of these cannot be exposed to air. Sponges, especially those never uncovered by low tides, should not be lifted out of the water at all; they should be kept submerged while being transferred from their habitat to the container in which they are to be transported. However, crabs, snails, clams, annelid worms, and most other animals travel well if just kept wet. Naturally, it will be essential to take back a supply of sea water in which to place the animals for observation or study with the microscope, and this water should be cooled before the animals are put into it. A refrigerator is handy for storing animals that are just wet as well as those in dishes of sea water.

A Plea for Conservation

This book has been written to help others enjoy the seashore life of our region. But what will happen if all the people who buy this book go out and start turning over rocks and digging up the mud flats? Pollution, the pressure of increasing population, and the destruction or modification of natural areas are already bad enough.

It is probably true that wholesale destruction of certain kinds of habitats brings more animals and plants to extinction than picking common wildflowers or digging clams. However, our natural heritage needs all the protection it can get. Each of us, in his own personal involvement with the environment, should do everything he can to offset the greed and carelessness of others.

Those of us in educational work ought to be exemplary as conservationists. Unfortunately, we are the ones who know where the rarer animals are and are most likely to collect in quantity for class use. We also sometimes unleash classes on beaches without first providing proper instruction in matters of conservation. Clam diggers, fishermen, curio collectors, and divers with spears are often none too virtuous, either. Prizes for the biggest octopus—or for the biggest or most of anything, for that matter—are strictly out of the Dark Ages.

The marine fauna and flora of one large part of our area enjoys a type of protection that perhaps should be extended to some other regions. By a law of the state of Washington enacted in 1923, the waters of San Juan County and some contiguous territory were set aside as a biological preserve. Collection of biological materials from this area for other than food purposes must be approved in advance. Of course, empty shells found on the beach can be taken home, but making curios out of live animals is unlawful.

For the benefit of those who use the seashore for recreation, gathering food, or learning, a few rules will be offered in the hope that our environment will get better before it gets worse.

1. Don't catch or dig up more than you really need or want. This idea should be extended to collecting for classroom study, too. One live specimen of a kind brought back to the laboratory may serve an entire class, especially if the class is not prepared to make detailed studies requiring several specimens.

2. Make as much use as you can of the fauna and flora of floating docks, thus taking some pressure off natural areas.

3. Avoid collecting altogether in unusual natural areas, because certain animals or plants that inhabit them are not often seen elsewhere in the same general region.

4. On a field trip, do as much studying as you can right at the shore, thereby sparing the animals unnecessary abuse.

5. If you bring animals back for study or for an aquarium, keep them cool and do not overcrowd them. It is better to transport them just wet than to crowd them in too little water.

6. If you cannot return animals to a habitat of the same type as that in which you found them, make all the use you can of them before they perish. Do not let the collection be an end in itself.

Some animals can be preserved in such a way that their usefulness may be extended beyond the time they are studied alive.

7. When you turn over a rock, do it gently, being careful not to crush any animal that is beside the rock or that moves suddenly as its hiding place is uncovered. Always put the rock back the way it was, again being careful of animals underneath. It is generally better to move them aside before you turn the rock over again, as they will soon find cover; but if you do not think they will, put them under some seaweed or in a little puddle or channel, if there is one. When the tide comes back in, they will probably get along all right.

Leaving a rock "belly up" is an almost sure way to kill most of the animals that are living on its underside, and perhaps also the animals and plants on its upper side. It may be a long time before the same kinds of organisms can establish themselves on it again.

8. If you dig clams or other animals in a sand flat or mud flat, fill in the holes. By leaving unnatural piles of mud or sand next to the holes you have dug, you may kill many small clams or other animals whose burrows can no longer reach the surface.

9. Obey the fish and game laws with respect to open season, bag limits, and size and sex of the animals taken for food. These laws have been developed on the basis of what we know about the biology of the animals they are supposed to protect.

10. If you teach about animals and plants, teach also conservation and a reverence for life. Good citizenship and a love of nature will have much to do with what we leave to succeeding generations.

2. SOME INSTANT
ZOOLOGY AND BOTANY

IT is difficult to explain, in just a few words, why clams, snails, chitons, and octopuses all belong to one group, and then to show how they differ among themselves. Oversimplifications can be misleading, especially if they sidestep details of internal anatomy, reproduction, and embryology. However, if a few outstanding features of each major group can be pointed out, the rest of this book will be rendered more useful.

The cardinal groups of animals are called phyla. Most botanists refer to comparable categories in the plant kingdom as divisions, but the term phylum is also accepted and will be used here in order to be consistent.

Practically all of the phyla of animals, and the majority of plant phyla, are represented in the sea. Some of them, in fact, are limited to the marine environment. Even those phyla that are successful on land or in fresh water have certain subdivisions that are abundant in the sea. Therefore it seems best to provide a review of most of the phyla consisting of organisms that can be seen without the help of a microscope, and also some of the classes into which they are divided. As a rule, the strictly microscopic organisms and those groups that are not found intertidally or are composed entirely or largely of specialized internal parasites will be omitted. The vertebrates, represented in the sea by fishes, birds, and mammals, will also be excluded.

This chapter is intended to give the reader a general introduction to the names and characteristics of the phyla of invertebrates likely to be seen at the shore in our region. A brief summary will be given of the salient features—especially the more obvious and externally visible ones—of each, with further discussion of any subdivisions significant to this guidebook. A subsequent synopsis with accompanying pictures will help the reader to associate quickly a particular animal with the phylum and class to which it belongs. After a little experience, one should be able to find his way around the synopsis with some speed and come up with the right identification most of the time—except, of course, for obscure or aberrant types that only an experienced zoologist could place. Finally, there will be a brief characterization of the important groups of marine algae. The seaweeds may look simple enough, but their classification is based to a very large extent on microscopic details.

INVERTEBRATES

PHYLUM PORIFERA: The Sponges

Porifera is considered to be the simplest phylum of multicellular animals, so it should be easy to explain. Unfortunately, most sponges are vague as individuals because they just keep spreading, and this habit stands in the way of defining them cleanly. Basically, however, a sponge consists of a restricted variety of cells, not forming tissues or even definite layers, organized around a system of pores, canals, and chambers. The "body" of a sponge is to a large extent composed of inanimate material in the form of spicules of either calcium carbonate or silica; there may be a considerable accumulation of organic fibers as well. The spicules and fibers provide a framework over which and through which the living cells and water passages are arranged.

In our area, we have nothing quite like bath sponges of the good old days, whose skeletons are composed entirely of fibrous material. But there are plenty of other sponges, mostly growing as thin or thick encrustations. A few are vaselike and thus are simpler to explain because their growth is not so indefinite. Over the entire outer surface of such a sponge are thousands of microscopic openings leading into canals through which water is moved by the action of flagella (vibratile projections) on certain of the cells. These particular cells function also in feeding, using a delicate collar to trap tiny food particles, including bacteria. After the water has passed through the system of canals, it enters a central cavity, then leaves the sponge by way of the single large opening at the top. The encrusting sponges follow the same general feeding process but they have many excurrent openings, often on little, volcanolike eminences, and the system of canals and chambers becomes very complicated.

The feltlike texture of many sponges, as well as the bristly margins of the excurrent apertures of some species, is caused by spicules sticking out through the surface. Some of our species are bright red, orange, or yellow; brown, tan, green, violet, amethyst, and off-white are other common colors. Certain species are inconsistent with respect to their coloration.

PHYLUM CNIDARIA (COELENTERATA): The Cnidarians or
Coelenterates

This phylum includes jellyfishes and polyplike animals: hydroids, sea anemones, sea pens, corals, and related organisms. It is impossible to define the phylum honestly without going into the numerous variations of the basic body plan. Unlike sponges, the cnidarians have a true mouth and true digestive cavity, which is basically just a sac, but may be subdivided by partitions. In colonial types, the digestive cavities of the separate polyps are continuous.

A cnidarian has two definite layers of cells, one covering the body on the outside, the other forming the lining of the digestive cavity. Between these is a basically noncellular layer called the mesogloea ("middle jelly"); however, cells or muscle strands derived from the inner or outer layer may sink into the mesogloea, and the amount of jellylike material in the middle layer varies from practically none, as in hydroids, to a great deal, as in most jellyfishes.

Some other traits of cnidarians can be mentioned here to strengthen the characterization of this phylum. Tentacles situated around the mouths of feeding polyps (or around the margins of the bell, in the case of jellyfishes) are provided with little capsules (nematocysts) containing threads that are shot out when the capsules are properly stimulated. The threads act as lassos or as piercing and poisoning agents mainly for the trapping of prey, but to some extent for self-protection. Cnidarians are routinely carnivores, feeding on crustacea, molluscs, fishes, and various other animals. The prey is taken into the digestive cavity and indigestible residues are ejected through the mouth. Representatives of various subdivisions of this phylum, such as certain of our sea anemones, carry symbiotic algae in their tissues; although they may benefit from the association, they remain basically carnivores.

Many cnidarians form colonies, frequently with more than one kind of polyp. Sea pens, for instance, which are closely related to sea anemones, consist of hundreds of polyps; some of the polyps resemble miniature anemones, others look more like tubes and serve as openings for sea water that "ventilates" the colony. In a colonial cnidarian there may also be polyps modified for reproduction, either sexual or asexual.

Finally, one other important characteristic of some cnidarians: alternation of two quite different phases in the life cycle. Most of our jellyfishes represent the sexual phase of a life cycle that also includes a polyp, or colony of polyps, which reproduces asexually.

PHYLUM CTENOPHORA: Comb Jellies

Comb jellies resemble jellyfishes because of their transparency and texture, for they are composed largely of jellylike material. However, they do not move in the same way as jellyfishes, which pulsate to force water out of the cavity beneath the bell. Instead, comb jellies have eight meridional rows of little "combs" (ctenes), which are paddlelike aggregations of large cilia. These combs beat rhythmically to propel the animals steadily instead of jerkily through the water. There may be a pair of long and extensile tentacles, which originate within deep sheaths on opposite sides of the body and have branches; they do not have stinging capsules, but are provided with sticky cells (colloblasts) that function in the capture of prey. Ctenophores, like cnidarians, are carnivores; ours feed mainly on small crustacea or upon one another.

PHYLUM PLATYHELMINTHES: The Flatworms

The flatworms include the parasitic tapeworms and flukes, as well as the largely free-living turbellarians. They are not necessarily flattened, however; many of the smaller species, especially, are cylindrical. In flatworms, the digestive tract (unless it is absent altogether, as in tapeworms) is a simple or branched sac with a single opening, the mouth. Between the digestive tract and the outside epidermis is a cellular layer in which the organs of reproduction and much of the musculature are located. The reproductive system may be surprisingly complicated for animals that are otherwise so lowly.

Turbellarians are abundant in marine environments, especially in sediment, on growths of seaweeds and colonial animals, and on rocks; but the majority are microscopic. Some are herbivores, feeding mostly on diatoms; others are carnivores, feeding on crustacea and other small animal organisms. They are characterized in part by being covered with cilia (flukes and tapeworms are not). The only turbellarians likely to be seen with the naked eye belong to a group called polyclads. They are usually very flat and two or three times longer than wide. The digestive cavity is much branched, with the mouth being near the center of the lower surface, and they are strictly carnivorous. Polyclads are most likely to be found on the undersurfaces of rocks, but may be overlooked because they are so thin and may resemble a gelatinous coating unless they happen to move. They glide through the use of their cilia, but some can also swim by fluttering undulations of the margins of the body. These worms usually show several to many little pepper-dot eyespots near the anterior end or around part or much of the margin of the body. They may also have a pair of tentacles at the extreme anterior edge or a bit away from the anterior edge.

PHYLUM NEMERTEA: The Ribbon Worms or Nemerteans

In general body texture, the nemerteans are much like turbellarian flatworms, being soft and covered with cilia. However, they are characteristically slender, highly contractile worms, somewhat resembling rubber bands but not at all rubbery in texture—in fact, they are often fragile, breaking apart when handled or pulled on. They are usually at least slightly flattened and may have eyespots on the anterior part of the body. They are considered to be more advanced than flatworms because they have a complete digestive tract, with a mouth at one end and anus at the other, and also a circulatory system consisting of definite blood vessels. However, the reproductive system of nemerteans is very simple compared to that of flatworms.

A unique feature of nemerteans is the proboscis. When withdrawn, this is turned into itself, like the finger of a glove that has been poked in, and is contained in a fluid-filled cavity surrounded by a muscular sheath. When the muscles of the sheath contract, hydrostatic pressure within the cavity forces the proboscis out. Sometimes it emerges through its own pore at the tip of the head region, but in certain groups of nemerteans it comes out through the mouth, even though its origin is unrelated to that of the digestive system. The proboscis, being either sticky or provided with thornlike stylets and a venom gland, is used to capture prey, often swallowed whole.

PHYLUM ANNELIDA: The Segmented Worms

The common earthworm belongs to the phylum Annelida and shows one of its cardinal characteristics: the division of the body into distinct segments. In some annelids, most or at least many of the segments may be essentially identical, even with respect to their internal organization. In others, segments in one region of the body may be quite different from those in another portion. Here again one faces the problem of trying to define a group of animals briefly, when the only way to understand them is to study representatives of many of the diverse groups.

The digestive tract of annelids is complete, with mouth and anus at opposite ends of the body, and there is a circulatory system. In addition, a feature not seen in the preceding groups shows up here: the body cavity, or coelom. The coelom is typically well developed and forms a fluid-filled space between the digestive tract and the outer body wall. Some of the organs, as those concerned with reproduction, excretion, and regulation of water balance, lie in this cavity. As it is lined by an epithelial layer, called the peritoneum, it is entirely comparable to our own body cavities, through which the digestive tract runs and in which various other internal organs— liver, pancreas, lungs, and kidneys—are located. The body cavity in annelids also serves as a kind of skeleton against which muscles can operate, so it is important in burrowing, crawling, and swimming, as well as in extension and retraction of certain structures used in feeding.

Of the three classes of annelids, one—the Oligochaeta, which includes the earthworm—consists mostly of terrestrial and freshwater animals, although there are some marine species. The leeches, or Hirudinea, are best represented in fresh water, but there are some marine forms, and even a few on land. The Polychaeta constitute by far the largest group and are almost all marine, so they will serve as the primary representatives of the annelids in this book. There is much diversity within the Polychaeta. Burrowing types form a number of distinct groups, as do those that build tubes of one sort or another. There are also many crawlers and swimmers. Structural specializations are especially evident in the anterior part of the body, where there may be tentacles, featherlike cirri, jaws, trap doors to close tubes, and so on. Most polychaetes have fleshy flaps of tissue on the sides of the segments; these flaps and the bristles that arise from them also show modifications that can be correlated with life styles. A number of entirely different types of polychaetes will be considered in this book, and the brief descriptions of their specializations for feeding, burrowing, and other functions will help one appreciate what a remarkably diversified group this is.

PHYLUM SIPUNCULA: The Peanut Worms

Sipunculans could be confused with certain polychaete annelids or with sea cucumbers. However, in contrast to annelids, they show no signs of segmentation and have no bristles. They resemble only those sea cucumbers that lack tube feet, and such types at least have longitudinal lines indicating division of the body into five sectors. In annelids and most sea cucumbers, the anus is at the hind end; but in sipunculans it is on the dorsal side of the body, closer to the anterior end.

The body of a sipunculan is divided into two vaguely defined regions. The slender and mobile anterior portion, called the introvert or "neck," can be completely withdrawn into the more bulbous posterior part. The neck may have some denticles in the skin; and the mouth, at the anterior tip of the body, is encircled by tentacles, which are usually bushy, but in our most common intertidal species are inconspicuous and unbranched. The body wall is tough and rubbery, and when the animal is contracted, the strength of the wall coupled with the high hydrostatic pressure within it makes it almost impossible to squeeze the sipunculan.

In addition to being bent back on itself, the digestive tract is extensively coiled, so that it is quite long in proportion to the body. Most sipunculans feed on detritus, using the tentacles to trap particles in a mucus film.

PHYLUM MOLLUSCA: The Molluscs

The phylum Mollusca is a very large group, successful in the sea, in fresh waters, and even on land. As a rule, the body of a mollusc is rather soft, and a portion of the body wall grows out around some or much of the rest of it as a sort of flap or tent, referred to as the mantle. When there are gills of the type peculiar to molluscs—called ctenidia—they are situated in the mantle cavity. The excretory organs and the anus also usually open into this cavity. A shell, two shells hinged together, or eight shells in a row may be present, and these are secreted by the mantle. However, in many molluscs, as sea slugs, there is no shell, or just a remnant of a shell. Internally there is a body cavity, but it is much reduced, being restricted to the cavities of certain organs—the gonads, a sac (pericardium) around the heart, and the excretory organs. Now that molluscs have been defined as a group, the major subdivisions found at the seashore can be described.

The chitons (subclass Polyplacophora) constitute most of the class Amphineura. (The other amphineurans are rare, wormlike animals not found at the shore.) Chitons are usually somewhat elongated, and their upper surface is covered by a series of eight separate, overlapping shells. Chitons cannot withdraw into their shells, but can only clamp down tightly to the rock, so that little of the body not protected by the shells is exposed. In the mantle cavity, on either side of the long, broad foot, is a series of gills. The head is not very distinct, but it is recognizable; there are no tentacles. The anus is at the end opposite the mouth. Chitons feed principally by rasping the substrate with the radula, a structure that looks like a toothed ribbon, which when not in use is in a sac off the digestive tract, just behind the mouth.

The Gastropoda—the snails and slugs—have a more definite head than chitons and usually tentacles of at least one kind. When they have a shell, it is single and either coiled, conical, or something like a cap. The body is generally thoroughly protected, although clamping to a rock may be necessary if the shell is not of a type into which the animal can withdraw completely. The foot is typically developed for crawling. The mantle cavity (which is missing or much reduced in some, as the sea slugs) may have one or two gills, or none. Certain gastropods have evolved lunglike structures for breathing air. These are characteristic of most land snails and slugs, and of a good many freshwater snails that have apparently gone back to the water after a long period on land. Only a few seashore gastropods have the habit of breathing air.

Gastropods have varied food habits and mechanisms for feeding. Jaws and a scraping radula are characteristic of the herbivores, and specializations of these structures are used also by the carnivores and scavengers. A few gastropods are filter feeders, which sort out microscopic food from water entering the mantle cavity. The anus is not often at the posterior end, unless the mantle cavity is missing; it generally opens into the mantle cavity somewhere on the right side of the body.

The Bivalvia—the bivalves—have little in the way of a head, even less than the chitons show. The body is enclosed by two valves that usually protect it rather completely. There is ordinarily a large foot adapted for burrowing in softer substrates, and between it and the mantle some extensive gills are characteristically located. In most bivalves, these are not so much organs of respiration as organs of feeding. The activity of cilia on these gills causes water to be drawn into the mantle cavity and then moved out again, usually by way of two siphons that are extensions of the mantle cavity. As water passes over the gills, microscopic food is trapped in mucus and then moved along ciliary pathways to the mouth.

The modern Cephalopoda, represented locally by squids and octopuses, are remnants of a once magnificent group. Few of the surviving members, as the chambered nautilus, have an external shell, although cuttlefishes have a rather strong internal plate useful to canaries for conditioning their beaks. Squids have a soft internal remnant of a shell, and octopuses do not have even that. The anterior part of the body of cephalopods is differentiated into eight muscular arms in octopuses, ten arms (two distinctly different from the other eight) in squids. The mantle cavity faces forward, and its wall is highly muscularized. By forcing water out of the mantle cavity, the animal can swim by jet propulsion. The jet emerges from a funnellike siphon on the ventral side of the mantle cavity, and as this siphon is mobile, the animal can control to some extent the direction in which it swims. There is a pair of large gills in the mantle cavity. The head is equipped with eyes that are remarkably well developed for an invertebrate. In octopuses, as a matter of fact, the eyes are similar to those of higher vertebrates in complexity and general organization. The nervous system as a whole is likewise very advanced. All squids and octopuses are carnivores, using a pair of jaws to subdue the prey that they capture.

PHYLUM ARTHROPODA: The Crustaceans, Insects, Spiders, and
  Their Allies

Arthropoda is the largest of all phyla, so it is naturally quite diversified. The success of arthropods is evident not only from the
fact that there must be over a million different kinds of them, but
also because they have penetrated just about every habitat that
supports life.

The more important characteristics of arthropods that are visible
without dissection are the external skeleton, the tendency of the
body to be divided into well-marked sections, and jointed appendages. The exoskeleton may be thin or thick—it may even be calcified, as in crabs—but it is in any case relatively firm, relatively
impervious, and more or less unyielding. Thus, although it offers
protection, it restricts growth; so in order for an arthropod to increase in size, it must shed its exoskeleton and secrete a new one.

The strong demarcation of the body into divisions—usually
head, thorax, and abdomen—is generally accompanied by a loss,
to at least some extent, of the identity of individual segments. Such
a loss may also happen in the head region of an annelid, where
segments are often blurred; but in arthropods the segments of the
head are routinely run together, though the appendages derived
from them are perfectly clear. Another complication is that the
exoskeleton may grow over a considerable part of the body as a
carapace, as in certain crustaceans where the carapace forms an
essentially continuous covering over both head and thorax.

The presence of jointed appendages is related to the existence of
the exoskeleton. If the exoskeleton is firm, it follows that movement will be restricted unless the appendages are divided into artic-
ulating units. At the joints between the articles ("segments") of the
appendages, as well as between segments or groups of segments of
the body proper, the exoskeleton is thinner and more flexible than
it is elsewhere, so that muscles can operate on them. The muscles,
of course, are attached directly to the exoskeleton.

The three principal surviving groups of arthropods are the Crustacea, the Arachnida (spiders, ticks, mites, scorpions), and the In-
secta. Most of the lesser groups—millipedes, centipedes, and so on
—can be linked closely to one of the major assemblages.

Insects, which constitute the majority of known arthropods, are primarily terrestrial and freshwater organisms; those that can be called marine are mostly at the fringes of the intertidal zone. Arachnids, except for mites, are not abundant in the sea either, but there are a couple of odd arachnidlike groups—the so-called horseshoe crabs and the pycnogonids—that are strictly marine. The crustaceans, however, are well represented in the sea, as well as in fresh water, and some are found on land. Examples of most of the groups likely to be encountered in shore situations in our area are illustrated later in this chapter.

PHYLUM BRYOZOA: The Bryozoans or Moss Animals

This phylum is large, and one of the more difficult ones for nonspecialists to deal with. Bryozoans form colonies of many essentially separate microscopic individuals and, although they are small, numerous details are packed into them.

The living portion of a bryozoan is termed the polypide, and the "house" it secretes around itself is called the zooecium. Special muscles withdraw the animal into its house, and others operate to force it out again by increasing hydrostatic pressure around it.

Bryozoa reproduce asexually as well as sexually; asexual reproduction builds up the colonies, often in a nearly symmetrical pattern. The colonies may be in the form of thin crusts (sometimes heavily calcified); bushy growths; branching stolons; calcareous, staghornlike masses resembling corals; and various other configurations.

A circle of tentacles, called the lophophore, surrounds the mouth, and the action of the cilia on the tentacles drives food into a U-shaped digestive tract that loops back to the surface not far from the mouth, but outside the lophophore. Many bryozoans, especially those that form bushy colonies, superficially resemble certain hydroids, mostly because of their rings of tentacles and hyaline appearance. However, there are no nematocysts on the tentacles of bryozoans, and the level of complexity of these animals is much higher than that of hydroids. Remember that the feeding polyps in hydroids are connected, so that their tissues and digestive cavity are continuous. Besides, when they are stimulated to contract, they shorten their tentacles and may turn them inward, and the polyp as a whole may contract considerably, but there are no special muscles to pull the animal into its house.

Furthermore, in hydroids, colonies are generally made up of feeding polyps and polyps specialized for reproduction; sometimes there are other types of polyps as well, such as batteries of stinging capsules. In bryozoans, the colonies are also frequently polymorphic, with individuals specialized for keeping the colony clean by sweeping it (vibracula) or for pinching strangers (avicularia). The latter have two jaws controlled by an array of muscles. However, the various types of individuals in bryozoans are more nearly separate and autonomous animals than just interconnected polyps.

PHYLUM PHORONIDA: The Phoronids

There are only a few species in the phylum Phoronida; these are assigned to just two genera, *Phoronis* and *Phoronopsis*. The phoronids live in tubes, and because they have a lophophore, they superficially resemble bryozoans. They are also superficially similar to sabellid polychaetes—the so-called feather-duster worms. However, phoronids are not segmented and have no bristles like those characteristic of polychaetes. Besides, the tentacles are never branched, and the way they are arranged, in a continuous double row having the general outline of a somewhat ornate horseshoe, is unlike anything seen in polychaetes. The digestive tract is U-shaped, so the anus is not at the end of the wormlike body; it is, in fact, close to the mouth, but outside the lophophore. There are a number of other peculiarities of internal anatomy and development that add to the distinctiveness of this phylum.

PHYLUM BRACHIOPODA: The Lamp Shells

Brachiopods look superficially like clams because they have a bivalved, calcareous shell. However, in a brachiopod the two valves are dorsal and ventral with respect to the rest of the animal, rather than being on the right and left sides of the body, as they are in a clam. In all of our local brachiopods, the valves are decidedly unequal; and a short, flexible stalk emerges through a hole or notch near the beak of the larger valve. (This is basically the ventral valve, though in nature the animal may be upside down.) The name "lamp shell" is given in allusion to the shape of many brachiopods, which resembles that of certain ancient oil lamps.

Brachiopods are close relatives of phoronids and bryozoans. They have a beautifully wrought lophophore, consisting of two diverging arms, each much coiled and with hundreds of tentacles used in trapping microscopic food in a mucus film. The food is then moved to the mouth by the action of cilia. Ciliary activity also brings water into the shell and then moves it out again by way of a gape at the broader end. The lophophore is supported by an exquisite little calcareous loop on the lower valve, which can be seen in some empty shells. The loop is so delicate, however, that it generally disappears before the shell as a whole shows signs of wear.

PHYLUM CHAETOGNATHA: The Arrow Worms

The arrow worms constitute a small group of almost strictly planktonic marine animals. They are slender, slightly flattened, and almost transparent, and thus are difficult to see unless they are in just the right light and against a dark background. They are characterized externally by a group of bristlelike jaws on each side of the mouth, a pair of eyespots on the top of the head, a horizontal tail fin, and two pairs of lateral fins. The anus is at about the same level as the second pair of lateral fins. Most arrow worms are small, our only common species being about two centimeters long. They tend to lie motionless unless stimulated to move by being touched or by the prospect of something to eat nearby; swimming is accomplished by flexing the body as a whole. Copepods, fish larvae, and other small organisms are captured by the bristly jaws.

PHYLUM ECHINODERMATA: The Echinoderms or Spiny-skinned Animals

This phylum can perhaps be most easily defined with reference to the characteristics of a sea star, a representative of the class Asteroidea. Attention is called, first of all, to its radial symmetry: a sea star with five arms can be cut into five essentially equal parts. Two other important features of echinoderms are their protruding, calcareous skeletal structures and mobile tube feet. The spines— sharp or blunt—that show on the upper and lower surfaces of most sea stars are not really external, for they are formed in the body wall, not on the outside of it. In a sense, they are like the tips of icebergs, because deeper in the body wall there are many skeletal elements that do not show.

The tube feet, arranged in one or more series on each side of the groove underneath each arm, are muscular and usually have tips something like suction cups. Their fluid-filled cores are continuous with a system of canals constituting what is called the water-vascular system. This, in terms of its origin during development of the animal, is related to the body cavity, but eventually becomes almost wholly separate. (In most sea stars, the water-vascular system retains a connection with the outside, by way of a calcareous sieve on the upper surface of the body, just a bit off center.) When fluid is forced into a tube foot, by contraction of the muscular wall of a little internal reservoir, its tip becomes less cuplike. When fluid is withdrawn, it becomes more cuplike, and thus effective in clinging to a firm substrate. In any case, the locomotion of a sea star and its ability to hang on tightly to a rock or to open a clam enough to start feeding on it depend on the operation of its tube feet.

Another significant structural specialization found in certain sea stars is the pedicellaria. The pedicellariae, each consisting of a pair of calcareous jaws on a short stalk, are usually in clusters on the upper surface. They close in response to the stimulus of contact with foreign objects, including small animals, that might otherwise settle on the surface.

This description of a sea star will serve as a basis for comparison with the other three groups of echinoderms found at the shore. (One group, the crinoids, will be omitted, as these are found locally only in deep water.) Brittle stars (Ophiuroidea) are superficially like sea stars, but they move by the writhing of their snaky arms. There are tube feet along the undersides of the arms, but they are used for feeding, not attachment. Pedicellariae are absent. The arms are distinct from the central disk, not just blending into it as in sea stars. Brittle stars, on the whole, feed principally on detritus and have a variety of methods for tangling food up in mucus before swallowing it.

Sea urchins (Echinoidea), like brittle stars and most sea stars, display a distinct, five-part radial symmetry. However, they have an internal shell, or test, which is solid, though composed of many separate plates. The mobile spines, shaped like golf tees, are articulated to bumps on the test. The tube feet, emerging through pores on the test, are used for locomotion and for catching pieces of seaweed and detritus and passing them down to the mouth on the lower surface. A rather remarkable chewing apparatus is associated with the mouth: called Aristotle's lantern, it consists of five teeth whose sharp tips converge. The teeth are used to chop up the food brought to the mouth. The pedicellariae of sea urchins have three jaws instead of two, as in sea stars.

Sand dollars also belong to the Echinoidea. They are aberrant sea urchins, being not only much flattened, but having the anus displaced from the top of the test to the lower surface just inside the margin; moreover, the spines and tube feet of sand dollars are small. These animals feed on small particles moved to the mouth to a large extent by action of cilia. Locomotion is effected by activity of the spines.

Sea cucumbers (Holothuroidea) are somehow more difficult to explain. They are basically radially symmetrical, but are elongated; and the five sectors are often unequal, either in actual size or in the extent to which the tube feet belonging to them are developed. Tube feet may be lacking altogether in certain sectors, so that the animal assumes a bilaterally symmetrical appearance. The feather-like or otherwise much-branched tentacles around the mouth of most sea cucumbers are tube feet specialized for feeding, serving mainly to trap relatively small detritus. In some burrowing sea cucumbers, these are the only tube feet. Sea cucumbers lack pedicellariae, and the skeletal elements tend to be isolated perforated plates in the body wall. In a few, some of these may protrude as tiny hooks or anchors that can catch the skin; and in some others there is a definite coat-of-mail covering the body.

PHYLUM CHORDATA: The Chordates (Including Sea Squirts)

The chordates are tied together by three especially important traits. First, the principal nerve cord and its anterior enlargement, the brain, are dorsal in position instead of ventral, as in invertebrates generally. Second, a rodlike structure, called the notochord, is located beneath the nerve cord, at least during earlier stages of development. Finally, there are outpocketings of the pharynx, which may or may not break through to the outside to form gill slits.

One small division of the chordates, the Cephalochordata (not represented in our area), shows all of the above characteristics nicely. The cephalochordates are filter feeders, using the perforated r harynx to process water for microscopic food and also for respiration. Another division, the Vertebrata, is composed of the only animals in which the nerve cord is surrounded by a vertebral column of cartilage or bone. The vertebrates include lampreys, sharks, and bony fishes as well as the amphibians, reptiles, birds, and mammals. In those forms in which gill openings develop and persist, these function primarily in respiration, for the method of feeding is no longer a water-filtering process. The notochord may survive into adulthood, as it does in lampreys, but in the higher groups it disappears during development. The dorsal nerve cord is fully characteristic of all vertebrates.

The Urochordata, or tunicates, includes the chordates with which this book will be principally concerned: the ascidians, or sea squirts. The definition of the urochordates will be based on the structure and development of these animals; however, there are two other general types of urochordates, both represented by plank-tonic species, that deviate from the ascidian pattern.

Some ascidians are solitary, and most of the larger species to which the term "sea squirt" is applicable are of this type. Social ascidians are those connected, at least for a time, by creeping stolons. The stolons are essentially runners from which new individuals arise. Compound (or colonial) ascidians are those that form masses containing several to many specimens embedded in a continuous matrix that has the character of a stiff jelly. The matrix in which the separate, small individuals of a colony are embedded, and much of the body wall of solitary and social ascidians, is called the tunic. It consists largely of a carbohydrate substance called tunicin, which is chemically close to cellulose of plants, with which we are all familiar in the form of wood, cotton, and paper.

In its development, an ascidian goes through a tadpolelike stage that has a dorsal nerve cord and a notochord, though the latter is limited to the tail region. The tadpole does not feed, but it nevertheless has a pharynx with perforations. After a very brief life on its own, the tadpole settles and metamorphoses into the attached adult phase, whereby the body becomes completely reorganized. The tail, together with its notochord, is resorbed. There is nothing now that can be called a head, though the cerebral ganglion survives in the upper part of the body, which ranges in shape from something like a low hemisphere to a cucumber. Two openings become obvious, and these may be on distinct elevations, rather like clam siphons. One of them brings water into the pharynx, where microscopic food is trapped in mucus. The water passes through the many perforations of the pharynx into a cavity called the atrium, and then leaves by way of the other opening. The intestine eventually opens into the atrium, so that residues from the digestive tract are carried out by the same stream of water. In some ascidians, the atrial cavity serves as a brood chamber for developing tadpoles, but in others the eggs and sperms liberated into the atrium leave the body and take their chances in the sea.

In compound ascidians, in which asexual reproduction is accompanied by deposition of additional matrix material, the incoming openings of the individuals are separate. The atrial openings may also be separate, but generally the atria of several individuals communicate first with a common chamber, which then has an aperture to the outside. When this is the case, the individuals are organized in circles around the common chamber.

ILLUSTRATED SYNOPSIS OF INVERTEBRATES LIKELY
TO BE OBSERVED AT THE SHORE

This section is intended to help one quickly recognize the general groups to which most of our obvious seashore animals belong. It is organized primarily on the basis of superficial similarities and differences. Thus, some of the nine major categories outlined include animals that are not closely related; conversely, animals that are related may be found under two or more of these headings.

The novice is urged not to be too hasty in deciding into which phylum a particular animal fits best. He should read the descriptions of any primary and secondary categories that are reasonably good prospects, and at the same time scan the pictures for characteristics that agree with those of the specimen in hand. Some phyla are so diversified that a few illustrations cannot do them justice. However, as one's understanding of important diagnostic features develops, he will find it increasingly easier to place almost any animal he finds into the right group.

1. Thin crusts, feltlike patches, spongy masses, or gelatinous coatings of nearly uniform texture

A. If thick (up to about 2 cm), feels spongy; whether thick or thin, usually has a feltlike texture due at least in part to microscopic siliceous spicules sticking through the surface; generally with some distinct openings, sometimes on volcano-like elevations, scattered over the surface; color extremely variable: whitish, tan, brown, green, gray, lavender, or red

Phylum Porifera, Class Demospongiae

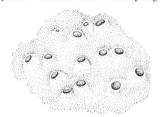

encrusting siliceous sponge

B. Texture crusty, brittle, frequently partially or wholly calcified; under magnification, seen to consist of numerous tubular or boxlike units into which the living individuals, characterized by long, ciliated tentacles, can be withdrawn completely; color of colonies usually whitish or silvery, but sometimes orange, pinkish, or brown

Phylum Bryozoa

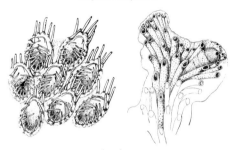

encrusting bryozoans

C. Lumpy or stalked growths, or growths of nearly uniform thickness, usually with the texture of very firm jelly and with a slick surface; with regularly spaced internal bodies (often yellow or orange), which are the individual animals embedded in the matrix, generally arranged in circles around a common opening; color of colonies pinkish, purplish, or brownish, but sometimes nearly white

Phylum Chordata, Subphylum Urochordata, Class Ascidiacea

compound ascidian

2. Fuzzy, featherlike, beardlike, or bushy colonies that are at least somewhat flexible; feeding individuals characterized by a circle of tentacles around the mouth

A. Branching slightly from a creeping stolon, or branching extensively into featherlike or bushy colonies; feeding polyps located at the tips of the branches or applied directly to one or both sides of the branches; tentacles not ciliated; in addition to feeding polyps, colonies may have polyps specialized for production of medusae

Phylum Cnidaria, Class Hydrozoa

hydroid

B. Branching into bushy growths, sometimes with spiral tendencies, but never in the pattern of a feather; colonies consisting almost entirely of separate tubular or boxlike units, frequently with spiny elaborations, into which the tentaculate individuals can withdraw completely; tentacles ciliated; colonies may have scattered nontentaculate individuals, the most common type being that with two jaws resembling those of a bird's beak; an extremely varied group, impossible to define briefly

Phylum Bryozoa

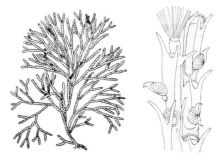

bushy bryozoans

3. Fixed to the substrate, but not wormlike and not secreting tubes; appearing to be individuals rather than colonies (though they may aggregate, settle on one another, produce buds, or brood young at their bases)

A. Vaselike or elongated, with a single opening at the upper end; feltlike texture, due partly to calcareous spicules protruding through the surface; sometimes producing buds that eventually develop an opening like that of the parent; body as a whole not contractile, though the opening may close slowly if stimulated

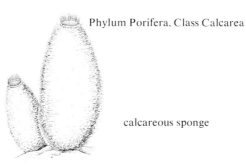

Phylum Porifera, Class Calcarea

calcareous sponge

Phylum Cnidaria, Class Anthozoa

B. Body with a cylindrical column, at the free end of which is a nearly flat disk bordered by a few to many tentacles; the tentacles and the rest of the body very reactive and contractile, so that the animal becomes approximately hemispherical when poked

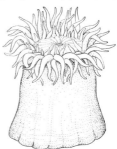

sea anemone
(cup corals similar, but have a column supported by an external calcareous skeleton)

C. Shape variable: hemispherical, more or less cylindrical and abruptly cut off, peanutlike, or globose and stalked; rather solid and firm; texture of surface variable: transparent and almost gelatinous, smooth and polished, translucent and like cartilage, or tough and leathery, sometimes with hairlike outgrowths; with two openings, either on distinct, siphonlike stalks or on little elevations of the surface, the size and shape of the openings and the siphons subject to muscular control

Phylum Chordata, Subphylum Urochordata, Class Ascidiacea

solitary ascidian

Phylum Arthropoda, Class Crustacea, Subclass Cirripedia

D. With a volcanolike shell attached by its base to the substrate, or with a leathery stalk, at the top of which is a laterally flattened portion protected by five or many calcareous plates; when active, extending plumelike appendages

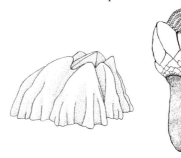

acorn barnacle   goose barnacle

A. Very flat (usually only about 1 or 2 mm thick), and about two or three times as long as wide (length generally 1 to 3 cm); eyespots near the anterior end or around the margin of the body; sometimes with a pair of tentacles; glides over firm substrates, but may also swim by undulations of body margins

Phylum Platyhelminthes, Class Turbellaria, Order Polycladida

polyclad flatworm

B. Usually at least slightly flattened; slender, many times longer than wide, something like a thin or thick rubber band, but very soft and very extensile; often with eyespots; no evidence of segmentation; sometimes fragile, breaking up into pieces while being disengaged from the substrate; glides over firm surfaces or through sediment, or burrows in sand or mud; may secrete a tube

Phylum Nemertea

ribbon worm

C. Elongated (usually at least ten times as long as wide); soft or fairly muscular, divided into many distinct segments, mostly much like one another (but in some, the body may be differentiated into two or more somewhat separate regions); with fleshy flaps (parapodia), sometimes lobed, on either side of most segments, and with groups of bristles associated with them; may have simple or branched tentaclelike or gill-like structures associated with the head region or with other parts of the body; head region may also

Phylum Annelida, Class Polychaeta

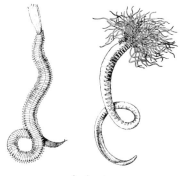

polychaetes

35

have enlarged bristles or other specializations; may crawl about freely, live in close association with other animals, burrow in sand or mud, or build a calcareous, muddy, parchmentlike or concretelike tube

D. Elongated, cylindrical body somewhat resembling that of some annelids; not segmented and without fleshy lateral flaps or bristles; delicate, unbranched tentacles arranged in the pattern of a horseshoe in which the free ends are spiraled; secretes a parchmentlike tube, generally with some foreign material adhering to it

Phylum Phoronida

phoronid

E. Body divided into two somewhat distinct regions: a slender, mobile, necklike anterior portion and a more nearly bulbous posterior portion; anterior portion can be introverted, but when extended may show tentacles (very small and unbranched, or larger and bushy) surrounding the mouth; rubbery, firm, resisting pressure of the fingers when tightly contracted; skin tough, almost leathery; no seg-. mentation

Phylum Sipuncula

peanut worm

F. Like a slender cucumber; soft, translucent, showing longitudinal lines indicating organization into five equal sectors; no segmentation; with ten tentacles, branched like feathers, around the mouth; clings to skin of fingers because of microscopic anchorlike spicules protruding from the body wall; burrows in sand

Phylum Echinodermata, Class Holothuroidea

burrowing sea cucumber

G. Slender, transparent, looking like a sliver of ice; about 2 cm long; horizontal tail fin and two pairs of lateral fins; two eyespots on head; jaws consisting of a number of stiff bristles; in plankton, generally motionless, but capable of rapid flexing movements

Phylum Chaetognatha

arrow worm

5. Jellyfishes or jellyfishlike animals, transparent or translucent, swimming free

A. Shaped like a saucer, bowl, or tall bell; moving by pulsations; with unbranched tentacles arising at or near the margin

Phylum Cnidaria, Class Hydrozoa

With a shelflike rim (velum) inside margin of bell; mouth (which may be on a long stalk) without large, frilly lobes; diameter generally less than 10 cm

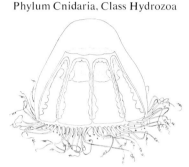

hydromedusa

Without a shelflike rim inside margin of bell; mouth with large, frilly lobes; diameter regularly exceeding 10 cm

Phylum Cnidaria, Class Scyphozoa

scyphomedusa

B. Globular to cucumber-shaped; not moving by pulsations; with eight meridional rows of glassy aggregates of thick cilia that propel the animal slowly and steadily; long tentacles, if present, only two in number, branched and retractable into sheaths

Phylum Ctenophora

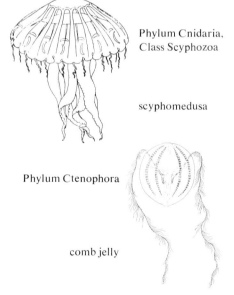

comb jelly

37

6. Sea stars ("starfishes"), brittle stars, sea urchins, and sand dollars—animals with radial symmetry (usually five-parted) and with externally evident calcareous spines, tubercles, or scales

A. With from five (the usual number) to over twenty arms, neither jointed nor sharply demarcated from the central disk; tube feet on lower surface of arms generally with suckerlike tips that can adhere tightly to firm surfaces and therefore are useful in locomotion; arms themselves not capable of rapid movements

Phylum Echinodermata, Class Asteroidea

sea star

Phylum Echinodermata, Class Ophiuroidea

B. With five arms that are jointed and rather sharply demarcated from the central disk; tube feet fingerlike and not capable of adhering to firm substrates; locomotion by relatively rapid movements of the arms themselves

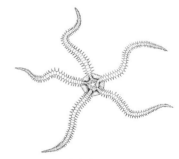

brittle star

Phylum Echinodermata, Class Echinoidea

C. With long, sharp, movable calcareous spines sticking out from a nearly globular test; tube feet slender when extended and with suckerlike tips; mouth, in center of lower surface, surrounded by five sharp-tipped jaws arranged something like those of a pin vise (but only the tips can be seen in an intact animal); anus in the center of the upper surface

sea urchin

D. Test disk-shaped, with short spines and small tube feet (at least some of which are tipped with suckers); radial pattern on upper surface of test eccentric and not perfectly symmetrical; jaws similar to those of a sea urchin, but very small; anus displaced to the lower surface, near the margin

Phylum Echinodermata, Class Echinoidea

sand dollar

7. Shaped like a cucumber, with branched (bushy or moplike) tentacles around the mouth, capable of being completely retracted; tube feet (those functioning in locomotion and attachment have suckerlike tips) may be in five equally developed and equally spaced longitudinal sets, or in unequally developed and unequally spaced sets, in which case the division of the body into five sectors is not clear externally; calcareous skeletal elements embedded in the tissue of the body wall and not evident externally (exceptions: burrowing sea cucumbers, which have tiny anchorlike spicules sticking out of the surface of the body wall, but no tube feet; certain bizarre types in which the lower surface of the body is flattened and the upper surface is covered by scalelike calcareous plates)

Phylum Echinodermata, Class Holothuroidea

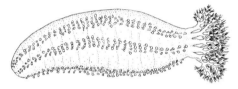

sea cucumber

burrowing sea cucumber

8. Molluscs and mollusclike animals (such as snails, slugs, clams, squids, and octopuses)

A. Body protected dorsally by a series of eight calcareous plates bordered by a margin of tough flesh that may be scaly or bristly (in one species, it completely covers the plates)

Phylum Mollusca, Class Amphineura, Subclass Polyplacophora

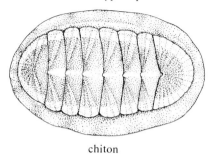

chiton

B. With a coiled, conical, or cap-shaped shell into which the animal can generally withdraw at least partially

Phylum Mollusca, Class Gastropoda

snail   limpet

C. Sluglike, without a shell (or with a shell that is strictly or largely internal, and in any case much too small for the animal to withdraw into)

Phylum Mollusca, Class Gastropoda

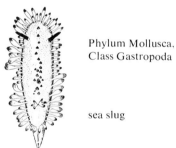

sea slug

D. With a shell of two calcareous valves hinged together; generally burrowing in sand, mud, clay, rock, or wood, but may be attached to a firm substrate by threads of organic material or permanently attached by one valve (this valve may or may not have a hole in it, but it remains stationary)

Phylum Mollusca, Class Bivalvia

clam

Phylum Brachiopoda

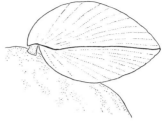

E. With a shell of two calcareous valves hinged together; attached to rock or shell by a tough but flexible and movable stalk emerging through a hole in one valve near the hinge

lamp shell

Phylum Mollusca, Class Cephalopoda

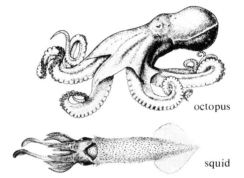

F. Octopuses (with eight more or less equal arms) and squids (with ten arms, of which two are longer than and different from the others)

octopus

squid

9. Shrimps, crabs, hermit crabs, and other animals sharing at least some of the same traits: jointed legs and jointed antennae; a body showing evidence of segmentation (usually at least in the abdominal region); a stiff or hard external skeleton

Phylum Arthropoda, Class Crustacea

A. Subclass Ostracoda

B. Subclass Copepoda

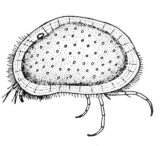

ostracod

copepod

C. Subclass Cirripedia

acorn
barnacle

goose
barnacle

D. Subclass Malacostraca

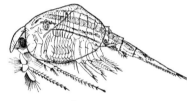

leptostracan

mysid

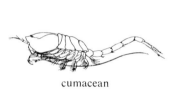

cumacean

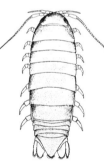

isopod

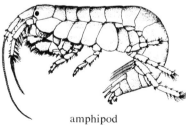

amphipod

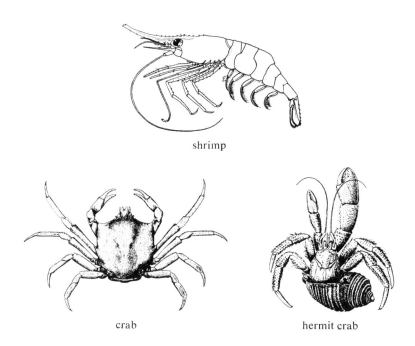

shrimp

crab

hermit crab

ALGAE

Not all algae represented in marine habitats can be called sea-weeds. The diatoms, for instance, are one-celled, even though their scummy or filamentous growths may be visible to the unaided eye. They will be considered briefly in this review, but other strictly microscopic groups will have to be excluded.

The classification of algae is based to some extent on pigmentation, hence the names blue-green, green, brown, and red algae. However, general structure, patterns of reproduction, and food storage products are also important. Many of the seaweeds this book will help to identify have alternate stages that are different from those described and illustrated. These alternate stages are frequently microscopic, or at least not easily noticed, and may be short-lived. There are a number of basic life histories and many variations on these themes. Although they are fundamental to the classification of algae, they will not be discussed here.

PHYLUM CYANOPHYTA: The Blue-Green Algae

Most blue-green algae are colonial, forming scummy growths or slick coatings over wet soil, seepage areas, and at the bottoms of shallow pools; a few are free-floating. The colonies are generally composed either of more or less single cells scattered through a gelatinous matrix or as masses of filaments, each consisting of single rows of cells surrounded by a gelatinous sheath. In either case, the individual cells are routinely smaller than those of most other algae. When viewed under a microscope with transmitted light, they are usually blue-green in color, since the chief pigments are chlorophyll (green) and phycocyanin (blue). However, other pigments—even the red phycoerythrin, which we think of as being the property of the Rhodophyta—are present in varying amounts, and sometimes to a degree that the coloration is decidedly something other than blue-green. The colonies as a whole show considerable variation in color, too, partly on account of the actual pigmentation, but also because of contamination by other algae or physical attributes such as the amount of matrix. Dark blue-green, olive, brown, and nearly black are common colors.

Blue-green algae are very simple organisms in terms of the structure of their cells. They do not have definite nuclei, though they have nuclear material, and this is one reason why some specialists think of them as being more closely related to certain bacteria than to other algae.

Blue-green algae are better represented in fresh water and in wet terrestrial situations than in marine environments. However, they should be mentioned in this guide because they are a regular feature of cliffside seepage areas just above the high-tide line; and in estuarine situations and salt marshes, they may coat the bottoms of shallow pools. One genus, *Calothrix,* is abundant in the upper reaches of rocky intertidal areas, where it forms very thin patches that dry out to a dull black.

PHYLUM CHLOROPHYTA: The Green Algae

Interpreted broadly, this group includes many one-celled species as well as others forming fuzzy, ropy, or stringy growths that cannot really be identified without the help of a microscope. In marine habitats, however, there are a number of distinctive larger types.

The green algae are indeed usually green, for their chlorophyll is not normally masked by other pigments. However, they may in some cases be a bit on the yellowish or brownish side. Most of the green seaweeds of our region fall into three general categories with respect to superficial appearance. Some grow as flexible or stiff filaments, often just one cell thick, and sometimes not even divided into cells; these are the ones most nearly like the filamentous algae of fresh-water habitats. *Cladophora, Spongomorpha,* and *Derbesia* fit into this category. Then there are types like *Ulva* and *Monostroma,* which form extensive thin sheets one or two cell-layers thick, and *Enteromorpha,* in which the microscopic appearance is about the same, though the thalli are in the form of hollow tubes instead of sheets. Finally, there are a few, such as *Codium,* that are thick, almost spongy growths consisting of many fine filaments woven together.

One odd alga common in salt marshes and on wet soil in terrestrial situations should probably be mentioned here, though it is not one of the Chlorophyta. This is *Vaucheria,* which forms feltlike mats of fine filaments that are not divided up into cells. In this respect, as well as in general color, it resembles certain green algae. However, when its pigments and storage products are analyzed, and when details of the structure of its reproductive cells are considered, it appears to be more closely related to a small group called the yellow-green algae.

PHYLUM BACILLARIOPHYTA: The Diatoms

As individual plants, the diatoms are usually one-celled. However, there are some that form filamentous colonies and may be confused with small brown seaweeds. Generally, they make a thin, scummy brown growth, often quite cohesive, over the surfaces of rocks, shells, wood, mud, other algae, and even on animals that are sessile. There are also many planktonic species. In short, one finds diatoms just about everywhere in seashore situations, and commonly in freshwater habitats as well.

The two outstanding characteristics of the diatoms are a cell wall composed largely of silica and an olive or yellow-brown coloration. The chlorophylls are masked to some extent by various other pigments, including fucoxanthin, which is found also in the brown algae.

Diatoms are extremely important as food for many animals, large and small. They are beautiful when studied under a microscope, because of the way in which the silica shell is sculptured with ribs, pits, pores, tubercles, spines, and other elaborations. The gliding style of locomotion of many diatoms is also engaging.

PHYLUM PHAEOPHYTA: The Brown Algae

The brown algae predominate in the intertidal region, and are also plentiful below the low-tide line. Most of the coarser seaweeds that we call kelps belong to this group. The presence of the pigment fucoxanthin, in addition to chlorophylls, usually results in a brown, golden brown, or olive coloration; a few encrusting species are nearly black, especially after they have dried out a bit.

The brown algae are highly varied in form. Some grow as essentially microscopic filaments just one cell thick. Others may have a fleshy stalk from which one or more broad blades arise. And there is about every imaginable form in between: thin hollow sacs, compact brainlike masses, feathery growths, and so on. A feature of many kelps is a holdfast consisting of a mass of stubby, rootlike structures. This type of holdfast, looking like something fished out of a jar of mixed pickles, is limited to the brown algae. Float bladders are another distinctive characteristic of many representatives of this group.

PHYLUM RHODOPHYTA: The Red Algae

In terms of numbers of species, there are more red algae than brown algae. However, a large proportion of them are small and delicate, and may go unnoticed; few red algae begin to approach the larger brown kelps in size. Also, red algae become progressively more abundant in the lower intertidal region and subtidally until they dominate the algal flora of deeper water. Their red pigment, phycoerythrin, functions together with chlorophyll in photosynthesis and absorbs green and blue components of the spectrum. As light of these shorter wave lengths is more effective in penetrating water than light of longer wave lengths, some red algae can live at depths where no other kinds of algae can survive.

If green algae are green and brown algae are at least close to brown, then one might hope that the Rhodophyta will be red. Usually they are. However, they not only have phycoerythrin, but also a variety of other pigments, including chlorophylls. The mixtures of these pigments, coupled with physical structure of the surface, result in a variety of colors, including pinkish red, brownish red, purplish red, and olive. Some red algae are so dark as to be nearly black, especially if they have dried out appreciably. Species that are olive or very dark might easily be mistaken for brown algae.

The red algae come in many shapes and styles of organization. Some grow as simple or branched filaments, perhaps just one cell thick, often with a feathery pattern of branching. Other red algae form broad thalli ranging in texture from thin membranes to thick, rubbery, and sometimes warty sheets. One important group found in the lower zones of rocky intertidal areas consists of coralline types. These are impregnated with calcareous material to the point that they are rather hard. Some coralline algae spread out as thin coatings, others form branching growths that are markedly jointed.

3. ■ ON AND AROUND FLOATING DOCKS AND PILINGS

THE relatively quiet waters of Puget Sound and the San Juan Archipelago are perfectly suited for boating and related recreational activities. The immense interest in boats has brought on the development of dozens of yacht clubs and public and private marinas with docking facilities constructed of heavy planking supported by floats of wood, Styrofoam, fiberglass, or concrete. Though man-made, and sometimes constructed partly of synthetic products, these become biologically favorable environments for many kinds of seaweeds and invertebrate animals once they are colonized by pioneering organisms.

Almost any extensive docking facility has some sections that have not been in the water long enough to be well colonized by marine organisms. However, floats that have been in place for at least a few months will almost certainly have a characteristic fauna and flora, depending on a number of variable conditions. Certain sections may be roofed over and thus shaded; others may be exposed. The salinity may be equal to that of the open sea, or it may be much reduced, at least at certain seasons of the year, by the influx of fresh water from a river or large streams. In any case, considerable variation may be expected in different portions of one set of docking facilities, and certainly between docks placed in ecologically different situations.

Generally speaking, floats exposed to considerable illumination tend to be monopolized by a few species of seaweeds. Partially or completely shaded areas are apt to have more interesting assemblages of animals and some delicate algae. However, any group of floating docks should have portions that offer an excellent introduction to the animal and plant life of the sea. As these docks are built to rise and fall with the tide—a matter of considerable importance in a region where the tidal amplitude is large—study and collection of material may be made at almost any time. This is a distinct convenience, especially in the winter, when the only very low tides come well after dark in our region. Moreover, many of the animals and plants on floats are those normally found at lower levels of the intertidal zone. They can live close to the surface, yet not be in danger of exposure.

Anyone who has been given permission to use floating docks to indulge his enthusiasm for study of marine life is expected to treat the facilities with respect. It is one thing to scrape off carefully a few organisms, and something else to rip out pieces of Styrofoam, pull on hoses that may be functioning as a system of water pipes, clamber over boats, and make a mess on the planking. Many marinas employ caretakers to minimize vandalism, and sometimes the amateur or professional biologist will have to make a convincing case for permission to use the floats.

Floating docks are usually placed in protected situations. During much of the year, especially from late spring to early autumn, there is little wave action and only slight turbidity. The visibility is therefore excellent, facilitating observation of animals and plants on the floats themselves, as well as jellyfishes and other animals swimming near the surface. The planking is not often more than a foot or two above the water line. If you find it easier to get a good look at the sides of the floats by lying on your belly, wear old clothes and watch out for splinters. If you wear glasses, it would be a good idea to equip them with something that will keep them from falling off when your head is down.

A thin film of oil is frequently present on the surface of the water. Much of this unfortunate nuisance is due to carelessness in handling fuel and crankcase oil, but some of it results from the operation of two-cycle engines, which always leak a little fuel. In any case, it is difficult to lift animals into a bucket without bringing up some of the oil with them. Although the toxicity of certain components of the film of oil may discourage some animals from settling permanently on the floats, species that luxuriate are probably little affected.

The more obvious elements in the complex embroidery of attached organisms on floats are certain seaweeds, sponges, hydroids, sea anemones, tube-dwelling polychaete annelids, barnacles, mussels, and ascidians. Green sea urchins, sea cucumbers, and sea stars are among the less mobile animals. Shrimps, certain other crustaceans, and small fishes may dart in and out of the heavy growths. But these are just the organisms that can be seen in a quick reconnaissance. Sharp eyes—and eyes that are trained—will soon discover many other creatures, and a hand lens or low-power dissecting microscope will reveal an astonishing variety of animals and plants in a colony of hydroids or in a small clump of worm tubes. Some of the organisms are so dependent upon others that they form constant associations with them.

When it comes to truly microscopic organisms, the variety becomes frustrating. Even a specialist on protozoa or small turbellarians would find species that he could not identify and that have never been described or given names, although they may have been seen many times before by other professional biologists. Many kinds of bacteria are present. Even though the variety of life on floats may seem to be relatively restricted when compared with that on a rocky coast exposed at low tide, the number of kinds of animals, plants, and microorganisms is enormous and the web of life is exceedingly complex. Moreover, there are seasonal changes, variations in annual cycles and patterns of succession, and occasional surprises. A dock that a biologist has visited regularly for years may suddenly show a good growth of some species that he had never noted there before.

This chapter will cover most of the conspicuous animals and seaweeds colonizing floats in this area, as well as some of the animals that can be seen swimming near the surface at certain times of the year. Attention will also be called to related species that, though they may not be common, may be noted by the more careful or experienced observer. Finally, it will be useful to mention some of the animals that live in tight associations with other animals, in what may be called symbiotic relationships or specialized predatory relationships. Thus there will be times when a particular animal is discussed out of order with respect to its position in the system of classification, simply because it is more appropriately considered in connection with the animal on which it is somehow dependent.

PROTOZOA

In the film of microscopic organisms and detritus that coats the substrate and surfaces of some of the algae and sessile animals, protozoa of various sorts are usually abundant. Although they are important constituents of the fauna, it is impossible to discuss them exhaustively in this book because they are so diversified and cannot really be appreciated without extensive study. Moreover, microscopes of high quality, capable of magnifications of one hundred to one thousand diameters, are required for serious work with protozoa. There are two or three types of protozoans, however, that can be recognized with the aid of a hand lens and can be truly enjoyed with the help of a low-power microscope.

1. *Ephelota gemmipara,* a suctorian; photomicrograph. Not all specimens show such a conspicuous thickening of the upper part of the stalk. The fine filaments adhering to the stalk consist of bacteria.

Ephelota (fig. 1) is common on stalks of hydroids such as *Obelia* and *Tubularia,* but it will grow on a variety of other substrates, as worm tubes, tunicates, wood, and occasionally even exoskeletons of planktonic crustacea. *Ephelota* belongs to a group of protozoa called suctorians, whose adult stage is characterized by tentacles that pierce delicate prey organisms, usually other protozoa, and withdraw their juices. Most suctorians are sessile, secreting stalks by which they are permanently attached. The tough stalk of *Ephelota* may reach a length of nearly 1 mm, so the bulbous tentaculate portion is elevated well above the substrate. Large specimens often show a number of elongated buds on their upper surface, which develop cilia, become detached, and swim around until they find a suitable place to settle. They then lose their cilia, start to secrete a stalk, and develop tentacles. *Ephelota* is sometimes so numerous that it forms a rather conspicuous whitish fuzz. When first seen with a low-power microscope, these protozoans may be mistaken for small hydroids because of their general shape and their tentacles.

Foraminiferans are generally abundant wherever detritus accumulates. Most of them are truly microscopic, but some can be seen with a hand lens or even by the unaided eye. There are many kinds of foraminiferans in shore situations. The majority have calcareous tests, often resembling snail shells because of the way they are coiled. The tests are partitioned into chambers connected by openings, so the protoplasmic mass of a foraminiferan is continuous from chamber to chamber. Perforations of the test permit the long, slender extensions of protoplasm, called pseudopodia, to emerge through almost all parts of the test, as well as from the principal aperture of the largest and newest chamber. The pseudopodia trap very small organisms, including bacteria, and carry them by protoplasmic streaming into the main body of the organism.

A none too typical foraminiferan, but one very likely to be seen in material scraped from a float, is *Gromia oviformis* (fig. 2). Its

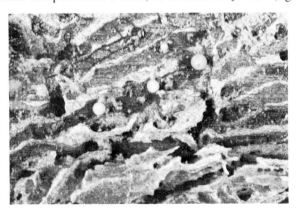

2. Tests of four specimens of *Gromia oviformis* on wood tunneled by the gribble. *Limnoria*

test is ovoid, of a light-brown color, usually somewhat shiny, and up to about 3 mm in diameter. Under favorable conditions (cool water is essential) it may be encouraged to extend its numerous long, slender pseudopodia, which it uses to trap bacteria, small diatoms, and other microscopic organisms. The pseudopodia radiate widely from the protoplasm that emerges from the aperture at one end of the test. They tend to remain single, but may occasionally join one another. (In most foraminiferans, the pseudopodia anastomose extensively, forming complex networks.)

SPONGES

The identification of sponges, many of which look much alike, is not an easy matter. On floating docks, however, only a few species are likely to be encountered. One of them, *Scypha* (fig. 3), is rather distinctive, forming whitish, vaselike growths attached to the substrate only at the base. Because of its relative simplicity, it is a good subject for studying the structure of a sponge. Note that its

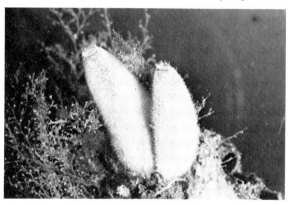

3. *Scypha,* a vaselike calcareous sponge

texture is bristly, since many of the calcareous, needlelike spicules, which constitute a loosely organized skeleton, protrude to the outside. Microscopic pores all over the surface lead into a complex system of canals and chambers. The chambers are lined by peculiar little "collar cells," so named because each has a ring of fingerlike projections that looks (under the highest magnification possible with a light microscope) like a transparent collar. These cells also have flagella, which create the currents that move water into and through the sponge until it finally enters a central cavity and then goes out by way of the single large opening (osculum) at the top. The collar cells are also the principal feeding cells of the sponge, trapping microscopic food on their collars and ingesting the particles after the fashion of amoebae. The constant movement of water through the sponge not only brings in food, but also supplies oxygen to cells remote from the surface and carries away waste products.

Two other sponges likely to be found on floats are encrusting types, *Haliclona* and *Halichondria,* which may form extensive patches. Both are very complex, having many oscula scattered over their exposed surfaces, and thousands upon thousands of microscopic incurrent pores obscured by the felt of protruding spicules.

Halichondria (fig. 4) is extremely variable in color and form. On floats, it is usually tan or yellowish and makes a mass about 1 or 2 cm thick. It frequently grows up over stubs of algae or worm tubes. The oscula are sometimes on eminences. It is called the crumb-of-bread sponge, in allusion to its texture when squeezed or broken between the fingers.

4. *Halichondria,* the crumb-of-bread sponge

Haliclona (fig. 5) is usually gray, pale amethyst, or lavender, sometimes a drab brown; it seems less opaque than *Halichondria.* Its oscula are usually on rather definite, volcanolike elevations.

Halichondria and *Haliclona* are classed as siliceous sponges because their spicules consist of silica. To get a look at the spicules

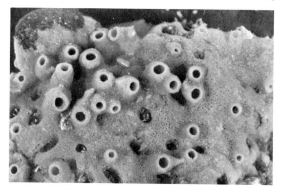

5. *Haliclona,* an encrusting siliceous sponge

of a sponge under the microscope, place a bit of the sponge in a commercial bleaching preparation consisting of sodium hypochlorite. The solution will destroy all of the organic matter, leaving a debris of spicules that can be washed in water and then mounted on a slide for examination. To determine whether a sponge has calcareous or siliceous spicules, place a bit of it into a drop or two of strong hydrochloric acid: siliceous spicules resist the acid, but calcareous spicules will be destroyed and bubbles of carbon dioxide will be given off.

CNIDARIANS

Hydroids

Among the invertebrates that form a conspicuous part of the fauna of floating docks are the hydroids. The more common types belong to the genus *Obelia,* several species of which are found in our region. At least two are regularly found on floats: *O. longissima* (figs. 6 and 7), which forms beardlike colonies 20 or 30 cm long, or sometimes even longer; and *O. dichotoma,* which grows as a delicate whitish fuzz about 2 cm high. In both species, and others that may occasionally be present, the colonies are branched; but the branching of *O. longissima* is of course very extensive. The feeding polyps have a crown of tentacles provided with stinging capsules, called nematocysts. These are formed within certain cells and explode when they are contacted by a small crustacean or other prey organism. The trapped prey is then brought by the tentacles to the mouth.

6. *Obelia longissima*, with two specimens of *Eubranchus olivaceus*, a sea slug that feeds on it

7. Portion of a branch of *Obelia longissima*, as seen with a microscope, showing feeding polyps and a reproductive polyp in which medusae are being formed

Hydroids, being cnidarians, have basically only two cellular layers, one lining the digestive cavity, the other lining the outside of the body. The jellylike layer between these definitely cellular layers is not as extensive as it is in some other cnidarians, especially jellyfishes. In *Obelia* the digestive cavity of one feeding polyp continues down the stalk to join that of others. The outer cellular layer secretes a thin, hyaline covering, called the perisarc, which in *Obelia* and other hydroids of the same general type envelops not only the stalks but also the feeding polyp.

At various points along the stalks are found club-shaped structures within which asexual reproduction takes place. The products of this budding process are little medusae (jellyfish), which eventually escape from the reproductive polyp by way of an opening at the top. When first set free, the medusae are only about 0.5 mm in diameter. They start to feed on crustacea and grow until they reach a diameter of nearly 5 mm. On their four radial canals they develop gonads—either ovaries or testes—and the eggs or sperms are released into the sea water by way of the digestive tract and the mouth. Eggs that happen to be fertilized develop into ciliated larvae called planulae. If a planula succeeds in settling on a suitable substrate, it is transformed into a polyp. This is the first stage, then, of the hydroid generation. As the young polyp grows, it puts out branches that terminate in new polyps. Eventually, reproductive polyps appear and another generation of medusae is produced.

A number of organisms from both the plant and animal kingdoms live on the stalks of colonies of *Obelia,* especially in the older and essentially dead portions. Diatoms, the suctorian *Ephelota,* and even other small hydroids may be among the adherent or tightly attached guests. Various kinds of small worms and crustacea may wander in and out, or they may remain in the coating of diatoms and sediment that sticks to them. There are two distinctive types of organisms, however, that are part and parcel of just about every *Obelia* colony: the caprellid amphipods and the little whitish and olive sea slug, *Eubranchus olivaceus.* The caprellids are more easily discussed later in this chapter, in the context of other crustaceans, but it should be pointed out that, as amphipods go, they are bizarre, with almost no abdomen and therefore little in the way of abdominal appendages. The thoracic region is somewhat sticklike, and the way its appendages are modified and arranged makes a caprellid look something like a praying mantis. These strange animals feed on detritus and diatoms.

Eubranchus (fig. 6), also to be dealt with a little later on, is quite another matter. It looks much gentler than a caprellid, but is a vicious predator that nips off the polyps of *Obelia.*

A hydroid that closely resembles *Obelia* is *Gonothyraea.* It is perhaps more likely to be found where the salinity is somewhat lower than that of full-strength sea water. In *Gonothyraea,* the medusae produced within the reproductive polyp move out of the opening and then remain attached to it. They reproduce sexually, but the eggs are retained by the female medusae until they have been fertilized and have developed into planulae. The planulae finally escape, settle, and become transformed into polyps.

A different group of hydroids, in which the perisarc—if this protective covering is present at all—does not extend to the feeding polyps. These are called athecate (*a* = not, *theca* = covering) hydroids, as differentiated from the thecate types discussed above. Two athecate hydroids are more or less regularly encountered. *Coryne* (fig. 8) is small—only about 1 cm high. The upper portion of its club-shaped polyp bears a number of scattered, knobbed tentacles, which are batteries of stinging capsules for capture of prey. Just below the tentacles, the polyp produces buds that develop into medusae. These eventually become detached and mature into sexually reproductive individuals. Before the medusa and polyp stages were recognized as belonging to the same life history, they were assigned to different genera, the medusa going under the name of *Sarsia*. Obviously, this sort of double nomenclature is biologically unsound if a particular hydroid can be definitely associated with a particular medusa.

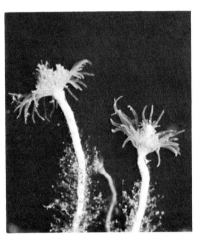

8. Hydroid stage of *Coryne tubulosa,* as seen with the aid of a microscope

9. *Tubularia marina*

Our largest athecate hydroid is *Tubularia* (fig. 9). Its polyps, on unbranched but generally crooked stalks up to about 5 cm long, may be 1 cm in diameter when the tentacles are extended. They are usually of a delicate orange-pink color. In Puget Sound and the San Juan Archipelago, the predominant species on floats is evidently *Tubularia marina;* in estuaries farther south, as in Coos Bay and

San Francisco Bay, *T. crocea* is the most common.

A careful examination of a polyp of *Tubularia* will reveal two entirely different sets of tentacles. One set forms a whorl around the moūth; the other set is at the base of the mouth cone. Between these rings of tentacles are stalked clusters of fruitlike bodies, which are comparable to the medusa-forming reproductive polyps of *Obelia* and *Gonothyraea.* However, the medusae produced by our *Tubularia* are buried in the tissue, and only a detailed study of cross-sections of the reproductive polyps will show that the medusae have a plan of construction similar to that of typical free medusae. These medusae, abortive as they are, do produce either eggs or sperms, and the eggs are fertilized within the female medusae. There they develop into planulae, which work their way to the outside but remain in close association with the polyp. They metamorphose into little polyps that already show the two rings of tentacles characteristic of mature polyps. This stage is called the actinula. When it is ready, the actinula drops away from the "parent" (remember that it is not produced directly by the hydroid stage, but indirectly by way of the abortive medusa generation) and settles on the substrate, generally in the same vicinity, and starts to grow into a mature hydroid.

On the lips of the tubes of two polychaetes—*Schizobranchia insignis* and *Pseudopotamilla ocellata,* both of a type called plume worms—is found an unusual little athecate hydroid called *Proboscidactyla flavicirrata.* Its feeding polyps have only two tentacles, and the integrity of the colony depends very much on its close association with the living plume worm. *Proboscidactyla* is discussed more fully later in this chapter, in connection with these polychaetes.

Jellyfishes

In the spring and summer, the waters of Puget Sound and the San Juan Archipelago show a superb fauna of jellyfishes. Some species are small, no more than 5 mm in diameter, but one species may be big enough to fill a washtub. The majority fall into the range between 1 and 5 cm.

What people generally call jellyfishes belong to two completely separate groups of cnidarians, the Hydrozoa and Scyphozoa. Hydrozoan medusae are regularly characterized by the presence of a membrane (velum) extending for some distance inward from the margin of the bell. The mouth may be on a rather long stalk (manubrium), but it is not provided with extensive lobes. The gonads are usually either on canals that extend radially from the central stomach or on the manubrium. Our largest hydrozoan medusae may come close to being 10 cm in diameter, but most species are much smaller than this.

The scyphozoan medusae of our region, when mature or approaching maturity, are relatively large—generally at least 10 cm in diameter. They have no velum, and the corners of the mouth are extended into long, frilly lobes ("oral arms"). The gonads lie in pouches off the stomach and are horseshoe-shaped in our more common species. There are other structural differences between medusae of the two groups, but the above should suffice for our purposes.

Hydrozoan medusae as a rule are produced asexually by hydroids and represent the sexual phase of the life cycle. There are exceptions to this rule, and the eggs of some hydrozoan medusae, after fertilization, develop directly into another generation of medusae. Scyphozoan medusae never come from hydroids, though most of them do have a polyp phase of a type called the scyphistoma (fig. 10). The scyphistoma resembles a little vase, but is provided with tentacles that enable it to trap small crustaceans and perhaps other animal organisms. Under certain conditions, the scyphistoma divides transversely into a number of lobed, saucer-

10. Scyphistomas of a jellyfish, probably *Aurelia,* on wood; some are in the process of dividing transversely into medusae.

shaped individuals, each a prospective jellyfish. In our area, scyphistomae are sometimes found attached to rocks, shells, or floats—especially old and decaying floats of wood. Once in awhile, a float will have what must be millions of scyphistomae on its shaded underside. These are judged, on the basis of the types of stinging capsules they have, to belong to *Aurelia*.

As might be expected, there are some scyphozoan jellyfishes in which the scyphistoma stage is obviated; sexual reproduction leads directly to another generation of medusae. However, most scyphozoans found in our area do go through the scyphistoma stage as far as is known.

Of the three or four scyphozoans likely to be seen in this region, the largest species is *Cyanea capillata*. It may be more than 50 cm in diameter and seems to be most abundant in the late summer. Specimens seen bobbing about in shallow water are often headed for disaster, being left high and dry when the tide recedes. The big blobs of jelly provide interesting conversation pieces. *Cyanea* is generally yellowish brown, though the coloration is sometimes absent and the animal just looks milky. There are eight groups of tentacles arising near the margin of the bell. Each group is approximately crescent-shaped, with its seventy or more tentacles arranged in four rather distinct rows. The tentacles are very extensile: in a medusa 50 cm in diameter, they may trail for 2 m or more. The margin of the bell is scalloped into eight notched lappets, and in the notch of each is a little sense organ called a rhopalium. The rhopalium is an organ of balance: it contains a crystalline mass, which gives it some weight, so that depending on the orientation of the jellyfish at the moment, the rhopalium either is or is not weighing down on the cilia of some sensory cells located on a little lobe beneath it. Information fed into the nervous system of the medusa from the various groups of sensory cells around the animal leads to appropriate righting reflexes. The frilly oral lobes are large and capable of great extension, and they are also richly provided with stinging capsules. Contact with either the oral lobes or marginal tentacles is not recommended. *Cyanea* seems to be the only reasonably common jellyfish in this area that can give a nasty sting. Some persons evidently are more seriously affected by it than others.

A scyphozoan that may occasionally occur in enormous numbers is *Aurelia aurita*. The huge populations are not surprising after one has seen the sheets of scyphistomae, thought to belong to this species, on some floating docks. However, in some years not a single *Aurelia* is seen by jellyfish watchers. *Aurelia* is generally from about 10 to 15 cm in diameter, but it can be larger. It is a rather flat medusa and nearly colorless, except for the horseshoe-shaped gonads, which may be tinged with violet, pink, or yellow. The margin of the bell is divided into eight lobes, each with numerous short and delicate tentacles. Sense organs of the rhopalial type, bordered on either side by small lappets, are located between the marginal lobes. The radial canals of the digestive tract are easily seen: they branch repeatedly as they move outward toward the margin, and some of the branches anastomose. The oral lobes are fairly large, but much less frilly than those of *Cyanea*.

Most of our hydromedusae fall into two rather distinct categories with respect to the shape of the bell, nature of the marginal sense organs, and parentage—that is, whether they are derived from thecate or athecate hydroids. To try to put the matter simply, medusae with bells as tall or taller than wide, with pigmented eyespots near the bases of the tentacles, and with gonads borne on the manubrium are usually derived from athecate hydroids, such as *Coryne*. Medusae with bells wider than tall, with marginal balance organs (statocysts) and no eyespots, and with gonads borne on the radial canals are usually derived from thecate hydroids, such as *Obelia* and *Clytia*.

Although hydrozoan medusae are not often seen here in winter, they start to show up by early April. In midsummer it is sometimes possible to find eight or ten species bobbing around all at once, some of them much more common than others. By late September, only three or four kinds can still be seen. Those mentioned here are just a few of the hydrozoan medusae visible almost anytime during the summer.

First to be considered are the medusae that have a small number of tentacles. Our only medusa with just two tentacles is *Stomotoca atra* (fig. 11). It is one of the tall-belled types, characterized by gonads on the manubrium which are organized as eight series of cross-foldings. The four radial canals are distinct. The bell is about 1.5 cm in diameter, about as high as wide, and somewhat pointed at the top.

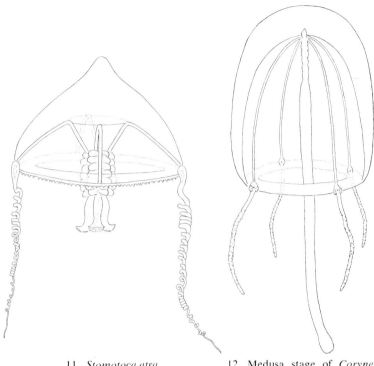

11. *Stomotoca atra*   12. Medusa stage of *Coryne tubulosa*

Species of *Coryne* (*"Sarsia"*) also have gonads on the manubrium, but they have four tentacles, with an eyespot at the base of each, and a bell that is decidedly taller than wide. *C. tubulosa* (fig. 12) is the more common of the two in our region. Its bell reaches a height of only a little more than 1 cm; but its manubrium, when fully extended, may be more than twice as long as this. *C. rosaria* is similar to *C. tubulosa,* but its manubrium rarely reaches beyond the edge of the bell. *Euphysa flammea* is similar, though it lacks eyespots at the bases of the tentacles; its rather short manubrium is beautifully colored, being carmine red throughout, or changing from red around the mouth to pink higher up.

Of the jellyfishes with numerous tentacles, the more common larger species are *Phialidium gregarium, Halistaura cellularia,* and *Aequorea aequorea.* All of these have relatively flat bells, and the gonads are on the radial canals. *Phialidium* (fig. 13) is the smallest of them, its bell being not quite 1.5 cm in diameter. The gonads are restricted to the outer portions of the four radial canals, and there are about sixty tentacles. The mouth opens directly into the stomach. This particular species of *Phialidium* is produced by a hydroid known as *Clytia*.

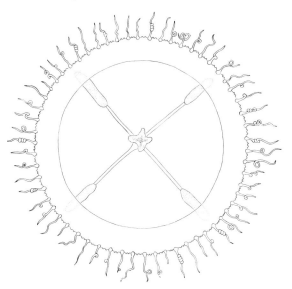

13. *Phialidium gregarium*

Halistaura resembles *Phialidium,* partly because the mouth is not on a stalk. It is larger, however, frequently exceeding a diameter of 5 cm. It also has many more tentacles—at least two hundred fifty—and the gonads are wavy and run the entire length of the four radial canals.

Aequorea (fig. 14) is our largest common jellyfish. It frequently attains a diameter of about 7 cm, and still larger specimens have been reported. In comparison with the other species just described, it has a very thick, gelatinous bell. There are about sixty radial canals, and the delicate gonads are under these. The tentacles, numbering over fifty in large specimens, are capable of great extension.

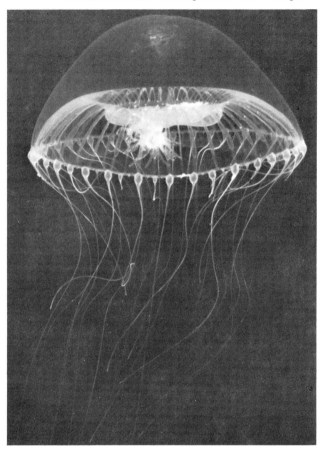

14. *Aequorea aequorea*

A few curiosities must certainly be included. *Melicertum octocostatum* (fig. 15) is an odd medusa, not much more than 1 cm in diameter, characterized by eight radial canals, each with a conspicuous wavy gonad. All around the margin, small tentacles alternate more or less regularly with about sixty larger ones, and the manubrium is proportionately stout.

Aglantha digitale (fig. 16) has a tall bell about 1.5 cm high and approximately one hundred tentacles. As in *Melicertum,* there are eight radial canals, but the gonads hang down like sausages inside

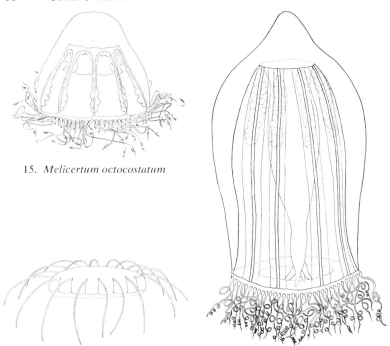

15. *Melicertum octocostatum*

17. *Solmissus*   16. *Aglantha digitale*

the bell. Unlike most of our jellyfishes, which move rather slowly
and by regular pulsations, *Aglantha* may appear to be motionless
much of the time; but when it does go into action, it almost leaps.
There is no hydroid stage in its life cycle; fertilized eggs develop
into another generation of medusae.

Just one more type, *Solmissus* (fig. 17), will be singled out for
special mention. The identity of the species occurring in our area is
uncertain; perhaps it is *S. incisa,* which has a wide distribution. It
is about 5 cm in diameter and something like *Aequorea* in profile
and consistency, but there is little similarity otherwise. The margin
is scalloped into about eighteen or twenty lappets, and the relatively stiff tentacles arise between these, well above the edge of the
bell. The mouth is very wide and opens directly into a large
stomach with a number of side pockets in which the gonads are
located; there are no radial canals. *Solmissus* is another one of the
hydrozoan medusae in which the hydroid generation is omitted.

Developing medusae are sometimes found on the floor of the stomach.

Most of our larger hydrozoan medusae are luminescent. If it is dark, and if one's eyes are adapted to the darkness, flashes of light emitted by jellyfishes and certain other animals bobbing near the surface will probably be seen. The best way to observe luminescence at close range is to take a jellyfish into an absolutely dark room, allow a little time for your eyes to become accustomed to the darkness, then touch or rub the animal. *Aequorea* is a good one to use for this purpose; its luminescent material is most concentrated around the margin of the bell.

Sea Anemones

The most common sea anemone attached to floats is *Metridium senile* (fig. 18; pl. II). In many situations, especially in estuaries where the salinity is reduced, it is the only one to be found. Small specimens are almost always white, but larger individuals—and

18. *Metridium senile*

they sometimes attain a height of 25 cm or more—may be white, tan, brownish orange, or related colors. Unlike most other sea anemones, which have rather thick tentacles, *Metridium* has hundreds of relatively small tentacles, arranged in lappetlike groups, and the number continues to increase as the animal grows. The majority of our sea anemones feed upon small fishes, crabs, shrimps, and other prey of considerable size, but *Metridium* feeds primarily upon small organisms. It is nonetheless a carnivore.

Metridium occasionally reproduces asexually as well as sexually. In sexual reproduction, it discharges eggs or sperms (depending on its sex) into the sea by way of its mouth. The eggs, once fertilized, develop into planula larvae, which settle and metamorphose into little anemones. Asexual reproduction, when it occurs, may be accomplished by fragmentation of the basal disk, with the pieces differentiating into small but complete anemones, or by an anemone pulling itself into two parts. It is not unusual to find specimens in which the basal disk is elongated and in which the column is already reorganizing with the prospect of forming two complete individuals.

In addition to *Metridium,* a different type of sea anemone, *Tealia crassicornis* (pl. III), may be fairly common. The oral disk and thick tentacles are usually greenish gray or olive gray, but diffuse red tints are often quite strong; in addition, the tentacles have some light bands. The column is sometimes an audacious mixture of red streaks and a light olive green background, or is sometimes almost uniformly red.

CTENOPHORES, OR COMB JELLIES

The comb jellies resemble jellyfishes because of their texture and transparency, but they are really quite different. Instead of pulsating, comb jellies propel themselves by the action of large cilia. The cilia are arranged in paddlelike aggregations (ctenes, or "combs"), disposed in eight meridional rows, called comb rows. (The phylum name, Ctenophora, means "comb-bearing.") Comb jellies are not strong swimmers and are therefore not really independent of currents. However, when observed in quiet water, they can be seen to make forward progress; if they happen to be of a type that has long tentacles, the tentacles will be trailing behind them. Although the unaided eye cannot distinguish the individual cilia, the cilia of a comb row collectively have a shimmering opalescence that is sometimes readily apparent.

Our most common comb jelly is the "sea gooseberry," *Pleurobrachia bachei* (fig. 19). It is probably present throughout the year in our area, but is rare in winter and not likely to be seen unless the plankton is sampled thoroughly. It begins to become common in the spring and generally reaches a peak of abundance in summer. Specimens are often washed up on beaches. If they have not been

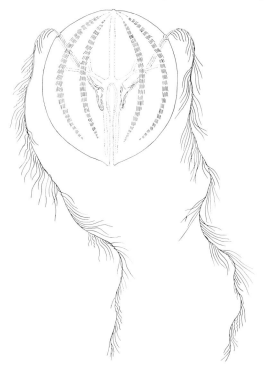

19. *Pleurobrachia bachei*

out of the water long, and if the day is cool, some of them will re-
vive if put into a jar of sea water.

Pleurobrachia is approximately egg-shaped, and a large specimen is about 1.5 cm long. The mouth is situated at one end—the
oral end—and opens into what can be called a stomach, from
which a number of canals constituting the rest of the digestive tract
arise. At the end opposite the mouth—the aboral end—there is a
complicated little organ of balance, in which a crystalline mass
rests on sensory cilia and is roofed over by a transparent dome also
consisting of cilia. Closer to the aboral end than to the oral end are
the sheaths in which the two tentacles originate and into which they
can be retracted. When the tentacles are extended, they may be
nearly 15 cm long, and their numerous fine side branches confer a
cobwebby appearance on the tentacles as a whole. As these tentacles are dragged through the water, adhesive "glue cells" (collo-

blasts) on them become discharged when they touch prospective prey organisms, such as copepods and other small crustacea. The tentacles then contract, bringing the trapped prey to the mouth. *Pleurobrachia* will usually survive for a number of days in a large jar of cool sea water and is uninhibited about extending its tentacles. If some copepods are added, it may eventually trap some of these and push them into the mouth.

Although *Pleurobrachia* is decidedly our most common ctenophore, a species of *Bolinopsis* is sometimes abundant, and *Beroë* is a pleasant surprise on occasion. *Bolinopsis* is distinctive because of its slightly compressed, helmet-shaped body, much of which consists of two oral lobes. The principal tentacles, comparable to those of *Pleurobrachia,* are short and originate close to the mouth; some other small tentacles lie in grooves leading toward the mouth. The comb rows are conspicuous, but four are shorter than the rest; none of them runs the full length of the body. *Bolinopsis* is beautifully luminescent. A large specimen is about 3 cm tall.

Beroë (fig. 20), when we are lucky enough to have it come in with prevailing currents, is impressive. It is shaped something like a cucumber and may be 7 or 8 cm long. The mouth and pharynx are capacious and can take in crustaceans of considerable size, as well as its own relative, *Pleurobrachia*. A striking feature is the honeycombed appearance of the body which results from the fur-

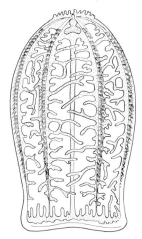

20. *Beroë*

ther division of the main branches of the digestive cavity into numerous ramifying and interdigitating diverticula. *Beroë* is another of the marvelously luminescent ctenophores.

FLATWORMS

There are many kinds of turbellarian flatworms crawling over seaweeds and over clumps of mussels, hydroids, and other animals attached to floats. Most of these turbellarians are less than a millimeter long and are not likely to be observed except with the aid of a low-power microscope. Some of them are herbivores grazing principally on diatoms, others are carnivores feeding on small crustaceans or other invertebrates. They fall into several rather separate groups, and our fauna of small turbellaria is essentially unknown. Few of the many species in this area have been named and described, and their habits and ecological relationships with other organisms are also in need of study.

Occasionally, a large turbellarian, belonging to the group called polyclads, will be found crawling over the surface of a float or will emerge from material brought back to the laboratory for sorting. Our largest species, not really characteristic of the fauna of floats but sometimes found on them, is *Kaburakia excelsa*. It reaches a length of more than 5 cm, but is only about 2 or 3 mm thick when extended and in tight contact with the substrate. Its usual color is tan or grayish brown. It has little black spots, consisting of pigment associated with its light-receptor organs, along the entire margin of the body, as well as on a pair of short tentacles situated near the anterior end, at the base of these tentacles, and in the region of the brain. Other polyclads that may be encountered on floats are about 1 or 2 cm long. Most of them do not have tentacles, and the pigmented eyespots are generally restricted to the region of the brain. The species shown in Figure 21 is typical.

All polyclads are carnivores, feeding on crustaceans, molluscs, worms, ascidians, and other invertebrates. They have a much-branched digestive tract, to which the name polyclad alludes. The mouth is usually near the middle of the ventral surface, and in most species there is a large, eversible, ruffled pharynx which can be extended like an umbrella over the prey. Digestion is generally begun while the pharynx is out, and a combination of ciliary and muscular activity brings partly digested food into the branched

21. A typical medium-sized polyclad
flatworm

digestive tract, where digestion is completed. As the digestive system of polyclads, like that of other turbellarians, is just an elaborately branched sac, indigestible residues must be voided through the mouth.

NEMERTEANS

It is unusual to find nemerteans just crawling around on exposed surfaces of floats. However, careful examination of clumps of algae, tunicates, mussels, tube-dwelling polychaetes, and other invertebrates may reveal one or more small species, mostly under 2 cm long. Occasionally a large nemertean may turn up in a bucket of material scraped off the floats. The most common large species encountered in this situation in our area seems to be *Tubulanus sexlineatus*. This worm may be about 50 cm long when fully extended, and its thickness is about a quarter of that of a pencil. Its background color of chocolate brown is interrupted by evenly spaced white rings and five or six longitudinal white lines (the specific name, *sexlineatus,* means "six-lined"), one of which runs right down the middle of the upper surface. *T. sexlineatus* inhabits a parchmentlike tube, and specimens in captivity soon secrete new tubes around themselves. Like nearly all nemerteans, this species is a predator, using its eversible proboscis to trap polychaetes and perhaps other animals.

POLYCHAETE ANNELIDS

Of the more obvious polychaetes, representatives of the two families of plume worms—the sabellids and the serpulids—are especially prominent. The sabellids generally construct leathery tubes, and the anteriormost part of the body (prostomium) is modified into a number of featherlike cirri ("tentacles" is a less desirable term for them) which, when they are expanded, collectively resemble a feather duster. On the inner face of the main stem and on each fine side branch of a cirrus is a broad tract of crowded, short cilia. Currents of water set up by some larger cilia bring tiny particles of food into the crown of cirri, and mucus on the ciliated tracts traps particles that are in a suitable size range. The film of mucus and food is moved down the side branches and then down the main stems of the cirri to a right and a left collecting groove that direct the film to the mouth.

As the tubes of sabellids are blind at their lower ends, these worms must have some kind of a system for transporting digestive wastes and reproductive cells out through the mouths of the tubes. Sabellids have ciliated tracts that move fecal material from the posterior end of the body forward to the open end of the tube. Eggs and sperms released into the space around the animal by sexually ripe segments are likewise carried forward by these ciliary tracts.

At least four species of sabellids are encountered on floats, but only two of them are apt to be common and regularly present. The most abundant species is invariably *Schizobranchia insignis* (pl. VI), whose cirri—colored red, orange, brown, gray, or greenish— fork dichotomously several times and thus are like branched feathers. Its tubes are up to about 20 cm long, and their diameter may exceed that of a pencil. *Schizobranchia* sometimes forms huge masses and thus provides a hiding place for some animals and a substrate to which others can become attached.

Pseudopotamilla ocellata (pl. VI) is a little smaller than *Schizobranchia*. Its cirri are characteristically a light tan color, though they may be banded with brown, and they have conspicuous, darkly pigmented eyespots. In structure, the cirri of *Pseudopotamilla* are distinctly different from those of *Schizobranchia* because they are simply featherlike; the main stems do not fork.

On the outside of tubes of *Schizobranchia* and *Pseudopotamilla,* right at the edge of the opening, there is generally a growth of a small hydroid, *Proboscidactyla flavicirrata* (figs. 22 and 23), in which the feeding polyps have only two tentacles. To really appreciate this little gem, one has to examine it with a low-power microscope. The feeding polyps, connected together by a stolon creeping

22. A group of feeding polyps of *Proboscidactyla flavicirrata;* photomicrograph

23. A reproductive polyp of *Proboscidactyla flavicirrata* producing medusae

over the surface of the tube, have their tall mouth cones raised well above the bases of the tentacles. Collectively they may resemble circles of ballet dancers in various poses. Also arising from the stolon are some simple, fingerlike polyps and reproductive polyps which bud off medusae from near their free ends. The medusae, as in other hydroids, represent the sexual generation. They mature after being set free, gradually developing about sixty tentacles, but are only about 1 cm in diameter when full grown. They are unusual because the four radial canals they start out with branch repeatedly, and the number of ultimate branches coincides with the number of tentacles.

Proboscidactyla may for the moment be considered a commensal symbiont, profiting by living in a situation where food of appropriate types is brought within its grasp by currents of water set up by its hosts. As the tube of *Schizobranchia* or *Pseudopotamilla* is enlarged, the hydroid keeps propagating itself to keep up with the edge, and the older part of the colony dies away. Experimental work on *Proboscidactyla* has demonstrated that close contact of the feeding polyps with the cirri of the sabellid host is essential to maintain a differentiated colony. In the absence of such contact, the colony deteriorates.

Two other sabellids likely to be found on floats are *Eudistylia vancouveri* and *Myxicola infundibulum. Eudistylia* (pl. VI) is larger than *Schizobranchia,* with tubes reaching a diameter of more than 1 cm. The cirri are simply pinnate, like those of *Pseudopotamilla,* and are richly colored by alternating bands of maroon and dark green.

Myxicola is quite unusual because its tubes consist of a transparent mucus and its cirri, which are practically colorless, are united for more than half their length by delicate membranes, thus forming a funnel. On floats, *Myxicola* tends to be scattered and solitary, and is most often found as a stranger among other sabellids or in clumps of ascidians.

The other group of tube-dwelling worms that invariably catches one's attention in visits to floating docks is the serpulids. They secrete calcareous tubes about themselves; and, although they have featherlike cirri similar to those of sabellids, they also have a device for closing the tube after withdrawing. This soft structure, called the operculum, is shaped something like a golf tee; it is, in fact, a striking specialization of prostomial outgrowths comparable to those that develop into cirri. Serpulids feed in much the same way as sabellids, trapping microscopic food on ciliary-mucus tracts and conveying it to the mouth.

Our only large serpulid is *Serpula vermicularis* (pl. VI). Its coiled or rambling white tubes, up to about 10 cm long, are readily recognized if they are not overgrown by other organisms. The cirri and operculum are usually red. It is common to find specimens that have two opercula functioning together to close the tube.

There may be several tiny serpulids of the genus *Spirorbis* (fig. 24) in a single square centimeter of a hard substrate such as fiberglass or concrete, unless this happens to be heavily overgrown by other colonizers. *Spirorbis* is also common on shells of mussels and other molluscs. There are several species in our area, but they all

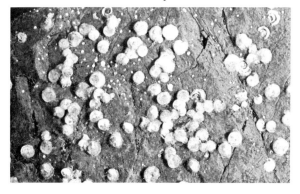

24. *Spirorbis*

look very much alike except to a specialist. The coils of their tubes are rarely more than 2 or 3 mm in diameter, but their cirri are usually reddish, so they look like miniature *Serpula*.

All serpulids and sabellids react quickly to touch, and sometimes also to sudden agitation of the water near them. They withdraw their cirri with great haste; but left alone, they will soon expand their flowerlike crowns and resume feeding.

When the holdfasts of seaweeds or clumps of worm tubes or other animals are detached, several species of polychaetes may be encountered. Two that are nearly ubiquitous in such situations— *Halosydna brevisetosa* and *Harmothoë imbricata*—are members of a group called scale worms (family Polynoidae). Most of the individuals found on floats are probably essentially free-living, although they are in hiding most of the time. Both species, however, are known to be involved in commensal relationships, especially with polychaetes of the family Terebellidae (sabellids seem not to harbor them within their tubes). They are carnivores, feeding on a variety of invertebrates, including other polychaetes.

H. brevisetosa (fig. 25) is the larger of the two, attaining a length of up to 5 cm. Its color varies, but it is generally gray or brownish gray, often with rather strong transverse bands. There are eighteen pairs of scales covering its dorsal surface.

25. *Halosydna brevisetosa,* a scale worm

H. imbricata is slightly smaller, rarely reaching 3 cm, and has only fifteen pairs of scales. It tends to be rather dark green or brown for the first few segments of the dorsal surface; behind this region, the coloration is generally a little lighter, with mottling of the scales, but without any distinct transverse banding. *Harmothoë* is one of the scale worms known to brood its eggs under the scales, releasing its young in a free-swimming stage called the trochophore.

BRYOZOANS

Some bryozoans may be confused with hydroids because they form branching colonies in which the individual animals have circles of delicate tentacles. However, bryozoans are much higher than hydroids on the evolutionary scale. Together with the phoronids and brachiopods, they constitute what is called the lophophorate phyla (the term "lophophore" applies to the group of tentacles). There are a number of reasons, based on our understanding of the internal and external anatomy of the animals in these phyla, for considering them to be closely related.

A close look at a bryozoan should dispel any illusions about its kinship to the hydroids. First of all, each individual, called a polypide, is enclosed within a separate "house," or zooecium. As the colony is built up by asexual reproduction, protoplasmic connections between polypides may persist, but these connections are at best tenuous. Recall that in hydroid colonies, the tissues and digestive cavity of one polyp are fully continuous with those of neighboring polyps. Also, when the polypide of a bryozoan is retracted, the entire animal is withdrawn into its zooecium by special muscles. In hydroids, the tentacles shorten and may bend inward—and in some species the whole polyp may contract until it is out of sight —but there are no special muscles for pulling it down into the theca. Other mechanisms are also involved in the withdrawal of a bryozoan. If the zooecium has an operculum for complete closure, as it often does, a special set of muscles operates this movement. In addition, there may be muscles that pull on the wall of the zooecium, or that operate in other ways, to effect an increase in hydrostatic pressure sufficient to force the lophophoral end of the polypide out again.

Of course, bryozoans have no stinging capsules, and they are basically filter feeders, not carnivores. Ciliary activity moves water through the lophophore, and particles of appropriate size and character are driven by cilia into the mouth. The digestive tract is

U-shaped and complete, leading to an anus located to one side of the lophophore.

The bryozoans discussed so far have been only feeding individuals. The colonies of many bryozoans are polymorphic, with some individuals specialized for functions other than feeding and reproduction. For instance, a type of individual called the avicularium resembles the beak of a bird, with muscles for closing one jaw against the other. A vibraculum is an individual modified into a vibratile process. Both the avicularia and vibracula seem to function in discouraging unwelcome settlers.

Bryozoan colonies come in many different forms. I have already mentioned the branching types that look something like hydroids. Some species form flat, encrusting growths or leaflike colonies that are connected to the substrate only at one point. Others form branching calcareous masses that superficially resemble certain corals, and one group has brownish cartilaginous colonies that may be mistaken for seaweeds. The classification of bryozoans is so complicated that a superficial review of it would be worse than none.

On the floats, the arborescent type is regularly represented by *Bugula* (figs. 26 and 27). It looks lacy and soft, but its actual tex-

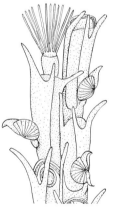

26. *Bugula*

27. Portion of a branch of *Bugula,* as seen with a microscope, showing an extended polypide and several avicularia

ture is brittle and gritty, for it is to some extent calcified. The pattern of branching is such that a colony of any size—a large one is about 4 or 5 cm high—exhibits a distinctly spiral configuration. Much of the colony consists of zooecia that no longer contain living polypides; but the upper portions should show plenty of active tentaculate individuals as well as the beaked avicularia. The dark brown bodies found in many of the zooecia are the remains of disintegrated organs.

Growing over the flat blades of brown algae, such as *Laminaria saccharina,* are silvery patches of an encrusting species, *Membranipora membranacea* (fig. 28). It is common only during the late

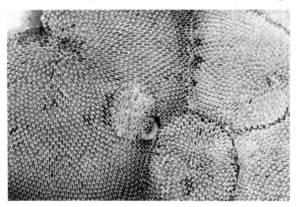

28. Contiguous colonies of *Membranipora,* with the sea slug *Doridella steinbergae* and its egg mass

spring and summer. The colonies are often nearly circular. The orderly asexual reproduction by the peripheral zooids arranges the zooids in radiating series that branch and rebranch. The opaque white lines (marking the thin, calcified walls of the zooecia) and more nearly translucent areas occupied by the polypides themselves form a pattern resembling fine lacework.

Some colonies of *Membranipora,* after being taken out of the water, have what look like little lumps of jelly of about the same color as the colony. If the colony is submerged in clean sea water and examined with a strong hand lens or a low-power microscope, the little blobs may prove to be one of the marine zoologist's delights, *Doridella steinbergae* (fig. 28). This is a tiny, flattened sea slug whose length does not quite reach 1 cm. Its color pattern—

white lines on a translucent and nearly colorless background—
almost perfectly matches that of *Membranipora*. A close look at an
active *Doridella* will reveal the two to four pairs of branched gills
on either side of the anus at the posterior end. *Doridella* is specialized for grazing on the polypides of *Membranipora* and rarely ventures off its pastureland. Its eggs are laid in little crescentic masses.

Corambe pacifica is also sometimes found in *Membranipora* in
our area. It has more gills on either side of the anus than *Doridella*
does, and there is a distinct notch at the posterior end of the dorsal
surface. Both *Doridella* and *Corambe* belong to a group of sea
slugs called dorids, which typically have a circle of gills around the
anus situated on the dorsal surface in the posterior part of the
body.

Another encrusting bryozoan, found at all seasons, is *Schizoporella bicornis*. Colored a dingy orange, it grows on shells of mussels
and barnacles as well as concrete and fiberglass. Its colonies are
much less regular and also thicker than those of *Membranipora*.
This particular species of *Schizoporella* is thought to have been introduced to this area with oyster spat from Japan.

Dendrobeania lichenoides (fig. 29) forms a flexible growth that
is somewhat leaflike. The older portion of the colony develops in
tight contact with the substrate, so there is a little stalk from which
the free foliar portion spreads out. *Dendrobeania* is usually pale
brownish white or tan, and on floats it seems generally to prefer to
settle on tubes of sabellid polychaetes. It is often mixed with *Bug-*

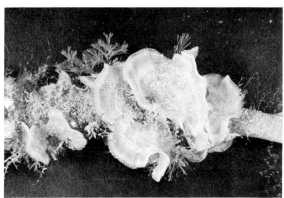

29. *Dendrobeania lichenoides*

ula, hydroids, sponges, and other organisms that have a liking for the same type of situation.

CRUSTACEANS

Among crustaceans that live in close contact with the substrate but are not permanently cemented to it, the copepods, amphipods, isopods, and certain shrimps are the more common. The copepods are mostly of a type called harpacticoids, which grub about for detritus and microscopic algae. They are small—generally under 1 mm long—and there are numerous species about which we know all too little. A picture of one of them (fig. 30) will show their general appearance.

30. Harpacticoid copepod

Ostracods have a bivalve shell, and thus may resemble tiny clams. However, their jointed appendages, which typically include three pairs of legs, antennules, and antennae, as well as mouth parts, show that they are crustaceans. Most ostracods are under 2 mm long. The shells are often sculptured or studded with bristles, and sometimes are opaque. Figure 31 shows a relatively delicate,

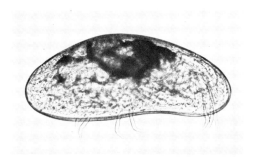

31. Ostracod

transparent species common on floats. There are many others in the sediment on worm tubes, colonies of barnacles, and similar situations.

Planktonic Copepods

A variety of smaller crustacea may be seen swimming near the surface. Some of them are large-eyed, truly planktonic amphipods or else other amphipods that have briefly cut themselves loose from the bottom or from the mat of vegetation on the floats. However, during late spring, summer, and early autumn, planktonic copepods are abundant. These belong to a group we call calanoid copepods (fig. 32), characterized by first antennae (antennules) that are long and have more than twenty articles, and by a body in which

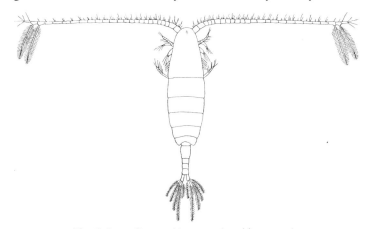

32. *Calanus finmarchicus,* a calanoid copepod

the posterior portion is distinctly set apart from the larger, anterior portion. In both these respects they are quite different from the harpacticoids found grubbing in sediment. Calanoids move jerkily, using their antennules and thoracic limbs for propulsion. The mouth parts and second antennae create currents from which microscopic food is strained. Calanoids are extremely important in the food chain, for they are herbivores, feeding on diatoms and other photosynthetic primary producers, and are in turn eaten by small fishes or by other organisms eventually eaten by fishes. Most calanoids are under 2 mm long, and when they are colorless they may be overlooked. However, those that store up red and orange carotenoid pigments from the plant food they consume are easily visible.

Amphipods

Amphipods (fig. 33) are plentiful among algae and other growths. Some actually feed on algae, and certain species may even build little nests from pieces of seaweed that they stick together.

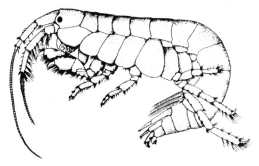

33. Amphipod

Those closely associated with seaweeds are often the same color: for instance, there are some on *Ulva* that are bright green. Most of the amphipods in shore situations are somewhat compressed laterally and have long antennules and antennae. The last three pairs of abdominal appendages are nearly as conspicuous as the seven pairs of legs. (The name Amphipoda was given to the group in allusion to the "legs" at both ends of the body.) No attempt will be made to characterize any of the look-alike amphipods we have. The largest on floats seem to be members of the genus *Amphithoë* and are about 3 cm long.

Where silt and detritus accumulate, as among growths of other organisms, some small amphipods of the genus *Corophium* (fig. 34) may form masses of soft, muddy tubes. The distinctive characteristics of *Corophium* include a body that is slightly flattened dorsoventrally instead of laterally, and proportionately stout antennae. Our species rarely exceed 1 cm in length, including the antennae. *Corophium* feeds by processing water for its detritus content. Certain of the abdominal appendages create currents, and the fringes of fine hairs on the legs farther forward strain out the

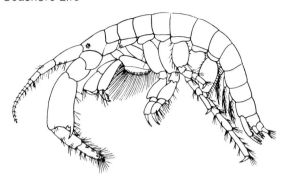

34. *Corophium,* an amphipod

food, which is then scraped off by the mouth parts. Although *Coro-phium* is found on floats almost everywhere, it is particularly abundant in estuarine situations where the salinity is reduced and silting is heavy.

Some strange amphipods of a totally different group, the sub-order Caprellidea, have already been mentioned in connection with *Obelia* and other hydroids. Caprellids (fig. 35) have no ab-domen to speak of, and the surviving abdominal appendages are vestigial. The thoracic segments are long and slender, and as a re-sult the legs are widely spaced. In some caprellids, certain legs are missing altogether, although the gills that typically grow from the bases of the legs survive as little fleshy pads or clubs. As in typical amphipods, however, the female has a thoracic pouch, covered by

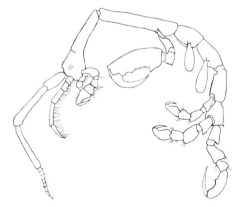

35. *Caprella equilibra* (male), a caprellid amphipod

some large, overlapping plates, in which the young develop. Because the body of a caprellid is so slender and the legs are so far apart, a brood pouch full of eggs or young is more noticeable than it is in most amphipods.

Caprellids are sometimes called skeleton shrimps, a name that suits them well. They remind one of a praying mantis, partly because of their general form and partly because of the appearance of their prehensile first and second legs. They remain motionless much of the time, attached by posterior legs and poised to grasp at food, which seems to consist mainly of diatoms and detritus. It is interesting to watch their looping movements: they attach by their front legs as they let go with their hind legs, then attach by their hind legs again.

Isopods

The most common and conspicuous isopod is *Idotea wosnesenskii* (fig. 85). It is about 3 or 4 cm long, and the color is generally olive green, but varies from rather bright green through brown to nearly black. The posterior quarter of the body (the abdominal region) is mostly unsegmented; its terminal portion is rather smoothly rounded, except for a tiny blunt tooth at the tip. When picked up, it may almost reflexly cling to a finger with its seven pairs of claw-tipped legs. On floats, *Idotea* hangs onto holdfasts, stalks, and blades of seaweeds, and to worm tubes and other objects. However, though it may be abundant in this general situation, it is still more common under rocks on the shore.

Wooden floats and pilings that have been in the water for a few years are usually riddled by burrows of a tiny isopod, *Limnoria lignorum* (the "gribble") (fig. 36) and those of a clam, *Bankia setacea* (the "shipworm"). Together or separately, the gribble and the shipworm cause an enormous amount of damage and could be called the "termites of the sea." (The shipworm is discussed more fully later in this chapter.)

The burrows of the gribble are small, as the animal itself, looking like a miniature sow bug, is only about 3 mm long. However, by the time a piece of wood has been worked over by a thriving population, it will be a spongy mess. The gribble's mouth parts rasp away the wood, and the small particles pass rather quickly through the digestive tract. Exactly how the cellulose is

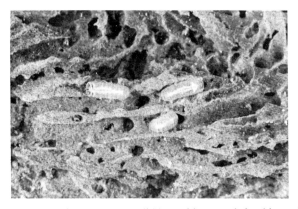

36. *Limnoria lignorum*, the gribble, and its tunnels in old wood

degraded into simpler compounds which might be of use to the animal, and how proteins and other essential foods are obtained, has never been satisfactorily explained. In any case, the burrows of the gribble expose more of the wood's surface to destructive bacteria and fungi.

An isopod sometimes found on floats and pilings is *Gnorimosphaeroma oregonensis* (fig. 86). It is a small species, only about 1 cm long, and is similar to the terrestrial pill bug in form and in its ability to roll up into a ball. Its color is basically a drab, mottled gray. *Gnorimosphaeroma* is most likely to be found living under mussels, among barnacles, or in cavities in wood mined by shipworms and the gribble, *Limnoria*. Large populations of it are usually an indication that the salinity is at least a little below that of full-strength sea water.

Shrimps

Clinging to seaweeds, and generally going unnoticed until they flop off when a bunch of weed is lifted, are the "broken-back" shrimps of the genus *Heptacarpus* (fig. 37). They range from about 2 to 3 cm in length and are characterized by a sharp bend in the region of the third abdominal segment. Like some other shrimps, and also crayfishes, they propel themselves backward by rapidly flexing their tails forward, so that they are momentarily almost U-shaped. Most broken-back shrimps have a translucent look and generally are colored green, olive, brown, or reddish brown, often with some opaque white markings or darker streaks, especially on the thorax.

Once in awhile, the relatively large, nearly straight-bodied shrimps of the genus *Pandalus* are seen gingerly poised on the floats or swimming by. These are the commercially important

37. *Heptacarpus,* a broken-back shrimp

shrimps of our region and may reach a length of 15 cm or more. The coon-stripe shrimp, *P. danae* (fig. 38), with rather strong brown, red, and nearly white markings, is perhaps the one most likely to occur around floats.

38. *Pandalus danae,* the coon-stripe shrimp

Crabs

The crabs on floats are chiefly those that look something like spiders, because of their proportionately long and slender legs. The kelp crab, *Pugettia producta* (fig. 149), is the largest of these, its carapace attaining a length of 5 cm or more. Its coloration is on the whole olive or olive brown, but there may be some attractive red or orange tones on the lower surface. The upper side of the carapace is smooth and does not normally accumulate growths of small seaweeds or sessile animals such as sponges or bryozoans.

Pugettia gracilis (fig. 215) is a smaller cousin of *P. producta*. Unlike the latter, its upper surface is somewhat roughened and almost always has some algae and animals growing on it, so that its reddish brown color may be almost completely obscured. Crabs that allow other organisms to grow on them, or that actually stick these organisms on their carapaces, are called decorator crabs. Even more inclined to be decorated is *Oregonia gracilis* (fig. 150). This species has a carapace that is almost triangular in shape, with its narrowed anterior end prolonged into two long, nearly parallel rostral horns. The color is mostly light tan, and is just about matched by the color of the sponges, hydroids, and bryozoans that are usually found on the carapace and frequently on the legs as well.

Barnacles

Two species of barnacles are regularly found on floats and pilings. One of them, *Balanus glandula* (fig. 67), is the most nearly ubiquitous of the barnacles on the Pacific coast, and is the one apt to be found on boats and in harbors where the salinity fluctuates a great deal. It also colonizes rocks, and its distribution in rocky areas is discussed in Chapter 4. A large specimen is about 1.5 cm across, and the height is usually about equal to, or a little greater than, the diameter. However, specimens in crowded masses tend to be nearly columnar. The plates of the shell, unless covered by diatoms or otherwise overgrown, are usually whitish and rather smooth.

Where the salinity approximates that of full-strength sea water, floats and pilings are frequently populated by *Balanus cariosus* (fig. 76). This species, like *B. glandula,* is common on rocks, and it will be discussed again in connection with intertidal situations. Its diameter may reach 5 cm. Specimens growing singly demonstrate the characteristic ridges and furrows of the shell plates; the ridges actually consist of poorly defined spines that point downward and tend to fuse together. When *B. cariosus* forms dense masses, it is forced to grow into a columnar shape, and the ridges normally present on the shell do not develop to any great extent. On floats, however, *B. cariosus* does not often become crowded and tends to be distinctly below the water line. *B. glandula,* on the other hand, forms sizable populations at or even slightly above the water line, and those above the surface are wet only when the water is agitated. On pilings, almost all of the barnacles that are at levels reached only by higher tides are *B. glandula,* unless *Chthamalus dalli* (fig. 66) is present.

Since barnacles are crustaceans, related to crabs, lobsters, and shrimps, it is logical that they should be remarkably specialized. In the so-called acorn barnacles, such as *Balanus,* the shell consists of a number of overlapping plates, and some other plates, controlled by muscles, close the opening at the top of the shell. All of the plates are secreted by a sort of mantle that surrounds the soft parts of the animal. The barnacle's counterparts of a crab's legs are six pairs of what look like rather soft, branched feathers, called cirri. As the cirri are rhythmically extended and retracted, they quite literally comb the water for microscopic food. The mouth parts collect the material strained out by the cirri and move it to the mouth.

Although adult barnacles might not easily be accepted as crustaceans, their life history includes certain developmental stages that positively establish the relationship. The first larval stage, called a nauplius, is similar to the nauplius of other groups of crustacea in having three pairs of appendages: the antennules, antennae, and mandibles of later stages. However, the barnacle nauplius is unique in having a pair of extensions, resembling handlebars, arising laterally from the anterior part of the carapace. After some changes and additions, accomplished between several molts, the developing barnacle arrives at the cypris stage. This has the appendages of the nauplius, some additional mouth parts, and six pairs of thoracic limbs. If this cypris settles on a suitable substrate, it fastens itself with the help of a cement produced by glands associated with the antennules. The bivalve shell of the cypris is lost, and the complex metamorphosis into a barnacle is completed. The limbs of the cypris survive as the food-catching cirri.

MOLLUSCS

Chitons

The chitons most likely to be found on floats are *Tonicella lineata* (pl. VII) and any of the three species of *Mopalia* of our region: *M. muscosa* (fig. 128), *M. ciliata* (fig. 129), and *M. lignosa* (fig. 130). All of these species are described in the section on rocky shores, as they are not often encountered on floats.

Limpets

Collisella pelta (Acmaea pelta) (fig. 77) is the only limpet one can expect to find on floats. It has a rather tall shell, in which the apex is nearer the middle than the anterior edge. The length reaches about 4 cm. As this species is typically found on rocky shores, it is discussed in more detail in Chapter 4.

Sea Slugs

Many species of nudibranch gastropods ("sea slugs") are known to occur on floats in our region, but only a few of these are "regulars." Some are inseparably linked to other invertebrates. Two of them, *Doridella* and *Corambe,* have been discussed in connection with the bryozoan *Membranipora. Eubranchus,* which lives on *Obelia,* will be mentioned shortly.

Hermissenda crassicornis (pl. VIII) is perhaps the most nearly ubiquitous of our nudibranchs. It is found in beds of eelgrass and in rocky intertidal areas, and is sometimes the prevailing larger species on floats. It belongs to a group of nudibranchs called eolids (or aeolids), characterized by the presence of numerous fleshy dorsal processes called cerata (in addition to the pair of club-shaped tentacles called rhinophores, on the head) and also by the absence of any plumelike gills around the anus. In *Hermissenda,* the cerata, set on a translucent and nearly white body, have an orange band close to their ends and are finally capped with white. The brown cores of the cerata are actually branches of the liverlike digestive gland, which go up into them. The coloration displays some other distinctive features. An orange band runs some distance backward from between the rhinophores, and there is frequently a similar band farther posteriorly. These orange bands are bordered by opaque white or electric blue lines which begin on the tentacles and run to the tip of the tail. A large *Hermissenda* is about 5 cm long when it is stretched out.

Although most nudibranchs are rather particular about what they eat, *Hermissenda* is not fussy. It consumes, among other things, hydroids, ascidians, other molluscs, eggs of various sorts, and pieces of fish. Some of the stinging capsules it ingests with hydroids end up in the tips of the cerata, where they are stored in an unexploded state. By pulling off one of the cerata, mounting it under a cover glass, and examining it with a microscope, one can observe the concentration of stinging capsules. Many eolid nudibranchs store these structures, and they probably have a protective function.

Aeolidia papillosa (fig. 39) is an eolid just a little larger than *Hermissenda* and about as adaptable as far as habitats are concerned. However, it is considerably more choosy about food and apparently eats anemones almost exclusively. On floats, of course, the variety of anemones available to it is restricted, but it will take both *Metridium* and *Tealia*. The body of *Aeolidia* is whitish and translucent, with some gray or brown spots, and usually has a large, triangular white patch, devoid of cerata, in the area in front of the rhinophores. The cerata are typically grayish brown, sometimes with white tips, but they can be almost colorless. They are so numerous and so crowded that *Aeolidia* looks like a shaggy little mouse.

39. *Aeolidea papillosa*

Colonies of *Obelia* (especially *O. longissima*) are generally inhabited by the tiny eolid, *Eubranchus olivaceus* (fig. 6). It is pale yellowish green and has both dark and light flecks. Its relatively few cerata are swollen and bumpy to the point of nearly branching.

Mature specimens are about 6 or 7 mm long. *Eubranchus* is a predator on *Obelia* and nips off the polyps as it wanders through its horn of plenty. Its little egg masses are regularly found along with it. A rather different group of nudibranchs, called dendronotids, are represented in our area by several species of *Dendronotus*. In dendronotids, the cerata are branched; and as the ultimate branches have sharp tips, the cerata in some species look a bit like thorny bushes. Around the rhinophores are sheaths with extensions in the form of simple or branched papillae. Unfortunately, only two species of these beautiful animals, *D. frondosus* and *D. rufus,* are found on floats; the rest are subtidal. *D. frondosus* (pl. VIII) is generally not over 4 cm long. Its color varies immensely, and specimens taken on floats are usually quite different from those collected in deeper water. The body as a whole may be almost completely white, with just some pinkish brown spots; it may be pale brown with yellow or white on the cerata and elsewhere; or it may be dark reddish brown with white or yellow markings. *D. frondosus* eats a variety of hydroids, including *Tubularia* and *Coryne* among the athecate types and *Obelia* among the thecate types. On floats it seems to prefer the latter, of which there is no shortage.

D. rufus is a large species, attaining a length of nearly 30 cm. It has from six to nine pairs of bushy cerata and several smaller cerata as well. The background color of the upper surface is usually white, with the branches of the cerata and of the rhinophores being dark reddish brown or dull magenta. In most specimens, there is a magenta line around the upper part of the foot. *D. rufus* feeds to a large extent on the scyphistomae of jellyfishes, and its presence on floats is a good indication that there are plenty of these little polyps, even if they are almost all on the underside.

The dorid nudibranchs, another large category, do not have true cerata into which branches of the digestive gland ascend. They may, however, have dorsal tubercles and other fleshy processes. Their hallmark is a circle of featherlike gills surrounding the anus, which is located on the dorsal surface in the posterior region of the body. A common and sometimes beautiful dorid found on floats, as well as in rocky intertidal situations, is *Archidoris montereyensis,* the sea lemon (pl. IX). Its color is basically yellow, but the exact shade and intensity vary. There are patches of black pigment on the tubercles as well as on the areas between them. *A. monterey-*

ensis commonly reaches a length of about 5 cm. Its diet seems to consist entirely of sponges, especially *Halichondria*.

Archidoris odhneri (pl. IX) looks something like an albino version of *A. montereyensis*, being absolutely white. Its food preferences are similar. Most larger specimens are between about 5 and 6 cm long.

Diaulula sandiegensis (pl. X) is another sponge eater, working on both *Halichondria* and *Haliclona*. Its basic color is generally pale gray, with several conspicuous rings or blotches of blackish brown superimposed on it. The dorsal surface is very firm and feels almost gritty because of the many small, hairlike projections of the skin. The six gills can be completely retracted. Large specimens may be nearly 8 cm long, but most fall into the range of 4 to 5 cm.

A dorid seen occasionally is *Acanthodoris brunnea*. Its body is rather stout, with a maximum length of about 2.5 cm. The background color of the dorsal surface is pale brown; over this, between and on the tubercles, are numerous flecks of blackish pigment. The anal gills and some little elevations on the surface of the body are tipped with pale yellow, but the most colorful part of most specimens is the bright yellow margin at the edge of the mantle. *Acanthodoris'* food preference is for bryozoans.

Mussels, Scallops, and Other Bivalves

The bivalves found on floats and pilings are firmly attached to the substrate by a byssus, secreted by a gland at the base of the foot. The foot of such bivalves is much reduced when compared with that of clams that burrow in mud or sand.

The prevailing bivalve on floats and pilings is *Mytilus edulis,* the edible mussel (fig. 90). Its byssus is composed of many brownish threads—looking more vegetable than animal in texture—extending out ventrally between the valves. The byssus threads are somewhat elastic, but hold the animal firmly to the substrate. The shell of *M. edulis* reaches a length of about 6 cm and varies considerably in color. Typically, it is dark blue-black or brownish black, but young specimens are often brown. Like almost all bivalves, *Mytilus* is a filter feeder. In an animal that is actively processing water from which the ctenidia, or gills, collect microscopic food, the exhalant siphon is just evident at the rounded, posterior end. There is no real inhalant siphon, as water enters by a rather broad gape on the ventral side, between the right and left folds of the mantle.

The dense masses formed by *M. edulis* provide protection and other biological necessities for many other organisms. The shells themselves serve as a substrate to which a variety of animals, as barnacles, hydroids, bryozoans, and ascidians, may become attached. On pilings, this mussel has a wide vertical range, and some populations are so high that they are out of water much of the time.

The jingle shell, or rock oyster, *Pododesmus macroschisma* (fig. 40), is tightly stuck to the substrate by a heavy, hard byssus that emerges through a hole in one of the valves. The valves are nearly circular, sometimes 10 cm in diameter. If the animal happens to have settled on a substrate that is not flat, the shells will be deformed to follow its contour; some are bent nearly to a ninety-degree angle. The flesh of the jingle shell, which can be seen if the animal is actively pumping water and the valves are separated slightly, is bright orange.

40. *Pododesmus macroschisma*

Scallops (*Chlamys*) are primarily animals of deeper water and tend to be concentrated on substrates in which gravel and shells predominate. They lie with the right valve against the substrate and may be cemented down to this by a byssus secreted by a gland on the much-reduced foot. There are no siphons, as the mantle margins are separate all the way around. When the shell is agape and the animal is actively processing water from which its ctenidia collect microscopic food, the sensitive tentacles projecting from the edge of the mantle will be evident, and the shining blue-green ocelli (or eyes) may also be seen just inside the edge. The ocelli are sensitive to changes in light intensity and are rather complicated, but they probably do not form images. When stimulated by certain predators, as a sea star whose tube feet have contacted the mantle, the scallop claps its valves together repeatedly and may succeed in propelling itself away from danger. Of the species of scallops in Puget Sound and the San Juan Archipelago, one—*Chlamys hastata hericia,* the pink scallop (fig. 145)—is rather frequently seen in intertidal areas and on floats. Its shell is about 6 cm high. It differs from *C. rubida,* with which it is mixed subtidally, in having its radiating ribs roughened by small, arched spines, and also in having rougher margins.

The destruction of wooden timbers by the gribble, a small isopod, was discussed in the section on crustacea. The gribble is often joined in this enterprise by the shipworm, *Bankia setacea,* a decidedly bizarre bivalve mollusc. It is often referred to as *Teredo,* but genuine teredos are rarely reported in our area.

The shipworm's burrows (fig. 41) may be large enough to take a pencil comfortably. Unlike those of the gribble, which are concentrated in the superficial layers of a timber, they go very deep. When the microscopic planktonic larva of *Bankia* settles on a suitable substrate and metamorphoses into a tiny clam, it commences working its way into the timber. It digs by rocking its roughened

41. Burrows of the shipworm, *Bankia setacea,* in an old piling. The pallets of a deceased inhabitant are shown in one of the burrows.

shell with respect to its foot, rotating on the foot periodically, and thus carves out a neat, tubular burrow. The wood it rasps away goes into the digestive tract. At least some of the cellulose is converted by an enzyme (cellulase) into simpler carbohydrates that the shipworm can use as food. However, much of what it swallows seems to be undigested and passes out the anus, to be carried away by the current of water moving out of the exhalant siphon. *Bankia,* although adapted to a way of life quite different from that of most clams, has preserved the system of filter feeding characteristic of its relatives. Its ctenidia process water by ciliary action, and food, in the form of microscopic organisms and other particulate material, is moved to the mouth by ciliary-mucus tracts.

When a timber burrowed by *Bankia* is cracked open, a number of live animals may be found in the deeper portions. (Even timbers that have been lying on the beach for a few days may have live shipworms inside.) Note that the burrows generally follow the grain and do not break into one another. The shells of *Bankia* are small in proportion to the rest of the body and resemble little shields with a filelike decoration. They abut the head of the burrow, where they can do the most good (or the most harm, depending on how one looks at it). The odd, calcareous, featherlike structures, called pallets, often found even in inactive burrows serve to close the burrow when the siphons are retracted. Like the thin, calcareous film lining the burrow, the pallets are secreted by the mantle.

Squids

Squids are almost never seen at floats during the daytime, and it is unusual for them to show up at night. Specimens that do come into the range of dock lights are usually immature, but almost all of them can be referred to one or the other of two species, *Loligo opalescens* and *Gonatus fabricii.* In both, the mantle (the conical part of the body behind the head) reaches a length of about 15 cm. In *L. opalescens* (fig. 42), however, the eight arms and two specialized tentacles are shorter in proportion to the length of the mantle than they are in *G. fabricii* (fig. 43). The tail fins of *Loligo* are also less ample than those of *Gonatus.* Most squids, including our species, feed on small fishes, shrimps, and some other swimming invertebrates. They use their tentacles for capturing prey, the arms for

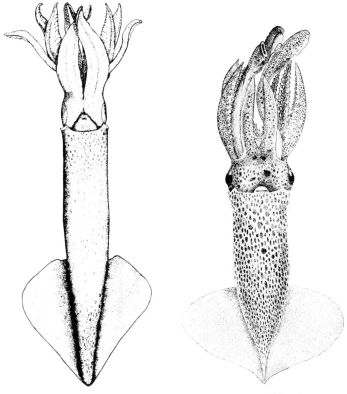

42. *Loligo opalescens*   43. *Gonatus fabricii* (an
                                  immature specimen)→

holding it securely, and the beaklike jaws for biting it until it is quiet and can be swallowed. Squids swim backward by jet propulsion, forcing water out of the mantle cavity through a funnellike extension of the latter.

Just about everything squids do is interesting, but the way they can change their pattern of pigmentation with respect to the substrate is particularly striking. When on a light background, a squid tends to contract its pigment-containing cells so that the pigment becomes concentrated in tiny, widely spaced flecks; the body as a whole thus becomes lighter. On a dark background, the pigment cells expand, diffusing the pigment over a larger area and making the body darker.

Once in a rare while, a giant squid, with a total length of 2 m or more, is washed up. It is usually dead for all practical purposes, but the pigment cells of the skin may still be reactive. This large species invariably proves to be *Moroteuthis robusta.*

ECHINODERMS

The fauna of echinoderms in our area is astonishingly rich, but little of it will be seen on the floats. At best, there are usually only two species of sea stars, two sea cucumbers, and one sea urchin.

Sea Stars

The sea stars found on floating docks and pilings are generally either *Pisaster ochraceus* (fig. 95; pl. XIII) or *Evasterias troschelii* (pl. XIII). Both are large: *Pisaster* regularly reaches a diameter of about 25 cm; larger specimens of *Evasterias* are usually in the range of 25 to 30 cm, but this species looks more graceful because its disk is smaller and its arms more slender. Within Puget Sound and the San Juan Archipelago, *Pisaster* belies its species name because it is represented almost exclusively by a vivid purple phase. The coloration of *Evasterias* is variable—it may be gray, gray-green, brown, or nearly red. It is never really purple, however. Both these sea stars are discussed in connection with rocky shores, but it is important to point out here that they are among the chief predators of the float fauna, taking a steady toll of mussels, other bivalves, and barnacles.

Solaster stimpsoni (pl. XIV) has been seen on floats, but it is evidently uncommon. It is usually found in the lower intertidal region of rocky shores and is therefore described in Chapter 4.

Sea Cucumbers

The principal cucumber on floats is *Eupentacta quinquesemita* (fig. 44), which is basically cream-colored and faintly tinged with orange or apricot. It attains a length of about 10 cm, but is usually hidden among masses of worm tubes or mussels. The tube feet are crowded and rather slender when fully extended; all five sets of them are well developed. The bushy tentacles around the mouth are modified tube feet and are interesting to watch. After an oral tentacle becomes more or less "saturated" with detritus and microscopic food organisms, it bends into the mouth as the accumu-

44. *Eupentacta quinquesemita*

lated material is licked off. Then another tentacle will do the same thing.

Eupentacta is among the many sea cucumbers that may become eviscerated when handled roughly or subjected to other forms of stress. A portion of the digestive tract and some other internal organs are simply ejected following a rupture of the body wall, usually at one end or the other. The missing parts are eventually regenerated. The eviscerative habit of *Eupentacta* (and of some of the other sea cucumbers in our area) works to the good fortune of a group of strange snails that live in the body cavity. These are modified to the extreme: they have no shells and look like soft, white worms. However, their affinities are betrayed by certain stages in their development, and especially by a type of larva called the veliger. The larvae would have no avenue of escape from the body cavity, and thus could not infect other sea cucumbers, if it were not for an occasional evisceration by the host.

Cucumaria miniata is a larger, reddish or reddish brown sea cucumber found on floats in some places. It is not common, so its description can be deferred until its typical habitat, the lowermost zone of the rocky intertidal region, is discussed in Chapter 4.

Sea Urchins

Of the several sea urchins in our area, the only one that seems able to survive on floats is *Strongylocentrotus droebachiensis,* the green sea urchin (pl. XVI). It is very abundant in rocky intertidal areas, as well as subtidally on various substrates. In favorable situations its test reaches a diameter of about 8 cm; on floats, where it is probably a bit out of place, it is rarely larger than 5 or 6 cm. This urchin feeds largely on algal growths, which it chews up with the aid of five sharp-toothed jaws. These jaws are organized into a beautifully unified structure called Aristotle's lantern.

In all of the echinoderms mentioned above, the eggs and sperms are discharged into the sea. If the eggs are fertilized, they develop into a distinctive planktonic stage that has bilateral symmetry instead of the radial symmetry characteristic of adult echinoderms. Presumably the animals on floats are derived from larvae that have merely settled and metamorphosed in this situation. These larvae, then, could have been derived from eggs shed by individuals living in completely different habitats many miles away.

CHAETOGNATHS

If the water surface is very quiet and the sun is shining brightly, you may see what looks like a sliver of ice, up to about 2 cm long, seemingly just suspended in the water. If you can capture it, you will probably find it to be an arrow worm, a member of the phylum Chaetognatha. *Sagitta elegans* (fig. 45) is the only species of this interesting group of marine animals found within our area, though others will be encountered in the open ocean. With few exceptions, they are strictly planktonic. Arrow worms are almost completely transparent, except for a pair of little black eyespots on the head, so they are next to impossible to see unless brightly illuminated from one side. However, they can be very numerous; and if a net is towed through the water for a few minutes, it may pick up many more than one might have expected on the basis of seeing a single specimen free in the water.

45. *Sagitta elegans,* an arrow worm

Arrow worms are an important link in the food chain, for they eat small crustacea and fish larvae, and serve in turn as food for other animals, especially certain fishes. *S. elegans* is more or less cosmopolitan and, along with some other organisms, has proved to be valuable for identifying water masses. In this respect it has helped researchers attempting to predict runs of herring.

Although much of an arrow worm's time is spent lying motionless, the prospect of a meal may cause it quite literally to spring into action. With powerful strokes of its finned tail, it quickly leaps a few lengths to where its sensory receptors indicate the prey is located, and its jaws, composed of stiff, sharp bristles, snap shut on the victim.

ASCIDIANS

Ascidians are filter-feeding animals that process sea water for the microscopic food it contains. By the activity of cilia, ascidians bring water through an incurrent opening (often on a siphonlike eminence) into a large perforated pharynx which functions as a kind of mechanical sieve. Fine particles and small microorganisms are trapped on ciliary-mucus tracts. The cilia then move the mucus containing the food to one side of the pharynx, and there the mucus is compacted into a string, which is directed by cilia into the digestive tract proper.

Around the pharynx is a cavity called the atrium, and the water entering the atrium from the pharynx leaves by way of a second opening, the excurrent (atrial) pore. The anus and ducts from the gonads (both testis and ovary are usually present in each individual) enter the atrium also, so wastes and gametes leave by the same pore as water that has been processed by the pharynx for the food.it may have contained.

The nature of an ascidian cannot be understood without an appreciation of its development. A larval stage, called the "tadpole," shows certain features that are lost or at least so much changed in the adult that they cannot readily be recognized. Some ascidians release their eggs and sperms into the sea as soon as they are ripe, and in these species the development of the tadpole takes place outside the body; others retain their eggs in the atrial cavity or in a pocket of the atrium that serves as a brood pouch, so that the tadpole develops there. In any case, the tadpole shows certain structures more clearly than the adult does. These structures are the notochord, a rodlike organ consisting of large, vacuolated cells running most of the length of the tail; and the nerve cord, which extends from the swollen anterior portion of the body into the tail, where it is dorsal to the notochord. The gut is blind and nonfunctional; and the pharynx, although it has a few gill slits already, is simple compared to what it will become after proliferation of many more openings. There are other complications of anatomy that need not be dealt with here. The main point is that the tadpole shows a plan of structure—pharyngeal slits, a notochord, and a dorsal nerve cord—somewhat like that in amphioxus and lampreys, and at least in embryos of other fishes and higher vertebrates. For this reason, ascidians have long been considered to be close relatives of vertebrates. But the relationship has been questioned, and we really do not know for certain if ascidians are evolutionarily tied to vertebrates.

The ascidian tadpole, when ready to develop further, usually has only a few hours to find a suitable substrate and to settle and metamorphose; otherwise it will die. By muscular activity of its tail, used in the fashion of a sculling oar, it drives its anterior end against the substrate. If it manages to stick in a favorable place (the adhesion is facilitated by some glandular papillae), the tail is resorbed and the body becomes completely reorganized. A tunic of a carbohydrate chemically related to cellulose is laid down around the animal. This tunic, although essentially a secreted layer, does have some living tissue and even blood vessels in it.

The heart of an ascidian has the curious ability to pump blood in either direction. It is a thin but muscular sac, which in the case of species with a transparent tunic may readily be seen without dissection. *Corella* is an admirable subject in which to observe the activity of the heart, whose contractions resemble the wringing out of a wet rag.

The ascidians found on floats can be divided into two groups:

46. *Ascidia callosa*

those that live singly (solitary ascidians) and those that form colonies consisting of several to many individuals embedded in a common matrix (compound ascidians). The colony of a compound ascidian is built up by asexual reproduction and coincident secretion of additional tunic material.

Solitary Ascidians

Of the five solitary ascidians to be considered here, two are particularly undistinguished in appearance. In both, the tunic is a translucent dingy brown and often supports a coating of diatoms and other small organisms. One species, *Ascidia callosa* (fig. 46), is more or less hemispherical, with its flattened lower side in tight contact with the substrate. The upper side shows two small elevations marking the incurrent and excurrent siphons. Larger specimens are about 3 cm in diameter. The other species, *Chelyosoma productum* (figs. 47 and 48), is very firm in texture and sharply truncate. The flat upper surface, on which both siphons are situated, is composed of thin, horny plates which are generally evident without magnification. Its diameter does not often exceed 2 cm.

47. *Chelyosoma productum*

Pyura haustor (fig. 49), like the two preceding ascidians, is broadly attached to the substrate, sometimes to another member of its own species. When extended, however, it is quite tall, reaching a height of about 5 cm. Its siphons are pronounced, smooth, and of a gorgeous pinkish red color. Over the rest of its body the tunic, usually brown or reddish brown, is thick, tough, and wrinkled. Bits

48. *Chelyosoma productum* (right) and *Distaplia occidentalis,* a compound ascidian (left)

49. *Pyura haustor*

of shell or other hard material may be embedded in it, and it may be colonized by various small organisms.

Boltenia villosa (fig. 50) is of a pale orange-brown color and is distinctly stalked, though the length of the stalk in proportion to the size of the body as a whole is variable. The most unusual characteristic of *Boltenia* is the presence of numerous hairlike outgrowths of the tunic. On floats, this species rarely approaches the maximum height (about 5 cm) attained by specimens found on

50. *Boltenia villosa*

rocky coasts, especially subtidally, but specimens up to 3 cm high are fairly common.

The most beautiful solitary ascidian on the floats is *Corella willmeriana* (fig. 51). Its tunic looks like ice, being colorless and generally free of encrusting organisms. Some of the internal organs—pharynx, digestive tract, and heart—can be recognized without having to be exposed by dissection. *Corella* may be attached to tubes of sabellids or mussels, but it is more often stuck to the float itself. It lives only about a year. Very large specimens, around 3 cm tall, are most likely to be found during the winter months. It is most striking when hundreds of individuals form tightly packed

51. *Corella willmeriana*

clusters, which resemble confections or sheets of lumpy ice. Such aggregations are more apt to be seen on the lower reaches of pilings exposed by very low tides than on floats.

Compound Ascidians

Of the compound ascidians found in our area, only two are regularly associated with floats. *Distaplia occidentalis* (fig. 48; pl. XIX) is more or less ubiquitous. Its colonies range from orange to purple in color, and are generally about the size of an olive, though they may be several times as big. Most colonies are shaped something like a mushroom. The individual zooids are small, but as they are of a light yellowish or orange color, they can usually be distinguished within the common tunic. Each zooid has its own incurrent siphon, but a single excurrent opening serves a circle of several zooids; the atrial cavities of these zooids are therefore continuous.

Distaplia reproduces sexually during the spring or summer. Each zooid produces only a few eggs at a time. The eggs are not released into the sea, but are retained in a sort of brood pouch derived from the atrial cavity, where they develop into the tadpole stage. Colonies of *Distaplia* are therefore useful sources of essentially typical ascidian tadpoles for class study.

A species of *Diplosoma* (probably *D. macdonaldi*) may occasionally be found by the sharp-eyed observer. It forms a rather thin encrustation on floats, seaweeds, and some sessile animals that provide a firm substrate. The color is grayish or brownish, but the colonies are translucent and appear nearly homogeneous despite the fact that they contain hundreds of zooids.

ALGAE

The algal flora on floating docks is not as varied as it is on rocky coasts, but it has some interesting surprises. A number of species found on floats are characteristically either subtidal or found only at lower levels of the intertidal region. Just a few species that are regularly encountered will be dealt with here, however. In addition to the algae large enough to be called seaweeds, there are many microscopic plants. Among these are diatoms, which are well represented on floats, generally forming scummy brownish growths over the primary substrate and over other organisms.

Some diatoms form filamentous colonies that might be confused

52. Branching filamentous colonies of a diatom, *Navicula ("Schizonema")*

with small brown algae. At least one of the species of *Navicula* common on floats in our area produces filaments that are somewhat flattened and dichotomously branched (fig. 52). When examined with a microscope, the filaments are seen to consist of separate diatom cells embedded in a transparent matrix (fig. 53).

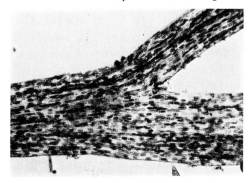

53. Portion of a colony of *Navicula;* photomicrograph

Green Algae

The green algae on floats range from semimicroscopic filamentous types to larger forms that can confidently be assigned to the right genus in the field. In many harbors, the sea lettuce, *Ulva lactuca* (pls. XXIV and XXVII) is decidedly the dominant alga. On floats exposed to considerable sunlight, it may grow so luxuriantly that there is little room for anything else. The thalli of *Ulva* are

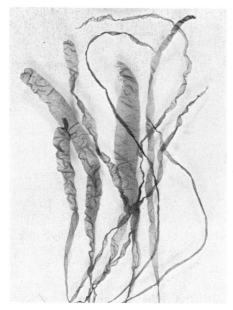

54. *Enteromorpha intestinalis*

thin, transparent sheets, often crinkly and with holes, bright green
in color. They are two cell-layers thick, a point that has to be established by microscopic examination of thin slices. An alga similar to *Ulva,* and often mixed with it on floats and in other habitats,

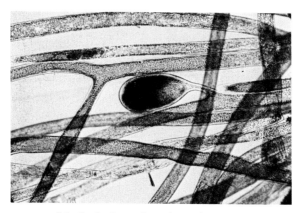

55. *Derbesia marina;* photomicrograph

is *Monostroma,* chiefly represented in our area by *M. fuscum.* However, as the genus name *Monostroma* implies, the thalli are only one cell-layer thick. When young, it forms a bright green sac, but this breaks open into a flat sheet, and as the thallus ages it may become more nearly olive green.

Enteromorpha intestinalis (fig. 54; pl. XXVII) is of the same general color as *Ulva,* but it grows in the form of tubes. It is tolerant of rather low salinities and is therefore the principal alga in some estuarine situations.

A semimicroscopic green alga sometimes common on floats is the spore-producing generation of *Derbesia marina* (fig. 55). It grows as rather stiff, blunt-tipped filaments that branch periodically. Here and there one may find the little ovoid structures within which the spores are produced. The spores, under appropriate circumstances, develop into the sexual stage, which was called *Halicystis ovalis* before its relationship with *Derbesia* was established. *"Halicystis"* forms little greenish globules, about 1 cm high, in the

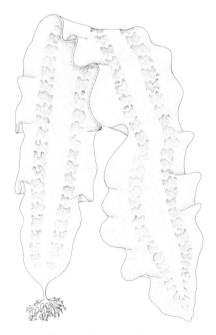

56. *Laminaria saccharina*

lower reaches of rocky intertidal areas, especially where there is an encrustation of coralline red algae. It liberates gametes, and the products of the union of these develop into the filamentous stage.

Brown Algae

In terms of total mass, the most conspicuous seaweed on floats is usually *Laminaria saccharina* (fig. 56). It merits being called a kelp, a term applicable to any large brown alga. The holdfast consists of a number of branching, rootlike structures and may provide a home or hiding place for a variety of worms and other invertebrates. The cylindrical stipe, which may be very short or more than 20 cm long, widens out gradually into the blade. This is usually several times longer than wide and is characterized by two series of blisterlike areas (bullations) running most of its length. (Very young plants, and some older ones as well, lack bullations.) The blades of large specimens may be over a meter long, but they are often badly torn.

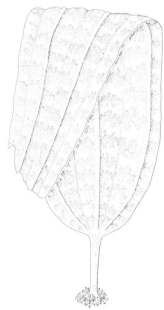

57. *Costaria costata*

A handsome kelp often growing with *Laminaria* is *Costaria costata* (fig. 57). Its broad blade has several strong ribs, but these are raised only on one side. The bullations between the ribs are conspicuous. The stipe is short, and the part that fans out into the blade is usually furrowed.

Quite a different sort of brown alga is *Desmarestia viridis (D. media)* (fig. 58). The thickest part of its main stalk is usually no more than about 5 mm in diameter, and the many side branches

58. *Desmarestia viridis*

are very slender. Large plants are about 50 cm long. Like all desmarestias, it cannot be trusted in a pail with other plants and animals because the cell sap that exudes from bruised tissue is strongly acid.

Red Algae

Polyneura latissima (fig. 59), characteristic of low tide levels on rocky shores, is one of the relatively few larger red algae found on floats. The broad primary blades coming off the holdfast may remain more or less entire, or they may branch once or twice; the branches often look as if they had been torn apart, and their tips frequently show some signs of wear. Considering the limited variety of red algae on floats, *Polyneura* is usually unmistakable because of its form and rich pink coloration. However, when a blade is viewed with light coming from behind it, a characteristic net-

59. *Polyneura latissima*

60. *Hollenbergia;* photomicrograph

work of veins shows up. The blades routinely reach a length of about 10 or 15 cm, but are occasionally a bit larger.

The more common red algae on floats are types that are small and finely branched. Members of one particular complex of genera —*Antithamnion, Antithamnionella, Hollenbergia,* and *Scagelia*—predominate. They are all quite similar and, for our purposes, an illustration of one species of *Hollenbergia* (fig. 60) and one of *Antithamnion* (pl. XXVI) will suffice. A strong hand lens, at least, will be necessary to appreciate the beauty of these delicate algae. They branch so frequently that it is difficult to trace the main axes of the colony. The branches consist of single rows of cells.

PILINGS

In central and southern California, where long piers have been built right on the open coast, the pilings support marvelous faunas and floras that can be studied at low tide. In our region, however, there are few pilings except in relatively calm waters, and just about everything that grows on them can be found on floats. They are nevertheless useful in showing us which animals and plants are successful at higher levels of the tidal range, and something of the mobility of predators that rise with the tide to feed on them.

Floating docks are generally linked to wharves or are at least connected to a set of pilings that provides stability. Thus where there are floats, there will probably be pilings close by, perhaps within arm's length. If this is the case, one can see, during an extremely low tide, a ten- or twelve-foot stretch of piling that was submerged a few hours before.

Nowadays, wooden pilings are subjected to a rather strict prophylaxis before they are pounded into place. Treatment with creosote and other preservatives, or ensheathment with metal or plastic, discourages destructive fungi, other microorganisms, shipworms, and *Limnoria*. It may be some time before a few hardy first settlers can stake out their claims and put the welcome mat out for their friends.

It is not necessary to review in any detail the animals and plants likely to be seen on pilings at the level of very low tides—those below about 0.0—because the fauna and flora on almost continuously submerged portions of piling are essentially the same as those found on floats. Above 0.0, however, the organisms that cannot stand much exposure are quickly thinned out. In the upper five or six feet of the tidal range one generally finds little in the way of seaweeds, and the more obvious animals are *Balanus glandula, B. cariosus,* and *Mytilus edulis.* Zonation is not likely to be very distinct, but *B. glandula* will probably reach upward farther than either *B. cariosus* or *M. edulis,* and its heaviest concentrations will also on the whole be higher.

In the middle and lower portions of the barnacle-mussel association, the limpet *Collisella pelta* is sometimes abundant. The sea stars *Pisaster* and *Evasterias,* if they have climbed the pilings to feed on the barnacles and mussels, may remain there after the ebbing tide has left them behind.

Nearer the low-water line, *B. glandula* and *B. cariosus,* as well as *Mytilus,* may still be quite successful, though their exposure to predation by sea stars is increased. Seaweeds, *Ulva* in particular, become more abundant close to the 0.0 level, and may practically cover the other organisms. In any case, most of the available space will be occupied. Between about 0.0 or —1.0 foot and the low-water line, *Metridium,* hydroids, *Serpula, Schizobranchia,* solitary ascidians, the compound ascidian *Distaplia,* and other sessile animals, together with seaweeds, usually luxuriate, especially during the summer months. As stated previously, just about anything that will grow on floats can be expected on pilings within a foot or two of the low-water line.

4: ROCKY SHORES

THE character of rocky shores in our region varies greatly; no two areas are quite alike. This variation is due in part to differences in geological origin. On any one of the large islands of the San Juan Archipelago, for instance, there will be a number of distinctly different rock formations in the intertidal zone. Most of the formations are of sedimentary origin, such as sandstone, shale, and limestone. Some, however, are of igneous origin, resulting from the action of heat within the earth; these include hard rocks of the type to which granite and basalt belong. Moreover, there are igneous intrusions into many of the sedimentary deposits.

Rocky shores differ also in topography and their situation with respect to prevailing climate, currents, and wave action. Some rocky shores are steep cliffs; others have a gentle slope. The flow of currents past them may be rapid or slow. Wave action within Puget Sound proper is often negligible, but some shores in the San Juan Archipelago receive relatively little protection and may experience considerable wave action during storms. In general, however, even the most intensive wave action in the archipelago during storms does not often equal that on the exposed outer coast in calm weather.

Many animals and seaweeds of the intertidal zone thrive only where the wave action is rather strong. Thus only a few areas in our region are suitable for certain species that are abundant on the open coast. The purple sea urchin, *Strongylocentrotus purpuratus,* to mention just one example, is rather uncommon except on shores that are somewhat exposed. On the other hand, quiet waters provide the right physical and biological encouragements for many other organisms. The characteristics of the shore are also important, for some animals can live only in crevices, under ledges, or under rocks.

As one works his way down a rocky shore from the high tide line to the low tide line, he will observe that the distribution of most of the more obvious animals and plants is not at all general. Even some of the organisms that have a wide vertical distribution are more abundant at certain levels than at others. This phenomenon, called intertidal zonation, occurs partly because some organisms are better suited than others to life under certain physical conditions.

Many animals and plants in the higher reaches of the intertidal zone must live out of the water for considerable periods of time. Thus, in winter they may be subjected to rain and to temperatures decidedly below that of the sea water; in summer they may have to survive long periods of exposure to sun and to relatively warm air, and perhaps will lose some of their water content. Though these organisms are certainly marine, they are adapted to a nearly terrestrial existence. Striking examples of such organisms are the periwinkles, little snails of the genus *Littorina*. If put into a jar of sea water, they will promptly crawl out and remain well above the water line. On the other hand, most animals and plants from the lowermost level of the intertidal zone are not adapted to withstand prolonged exposure, especially during warm and dry weather.

Zonation is not, however, entirely the result of adaptations to physical conditions. There are biological factors, especially competition and predation, that have to be considered. If a particular predator, for instance, can live comfortably at certain tide levels, then the population of a species on which it feeds will be kept in check. If the prey species can flourish at higher levels than the predator can, then it may become abundant at those levels. An actual case along this line is one studied in Europe, involving a snail of the genus *Thais* and certain barnacles belonging to *Balanus* and *Chthamalus*. The barnacles, especially *Balanus,* are capable of living over a rather wide vertical range, but predation by *Thais* keeps them in check over most of it. At higher levels, where *Thais* drops out, the barnacles grow thickly.

This same case also demonstrates something about competition for space. Although *Chthamalus* can live at levels lower than those at which it is normally abundant, it does not compete well with *Balanus*. The fact that it can prosper at levels too high for *Balanus* gives it an advantage in the uppermost part of the intertidal region. So, the distribution of both *Chthamalus* and *Balanus* results from the combined effect of the the competition between the two barnacles, the predation by *Thais,* and the ability to survive at progressively higher levels.

INTERTIDAL ZONATION

Discussion of the fauna and flora of rocky shores will be based on the zonation shown by some of the more conspicuous organisms. But, as the intertidal region is not one continuous, smooth sheet of solid rock, there will be sections dealing with life in crevices, in tide pools, and other specific situations. Some of the trophic relationships, as those of prey to predator, and various kinds of symbiotic associations, will also be pointed out.

To follow this basic framework it will be convenient to divide the intertidal region into four numbered zones: "1" will indicate the uppermost zone, "4" the lowermost. In many treatments of the subject of intertidal zonation, the term "supralittoral fringe" applies to our zone 1, and "infralittoral fringe" to our zone 4. The midlittoral zone, then, corresponds to our zones 2 and 3. For this introduction to rocky intertidal areas, it will be most instructive to use one in which the substrate is composed to a large extent of massive and more or less coherent rock formations (not just an accumulation of small rocks or boulders), and one that sustains a fair amount of wave action. Rocky shores of this type (the ones shown in Figures 61 and 62 are good examples) are found on the west and south side of San Juan Island and elsewhere in the San Juan Archipelago. What one learns from such a shore can be adapted to various other kinds of situations. One can expect, however, that generalizations formulated on the basis of observations of one particular area will be violated elsewhere. Moreover, in many places zonation is simply not well marked. Almost any exposed rocky shore on the open coasts of Oregon, Washington, or Vancouver Island will exhibit zonation that is much more dramatic than that shown by any topographically similar situations within Puget Sound or the San Juan Archipelago. Nevertheless, a good many characteristics of the zonation on the open coast will be seen in even relatively protected areas. Vertical bulkheads and sea walls generally show more pronounced zonation than is evident on slopes.

No matter how strong the zonation may be, two features found

61. A rocky shore exposed to a moderate amount of wave action (west side of San Juan Island)

on most rocky shores will tend to blur it to some extent. Permanent tide pools, especially larger ones, and gullies in which water sloshes up and down after waves break make it possible for certain organisms to live at appreciably higher levels than they would be able to do otherwise. Thus, although surfgrass *(Phyllospadix)* and coralline red algae are considered typical of the lowermost zone of the intertidal region, in tide pools and gullies they may be found well above this zone.

62. A rocky shore exposed to a moderate amount of wave action (west side of San Juan Island)

Zone 1: The Supralittoral Fringe

This zone is affected only by higher tides, and its uppermost portion may not often be wet except from spray or rain. To relate it to data given in a tide table, in the San Juan Archipelago its lower limit is usually about 7 feet above 0.0 (mean lower low water); in much of Puget Sound, its lower limit is about 9 feet above 0.0. Of course, it passes rather imperceptibly into the next zone below. Remember that a zone is characterized by an assemblage of organisms, not by the finite distribution of one species. In any case, zone 1 has relatively few obvious species, but those that do occur here may be present in large numbers.

Only a few plants are apt to be obvious. One of them is a black lichen, *Verrucaria* (pl. XXV), which forms slightly raised, encrusting growths. Lichens are symbiotic associations of microscopic algae with fungi, and most of them are strictly terrestrial. *Verrucaria* is one of the few that are close to being truly marine. It may be so abundant that its presence is obvious even from a distance, in the form of a horizontal black band. Other lichens are generally plentiful above the spray zone, and some of these may be richly colored. *Caloplaca* (pl. XXV), one of the common types in our area, paints the rocks orange.

Often contributing to the black band of the spray zone is a blue-green alga, *Calothrix*. Its encrustations are thinner than those of *Verrucaria* and less likely to be noted, especially when the rock on which they are growing is dark.

Prasiola meridionalis (pl. XXV) is a green alga that grows as little blades about 1 cm high. In Puget Sound and the San Juan Archipelago, it seems to be rather regularly present and may form extensive colonies. On the open coast, it is sometimes more or less restricted to rocks where there are colonies of sea birds and plenty of droppings.

Where there is seepage of fresh water onto the vertical face of a rock or out through a fissure, there will almost certainly be a growth of the bright yellowish green *Enteromorpha intestinalis* (fig. 54; pl. XXVII). As it dies, it turns white, so large splashes of this alga are often varicolored.

In depressions in rock that serve as miniature tide pools, there may be a bloom of various microscopic green algae and diatoms that makes the water look like thin pea soup. In this situation, look for a tiny bright red copepod, *Tigriopus*. Members of this genus are found in various parts of the world, almost always in this kind of place—pools that may not be refreshed for days at a time and may become brackish during periods of rain and hypersaline during warm summer weather.

One or both kinds of little snails called periwinkles will certainly be found in zone 1. *Littorina sitkana,* the Sitka periwinkle (fig. 63), commonly has a fat, almost globose shell which reaches a height of

63. *Littorina sitkana,* the Sitka periwinkle

a little more than 1.5 cm. It generally has some strong spiral sculpturing in the form of continuous ridges and furrows. The color is variable: some specimens are monotonously brown or gray, but others have lighter bands, especially.on the upper sides of the

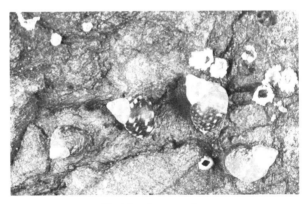

64. *Littorina scutulata*

whorls. The lighter areas, and occasionally much of the body whorl, may be a rather pretty yellow or orange. *L. scutulata,* the checkered periwinkle (figs. 64 and 71; pl. XXVI), rarely exceeds a height of about 1 cm, and its shell is more slender than that of *L. sitkana.* It does not have any significant spiral sculpturing. The color is brown to bluish black, usually mixed with some white in a checkerboard pattern.

Collisella digitalis (Acmaea digitalis) (fig. 65) is the only limpet likely to be found among *Littorina.* It is distinguished by its strong ribs, undulating margin, and an apex that is displaced so far anteriorly that it is nearly or fully as far forward as the edge of the shell. *C. digitalis* reaches a length of about 2 cm.

65. *Collisella digitalis*

Both of the littorines and *C. digitalis* are herbivores that scrape small algae from the rocks. They are often found clustered along cracks in which moisture collects and which therefore may support a growth of algae a little less depauperate than that on relatively smooth surfaces.

Two species of barnacles are characteristic of this zone. *Chthamalus dalli* (fig. 66) is a small species, its diameter at the base not often exceeding 5 or 6 mm. It is rather easy to recognize because of the way the contiguous margins of the four cover plates, when closed, form a cross-shaped configuration. Its color is characteristically brownish. The more nearly ubiquitous *Balanus glandula* (fig. 67) reaches a diameter of about 1.5 cm, and tends to be white.

66. *Chthamalus dalli*

In some rocky areas, the larger specimens are more abundant in zone 1 than elsewhere because snails of the genus *Thais,* which prey heavily on *B. glandula,* are mostly active at lower levels. As the barnacles are filter feeders, using their thoracic appendages to comb the water for microscopic food, those in the uppermost part of the intertidal region can feed only when the tide is high. Some are left high and dry for longer periods than others, and may not be wet except by spray for several days at a time.

In deep crevices and under ledges, generally so high that it is

67. *Balanus glandula*

only rarely drenched directly by sea water, is the isopod *Ligia pallasii* (fig. 68). Squeezing into cracks, so that it is sometimes almost impossible to extract in one piece, it behaves much like a cock-

68. *Ligia pallasii*

roach. The female is larger and proportionately wider than the male, attaining a length of about 2.5 cm. As in other isopods, overlapping plates on the underside of the thoracic region of the female form a brood pouch in which the young develop. *Ligia* is a scavenger, feeding mostly on decaying algal material.

Hiding under the lower edges of boulders is a large limpet that has an almost inflated look because the posterior and lateral slopes

69. *Notoacmea persona*

of its shell are so distinctly convex. *Notoacmea persona (Acmaea persona)* (fig. 69) sometimes reaches a length of about 5 cm and may be abundant in both zone 1 and zone 2, providing it has the habitat it likes. In any case, it tends to be somewhat gregarious, except at night, when it wanders to feed on the thin surface film of algae and diatoms.

Zone 2: The Upper Midlittoral Zone

In the San Juan Archipelago, this part of the intertidal region ranges from about 7.0 feet down to about 4.0 feet; in most portions of Puget Sound that are characterized by rocky shores, it is a little higher. Among the brown algae, one species, *Fucus distichus* (fig. 70), stands out. It is a substantial seaweed with a flattened thallus

70. *Fucus distichus,* the rockweed

that keeps branching dichotomously until it reaches a length of about 30 cm. The midribs of the branches are continuous and prominently raised. The holdfast is not much more than a thickened button. At least some of the terminal branches become swollen and warty; these are the sites of egg and sperm production. *Fucus* luxuriates in late spring and summer, and where it grows well, it may cover just about everything else.

A red alga especially characteristic of this zone is *Endocladia muricata* (figs. 71 and 72; pl. XXVI). It is small and rather delicate, forming tufts not often more than 3 cm high. The branches are cylindrical and studded with short tubercles crowned by a number of tiny spines. The color of the tufts ranges from dark

71. *Endocladia muricata* (left) and *Petrocelis,* with two specimens of *Littorina scutulata*

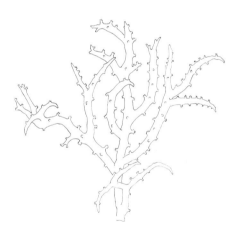

72. Portion of a clump of *Endocladia muricata,* greatly enlarged

brownish red to greenish brown or blackish brown; they become almost black when they dry out during summer low tides.

Cumagloia andersonii (fig. 73) is more common on the open coast than in our area, but when it is found, it is generally in zone 2. It is so distinctive and easily identified that it deserves mention. Its several stalks, growing from a small holdfast, are cylindrical or slightly flattened and look as though they had been inflated. They are typically under 5 or 6 mm in diameter and under 30 cm long.

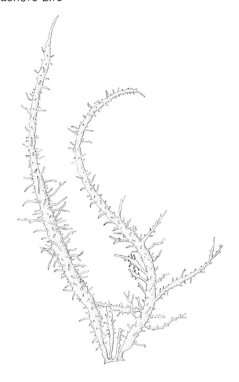

73. *Cumagloia andersonii*

Most of the many side branches arising from the main stalks are short. The coloration is on the whole rather light, most commonly greenish red or purplish red. This species is characteristically very slimy.

A common red alga that is especially noticeable on the upper surfaces of smooth boulders is *Bangia fuscopurpurea* (fig. 74). It is not at all pretty, growing as rather thin filaments of a rusty, purplish brown, or blackish color. Younger portions of these filaments are just one cell thick. As the tide ebbs, the filaments spread out over the rock in a way much too reminiscent of a few hairs artfully plastered down on a nearly bald head. *Bangia* seems to be mocking some of us.

The species of *Porphyra* found in zone 2 consist of single, thin blades. They are sometimes gray, sometimes brownish purple, and

74. *Bangia fuscopurpurea*

so iridescent as to appear oiled. *P. perforata* (fig. 75) is a rather distinctive kind, ruffled and perforated, especially near the edges. A really large thallus, if carefully spread out, may be nearly 1 m across.

75. *Porphyra perforata*

Among the green algae, *Ulva* (pls. XXIV and XXVII), which forms thin, green sheets, may occur in some abundance, at least in tide pools. However, it generally becomes more common below zone 2.

There are three general types of purplish, brownish, or blackish encrusting algae in this zone, and also in zone 3. Two of them, *Petrocelis* and *Hildenbrandia,* belong to the red algae; the third, *Ralfsia,* is a brown alga. However, they resemble one another to some extent, and beginners will have some difficulty in distinguishing them. In our area, *Petrocelis* (fig. 71; pl. XXVI) is generally the most widespread and obvious. Its coatings are about 2 mm thick and may be very extensive, being interrupted only by barnacles, *Endocladia,* and other attached organisms. When dry, the coatings are purplish black or purplish gray; but after becoming wet, they usually are more nearly brownish red. The genus *Petrocelis* has been recognized for a long time, but it now appears that the growths of the common species in our area constitute a phase in the life history of *Gigartina papillata.* This is somewhat similar to *G. exasperata* (fig. 117), which is discussed later under zone 4, but smaller (up to only about 15 cm long) and characterized by a blade that tends to split repeatedly. *G. papillata* is abundant on our rocky shores, especially in zone 3.

Hildenbrandia is similar to *Petrocelis* in habit of growth, but it comes closer to being really red when wet. It can be positively distinguished from *Petrocelis* only by microscopic characters. *Ralfsia* is quite different from both of the preceding. It forms small patches that are so thin they cannot be separated neatly from the rock with a fingernail. The color is usually brownish black when dry, reddish brown when wet.

All three of the encrusting algae just mentioned are sometimes called "tar spots." *Petrocelis* probably comes closest to looking like a deposit of tar.

Among the barnacles, *Chthamalus,* for all practical purposes, is out of the picture here. *Balanus glandula* (fig. 67), however, is abundant in zone 2, and so is *B. cariosus* (fig. 76). The shell of the latter has very prominent ridges, which give rise, especially near the base, to downward-directed projections. When *B. cariosus* is broken off the rock, it leaves soft tissue instead of the calcareous scar left by *B. glandula.* Large specimens have a basal diameter of about 5 cm.

Of the limpets, a few *Collisella digitalis* may be present, but *C. strigatella, C. pelta,* and *Notoacmea scutum* are more typical of this zone. In *C. strigatella,* the profile of the shell is very similar to

76. *Balanus cariosus*

that of *C. digitalis;* however, there are no ribs, and the margin is smooth. Internally, the shell is bluish white, instead of almost white, and generally lacks the large, brown, apical blotch characteristic of *C. digitalis*. The maximum length of *C. strigatella* is about 1.5 cm.

C. *pelta* (fig. 77) is an extremely variable species. It may be strongly ribbed and have a wavy margin, but even with these features it differs from *C. digitalis* in having its apex some distance

77. *Collisella pelta*

back of the anterior edge. Other specimens may have a smooth margin and no ribs. Large specimens attain a length of about 4 cm.

N. scutum (figs. 78 and 79) also grows to a length of about 4 cm,

79. *Notoacmea scutum,* in profile view

78. *Notoacmea scutum*

but its shell is low and shieldlike. It is never strongly ribbed, though it may be marked with very fine concentric, radiating lines.

The littorines so characteristic of zone 1 may be fairly abundant in zone 2, but some larger snails become conspicuous here. *Thais emarginata* (fig. 80) gets to be about 2.5 cm long and has strongly

80. *Thais emarginata*

developed spiral ribs; as a rule, heavier ribs alternate with more delicate ones. The ribs themselves are usually white, and the furrows between them are yellow, orange, brown, gray, or almost black. *T. canaliculata* (fig. 81) is on the average a little larger and a little more slender, reaching a length of about 3 or 4 cm. The spiral ridges are all much alike in caliber and distinctly set off from one another by deep furrows. The coloration on the whole is light, gen-

81. *Thais canaliculata*

erally whitish gray. *T. lamellosa* (fig. 82), with a shell that often exceeds a length of 5 cm, may be common, although it is more typical of zone 3. Specimens from protected situations usually have attractive axial frills, but those from exposed areas tend to be nearly smooth. The color is almost uniform, ranging from white to pale brown or gray.

All of the species of *Thais,* unlike the limpets and littorines, are carnivores and are the most important predators on intertidal barnacles. The interactions between these two groups of organisms have been the subject of a number of studies in Europe and America. In our region, *Balanus glandula* is preferred over *B. cariosus* as food, and the usual relative scarcity of the former, except at higher levels, is definitely related to the abundance of *Thais.* In situations where there are few or no *Thais, B. glandula* can enjoy a much wider vertical distribution.

Thais seems to drill a small hole into the shell of a barnacle where two wall plates meet, at the base of one of these plates, or at the edge of one of the valves that cover the animal when it is withdrawn. The proboscis, however, is too large to go through the hole, so probably some toxic substance is introduced through the hole in order to relax the muscles that close the valves.

The peculiar stalked egg cases of *Thais* (fig. 82), laid in large clusters on the undersides of rocks, are abundant in the spring and summer. Each pale translucent yellow case is about the size of a large oat. These cases are useful sources of developmental stages.

Another fairly large snail may show up in zone 2, at least in its

82. *Thais lamellosa* and its egg cases

83. *Searlesia dira*

lower portion. This is the spindle shell, *Searlesia dira* (fig. 83). On rocky shores it reaches a length of about 3 cm. (It grows larger in bays, where it lives at the lower edges of rocks set on gravel or mud.) The shell is gray on the whole, but a close inspection will reveal that most of the color is concentrated in the furrows between the rather fine spiral ridges. The dark pigment in the furrows that reach the lip of the aperture is visible within the aperture as a series of dark streaks. There are some low axial ribs on the upper whorls, but these are not continued on the body whorl. *Searlesia* has rather catholic carnivorous tastes, eating littorines, barnacles, worms, and other animals, and is said to specialize on animals debilitated by injuries or other misfortunes.

The hermit crabs must be close to the top of everyone's list of favorite seashore animals. The idea of living in an empty snail shell has been explored by several groups of invertebrates, including some other crustaceans, but hermit crabs have made a real success of it. As a hermit crab outgrows one shell, it must find another, sometimes running into serious competition for available homes in the right size range. Once the crab has solved its housing problem and has safely tucked away its soft, coiled abdomen, it will not look again for some time. On the whole, unoccupied shells, especially larger ones, are in short supply wherever hermit crabs are found, but the intensity of competition varies depending on circumstances. In any case, hermit crabs will fight for exclusive rights to empty shells, and this behavior can be observed in aquaria as well as in tide pools.

We have a rather interesting variety of hermit crabs in our area, but of the sixteen recorded species, only three are regularly found in the intertidal region. Some of the more peculiar species from deeper water just have to be mentioned, however. One of them, *Orthopagurus schmitti,* has a straight abdomen and lives in empty tubes of two kinds of polychaete annelids, *Sabellaria cementarium* and *Serpula vermicularis*. At least three other species sometimes live in masses of a hard-textured sponge, *Suberites*. They start out as juveniles in empty snail shells, but these become overgrown, except at the aperture, by the sponge. The shells eventually dissolve, and the hermit crabs live out the rest of their lives in lumps of *Suberites* many times larger than they are.

But, getting back to zone 2, the only hermit crab likely to be found here is *Pagurus hirsutiusculus* (fig. 84). The specific name alludes to its general hairiness, but other good characteristics by which most larger specimens can be recognized are the light and dark banding of the antennae and the white or pale blue band around the base of the next to last article (the "segment" just before the claw) of the second and third legs. In any case, *P. hirsutiusculus* is usually abundant in tide pools between and under rocks (especially those resting on coarse gravel), and under masses of seaweed. Larger specimens, with a body length of up to about 3 cm, prefer the shells of *Thais emarginata* and *Searlesia dira;* small specimens are most often found in shells of one or the other of our two species of *Littorina*. Too frequently, the fit seems much tighter

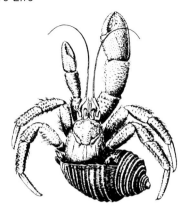

84. *Pagurus hirsutiusculus*

than it should be, so the little hermit cannot get its head under cover. This situation is typical for large males of *P. hirsutiusculus*. The majority of hermit crabs, including *P. hirsutiusculus*, feed largely on detritus, but they may scavenge on dead animal and plant material to some extent.

Where rocks lie on a gravelly or sandy substrate, and where decaying seaweed accumulates under their edges, two species of isopods are abundant. *Idotea wosnesenskii* (fig. 85) has already been mentioned in connection with the fauna of floats, but it prefers under-rock situations with plenty of vegetable debris. The coloration is generally uniform and ranges from brown through olive green to nearly black; dark olive green seems to be the most common shade. The length of large specimens is about 4 cm. *I. wosnesenskii* can cling tightly to rough rock—and to one's fingers

85. *Idotea wosnesenskii*

—by its seven pairs of clawed legs. It does not look like much of a swimmer, but it is remarkably agile and graceful when it does swim; the paddlelike appendages on the underside of its abdomen propel it with seeming effortlessness, while the legs are spread as if to take hold of any firm object that comes along.

Gnorimosphaeroma oregonensis (fig. 86) is smaller, only about 1 cm long. It is not much for looks, being pudgy and of a drab, mottled gray color; but it is rather distinctive among marine isopods because of its ability to roll up into a ball, like its garden cousin, the pill bug. *Gnorimosphaeroma* seems generally to be most abundant where there is considerable seepage of fresh water onto the shore.

86. *Gnorimosphaeroma oregonensis*

When the intertidal region is submerged, many kinds of fishes move in and out of it. As stated in the Preface, this book is not meant to include fishes, for there are other good guidebooks to cover the species commonly found in our region. However, it is impossible to neglect completely a few that are encountered regularly in the course of field work. At this particular point only the

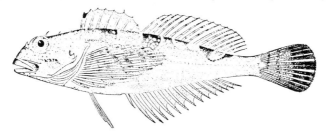

87. *Oligocottus maculosus*, the tidepool sculpin

tidepool sculpin, *Oligocottus maculosus* (fig. 87), need be mentioned. It is abundant in tide pools of zones 2 and 3, where other fishes are not so likely to be found. It is a typical sculpin, with a big head, large pectoral fins, and a tapering posterior portion. *O. maculosus* reaches a length of about 10 cm. The coloration is extremely variable, but greenish black tones predominate. Younger specimens are particularly undependable with respect to color, but as a rule they are more sharply marked—especially with white areas—than adults.

Zone 3: The Lower Midlittoral Zone

Mussels and Goose Barnacles

Between about 4.0 feet and 0.0, the flora and fauna show some characteristic elements. Where there is some real wave action—as is typical of the west side of San Juan Island and the southern part of Lopez Island—there will be beds of the California mussel, *Mytilus californianus,* and of the goose barnacle, *Pollicipes polymerus.* Neither of these will be found in Puget Sound proper, and they are absent from most islands of the San Juan Archipelago. Thus only the more exposed shores in the archipelago can come close to showing a lower midlittoral zone of the sort seen on the outer coast.

The California mussel (fig. 88) sometimes attains a length of

88. *Mytilus californianus,* the California mussel

about 20 cm, but specimens 15 cm long can be considered large. Like the edible mussel prevalent in quiet waters, it is tightly attached to the rock by means of a byssus and tends to be aggregated. The masses are sometimes several feet across. The California mussel has a good flavor when it is cooked by boiling or roasting, but it can be very poisonous. "Mussel poisoning" is caused by a toxin derived from a microscopic organism, a dinoflagellate called *Gonyaulax catenella.* When *Gonyaulax* is abundant in the plankton, it is ingested along with other organisms, and the toxin accumulates in the tissues of *Mytilus.* The paralyzing effect of this substance is somewhat similar to that of curare, which has long been used on darts and arrows by certain South American Indians. In California the beaches are routinely posted from late spring to early autumn to warn of the danger. The summer months are apt to be the only really dangerous ones, although the poison stored in the tissues may remain for some time after the *Gonyaulax* has disappeared from the diet of mussels. In any case, one should avoid gathering the California mussel for food in the summer months. Toxicity can be established by injecting laboratory mice with an extract of mussel tissue, but this is obviously not practicable for every lover of seafood. Cooking does gradually destroy the toxin, but even high heat over a long period cannot be trusted to do the job thoroughly. Other bivalves, including the littleneck clam of protected situations, store up the toxin at dangerous levels, but the California mussel is the worst offender on the open coast.

The beds of the California mussel accumulate a gritty mixture of sand and bits of shell. In this, and elsewhere among the tightly packed mussels, an interesting assemblage of other organisms is usually found. A little blackish sea cucumber, *Cucumaria pseudocurata,* only about 2 cm long, is more or less completely restricted to this situation. Then there are a number of polychaete annelids, including *Nereis vexillosa* (fig. 216). This reaches a length of about 15 cm, and its color is mostly a mixture of leaden grays with iridescent greens and blues and some reddish tones. If picked up, it wriggles to get away and may be excited enough to protrude its eversible pharynx, which is armed with a pair of blackish, pincerlike jaws and studded with numerous small denticles. If the worm does not spontaneously extrude its pharynx, try pressing gently, between thumb and forefinger, just behind the head. Nereids, as a group, are herbivores, and their big jaws are handy for tearing off pieces of algae.

The tight colonies of *Pollicipes* (fig. 89) often interrupt otherwise continuous beds of the California mussel or else alternate with them. The tough stalk of this barnacle is generally about 2 cm long and contains the gonads and an adhesive gland. The upper portion of the body includes most of the rest of the viscera and the appendages. It is protected by a kind of coat-of-mail consisting of a number of essentially separate calcareous plates of varying size.

89. *Pollicipes polymerus,* a goose barnacle

The feeding of *Pollicipes* differs from that of most acorn barnacles, such as the species of *Balanus.* The cirri do not beat regularly and rhythmically, but instead are spread so that water can rush through them. The catch includes small crustaceans and other planktonic organisms whose size on the average is larger than that combed out of the water by acorn barnacles. When sufficient food has accumulated on the cirri, they withdraw and the catch is transferred to the mouth parts.

If *Pollicipes* feeds by spreading its cirri to form a net, one might expect the cirri to face the incoming wave. However, *Pollicipes* typically takes advantage of the water running *off* the rock. For this reason, the specimens in a colony on one part of a large rock mass may be oriented in one direction, whereas some others not too far away may be oriented in a completely different direction.

Those situated in definite channels, regardless of which way these run, characteristically face the down-rushing water. Because *Pollicipes* feeds the way it does, some colonies are found much higher than the typical *Mytilus-Pollicipes* association. These colonies will almost invariably be in gulleys in which water breaking on the shore surges upward for some distance before it falls back.

Mytilus edulis, the edible mussel (fig. 90), is characteristic of quiet waters and of estuaries where the salinity is relatively low.

90. *Mytilus edulis,* the edible mussel

Over most of the area with which we are concerned, it is the only mussel found intertidally. It is not often observed on the exposed outer coast, where *M. californianus* is in its element, but one has only to locate a protected harbor and it will be present if there is rock or wood for it to settle on. In the San Juan Archipelago, in those few places where the California mussel does occur, the rocky habitat is not quite comparable to that on the open coast and the edible mussel is generally found along with it. It can easily be separated from the California mussel by its smaller size (the maximum length rarely exceeds 6 cm) and its relatively smooth shell; the California mussel typically has several strong ribs.

Chitons

Even if *Pollicipes* and *M. californianus* are absent, other animals help to define this zone. The black chiton, *Katharina tunicata* (fig. 91) is rather regularly present. It is up to about 7 cm long, and its eight shell plates are very nearly covered by the mantle. If you de-

91. *Katharina tunicata,* the black chiton

tach it (you may have to use the blade of a pocket knife or putty knife, so be careful with the animal), you will see that the undersurface is mostly a dull yellowish orange. The numerous separate gills characteristic of a chiton are arranged in a single row on each side of the broad clinging foot. Water enters the mantle cavity anteriorly, passes over the gills, then exits posteriorly. Like almost all chitons, *Katharina* is an herbivore, grazing on the film of diatoms and on other algae that coat the rocks.

Snails and Limpets

Thais lamellosa is common in zone 3; *T. emarginata* and *T. canaliculata* are also present, along with *Searlesia dira. Collisella digitalis* will not be found here, and *C. pelta* and *Notoacmea scutum* are generally less abundant than they are in zone 2.

Crabs and Hermit Crabs

Under loose rocks and in cracks, the crabs *Hemigrapsus nudus* (fig. 92; pl. XX) and *H. oregonensis* (fig. 93) will be found. Some-

92. *Hemigrapsus nudus*

93. *Hemigrapsus oregonensis*

times these two species occur together, but more often there is only one or the other. *H. nudus* is most likely to be present in exposed rocky situations, whereas *H. oregonensis* is typical of quiet water and of rocky habitats within estuaries. Both species of *Hemigrapsus* have a nearly rectangular carapace. *H. nudus* is usually rather reddish and has a number of distinct purple spots on the pincers of its first pair of legs; its legs in general are not particularly hairy. *H. oregonensis* tends to be grayish green and lacks purple spots on the pincers; its legs have conspicuous fringes of hairs. Both species can pinch hard if they have to, but they are primarily scavengers on animal matter.

Although *Pagurus hirsutiusculus* (fig. 84), characteristic of zone 2, is also found in zone 3, most of the hermit crabs one finds here belong to *P. granosimanus*. This species is about the same size as *P. hirsutiusculus,* but is almost hairless; moreover, the antenna is not banded. The shells used by larger individuals are mostly those of *Searlesia dira, Thais emarginata,* and sometimes *T. canaliculata.* Small specimens use littorines. *P. granosimanus* generally manages to find shells into which it can withdraw completely.

Where loose rocks rest tightly on an accumulation of sand or rather fine gravel, there will probably be porcelain crabs, *Petrolisthes eriomerus* (fig. 94). These are much flattened, sometimes blue, sometimes purplish red, with a nearly circular body up to about 2 cm across. Note that the antennae (these are longer than the antennules) are widely spaced and are lateral to the eyes. This characteristic, together with the fact that the fifth pair of legs is small and tucked under the body, sets these crabs apart from "true"

94. *Petrolisthes eriomerus*

crabs such as *Hemigrapsus*. They are actually more closely related to hermit crabs. When a rock hiding some *Petrolisthes* is lifted, they scurry wildly for cover. A curious trait of this crab and some of its relatives is the ease with which it can autotomize a leg that happens to be immobilized. Near the base of each leg is a groove-like ring that marks a feature quite comparable to the abscission layer between a stem and a leaf that is about to fall away. Thus if the leg is pinned down, the crab simply parts company with it and walks away, as a lizard might from a tail caught in the mouth of a predator. The wound does not bleed long, and within a few weeks the lost portion of the limb will be regenerated from the stub.

Lophopanopeus bellus (pl. XX), the black-clawed crab, is some-times common under rocks, especially those set on muddy gravel. This species is often mixed with *Petrolisthes*. The black-tipped claws constitute a reliable characteristic for identification, as the only other intertidal crabs with claws so marked are *Cancer orego-nensis* (pl. XXI) and *C. productus* (fig. 214); both have a number of almost equal and evenly spaced teeth between the eyes and widest part of the carapace, whereas *L. bellus* has just three teeth, all close to the widest part. The carapaces of large specimens of *L. bellus,* moreover, rarely reach a width much greater than 2.5 cm. This species varies a great deal in color, some specimens being red or nearly red and others ranging through browns and grays to almost white. Unfortunately, the coloration of most specimens taken within Puget Sound and the San Juan Archipelago could not be much duller, so they look like little gray or brownish gray stones. The hardness of the carapace adds to this illusion as does their behavior, for they go into "rigor mortis" when handled.

Sea Stars

The most conspicuous sea star of rocky intertidal areas is *Pisaster ochraceus* (fig. 95; pl. XIII). It is most appropriately considered at this point in our survey of the beach because its food consists to a large extent of the California mussel, when available. However, it also preys on the edible mussel, acorn barnacles, limpets, and other snails. It may even move into zone 2 with the rising tide and not move back down as fast as the tide ebbs. In any case, it shows a rather wide vertical distribution.

95. *Pisaster ochraceus*

P. ochraceus is a very stiff sea star, harsh to the touch, which commonly attains a diameter of about 25 or 30 cm. Its specific name implies that the color should be close to ochre, and it sometimes is. The ochraceous phase can better be described as being orange-ochre, but some specimens are brown. On the open coast, individuals having the orange-ochre color (pl. XIII) are mixed with those of a deep purple phase. In Puget Sound and in the San Juan Archipelago, almost all specimens are purple.

Like many other sea stars, *P. ochraceus* vanquishes its prey by a combination of the holding and pulling action of hundreds of tube feet, the ability to hump and pull with its arms in more than one direction, and mobility of its stomach. Part of the stomach can actually be extruded and spread over the prey or inserted into a crack between its shells. Among the clusters of spines that stand out on the upper surface are numerous microscopic, stalked pincers, called pedicellariae, which discourage settlement of other organisms. If you let the inner side of your forearm rest in solid contact with the upper surface of a *Pisaster* for a half minute or so, then draw it away, you may be able to feel that the pedicellariae have engaged the skin or some of the hairs.

Sea Anemones

The sea anemone *Anthopleura elegantissima* (pl. IV) is almost ubiquitous in zone 3 up and down much of the Pacific coast. It may range upward on the shore, however, if there are tide pools and depressions that hold water. It is typically found in situations where the rock to which it is attached accumulates some sand and fragments of shell; or perhaps it is fairer to say that where *A. elegantissima* colonizes rock, sand and shell will accumulate. The column of this anemone is studded with little tubercles, to which foreign particles adhere. When it is submerged, *A. elegantissima* stands about 4 or 5 cm high, so its tentacles are spread well above the sand that may be covering its lower portion. When the tide ebbs, the animals not in pools contract into gritty blobs (fig. 96); but the beds are still plenty wet, and if sat on or walked on, the anemones exude water through the mouth and through pores on the column. This species is beautiful in a delicate sort of way. The tubercles and some of the rest of the column are green or

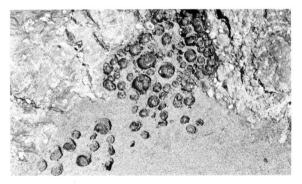

96. A bed of *Anthopleura elegantissima* attached to rock that is covered by sand

olive green, and the tentacles are generally a delicate pink. The green color is due largely to the presence of algal cells in the tissue. A discussion of this aspect of its biology will be postponed until the section on a related species, *A. xanthogrammica* (pl. IV), found in zone 4. In spite of its capacity to grow algae, however, *A. elegantissima* is a carnivore and probably feeds largely on crustacea.

Seaweeds

In covering the algae of zone 3, attention will have to be restricted to species that are either very common or very distinctive. Among the green algae, *Ulva* (probably mostly *U. lactuca*) is routinely abundant; and where it grows profusely, its thin, bright green sheets may cover large surfaces. *Spongomorpha coalita* (fig. 97; pl.

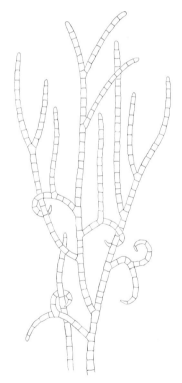

97. Portion of a growth of *Spongomorpha coalita,* as seen with the aid of a microscope

XXVIII) is quite a different type, composed of branching filaments of single cells. Some of the branches curve near their tips
and hook onto other filaments, so that a plant of *Spongomorpha*
forms almost ropelike complexes up to about 20 or 30 cm long.

There are many species of brown algae here. *Fucus* (fig. 70), already mentioned in connection with zone 2, may be present, but it
is not likely to be as important as it is higher up. *Hedophyllum sessile* (fig. 98) is almost always dominant in zone 3. It looks some-

98. *Hedophyllum sessile*

thing like a low-grade cabbage, but is composed actually of just
one large, thick blade that becomes partly wrapped around itself.
Most specimens are badly torn, in places almost all the way to the
base. Plants growing on the open coast are generally rather smooth,
but those in sheltered areas usually have a blistered look. Large
specimens are about 50 cm long.

Leathesia difformis (fig. 99) is an interesting brown alga—its
color is actually more olive than brown—which appears in the late
spring and hangs on until early autumn. It forms hemispherical or
globular masses somewhat resembling a brain because of the con-
volutions of its surface. Most specimens are 4 or 5 cm across.
Leathesia is sometimes attached to other algae, but usually it prefers rocks that have a coating of other small species.

Halosaccion glandiforme (fig. 100) is certainly one of the more
distinctive red algae of zone 3. The major part of its thallus con-

99. *Leathesia difformis*

100. *Halosaccion glandiforme*

sists of one to several hollow sacs growing out of a disklike holdfast. The sacs sometimes exceed a length of 10 cm, but they are generally smaller than this. As they are filled completely or nearly completely with water, desiccation of the alga is minimized when low tides coincide with warm, dry weather. Perhaps, by keeping the sacs turgid and erect, this internal water also helps to prevent mechanical abrasion. Although *Halosaccion* is a red alga, its color is more often yellowish brown or olive; some specimens are reddish purple, at least at the base.

Zone 4: The Infralittoral Fringe

This part of the intertidal region is exposed only by very low tides—those that bring the water level down into the range between about 0.0 and —3.5 feet. The fauna and flora of zone 4 are apt to be frustratingly rich for a beginner, so they will have to be approached selectively, with a view to laying a solid foundation on which one can continue to build as his background and interest deepen.

Surfgrass and Seaweeds

Some plants that are characteristic of this zone will be discussed first. The surfgrass, *Phyllospadix scouleri* (fig. 101), is not a true grass, but it does have flowers, and the family to which it belongs (Zosteraceae) is not far from the grasses. Its bright green leaves are narrow (generally under 3 mm wide) and usually about 30 to 50 cm long. They arise from short stalks produced by a fuzzy, creeping stem. The flowers are borne in tight, caterpillarlike clusters, and pollination takes place under water. When *Phyllospadix* grows in pools, or in channels that retain at least a little water, it may occur considerably higher than 0.0, but when it is at the mercy of the tide, its upper limit is generally close to 0.0.

101. *Phyllospadix scouleri,* the surfgrass

A narrow-leaved form of eelgrass, *Zostera* (discussed more fully in Chap. 5), is occasionally found in pools and channels on rocky shores, especially where there is relatively little wave action. It can easily be confused with *Phyllospadix*. The two genera may be positively distinguished during the summer by the arrangement of their flowers. In *Phyllospadix,* the pollen-bearing ("male") flowers and the flowers that ultimately produce seed ("female") are not only in separate clusters, but on separate plants. In *Zostera* (fig. 202), both types of flowers occur in the same cluster.

In late spring and summer, both *Phyllospadix* and *Zostera* frequently have a red alga, *Smithora naiadum* (fig. 203), attached to their leaves. *Smithora* grows as thin, purplish red sheets up to several centimeters long. It is a close relative of *Porphyra,* discussed in connection with zone 2.

A little lower than 0.0, there typically grows an assemblage of brown algae of the type called laminarians—members of the genus *Laminaria* and their close kin. When the tide drops to about − 1.5 or − 2.0 feet, a forest of these laminarians is exposed, their blades drooping from the stiff and often upright stipes (fig. 102). In many species, as in the easily identifiable *Laminaria setchellii* (fig. 103) of our region, the blades are cut into a number of strips. A laminarian with an entire blade (unless the blade has been lacerated) is *L. saccharina* (fig. 56). It grows luxuriantly on floating docks, so it has been mentioned in the preceding chapter. It is also abundant, however, in the lowermost zone of rocky intertidal areas. *L. groenlandica* is another large species that resembles *L. saccharina,* but its blades are regularly cut into three divisions.

Another large laminarian, *Costaria costata* (fig. 57), has also been discussed in connection with the algae of floating docks. Its

102. A "forest" of laminarians exposed at a very low tide. Floating farther from shore is the bladder kelp, *Nereocystis luetkeana*

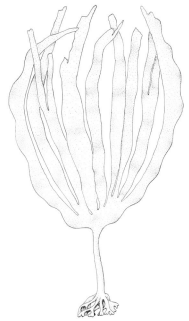

103. *Laminaria setchellii*

great blades, with five parallel ribs and a blistery texture, are truly handsome.

Egregia menziesii (fig. 104), the feather boa kelp (the common

104. *Egregia menziesii*

name alludes to a once-fashionable scarf made of feathers), is as easy to recognize as it is common and luxuriant. It has branching stipes about 2 or 3 cm wide and 5 m or more in length, which are rather strongly flattened, tough, and covered with little bumps. From either side arise numerous crowded blades of various lengths up to about 5 or 6 cm; some of the blades are swollen into floats about the size of a large olive. On the whole, *Egregia* is more or less olive or olive brown, but the stipe is sometimes very dark. On the open coast, this species is regularly found in what would correspond to zone 3; but its presence at this higher level on the more protected shores of the San Juan Archipelago is unusual.

A coarse, hard brown alga that is mostly subtidal is *Pterygophora californica* (fig. 105). Its stalk, arising from a holdfast of the type generally found in kelps, is almost woody; the plant lives for a number of years and the stalk forms growth rings much like the annual rings found in the trunks and branches of trees. The stalk is continued apically into a blade, below which several other broad blades branch off on opposite sides. The lower portion of the stalk,

105. *Pterygophora californica*

at least in older plants, is devoid of any such branches. Large specimens of *Pterygophora* may reach a length of about 2 m, of which about half is taken up by the stalk.

Alaria marginata (fig. 106) is closely related to *Pterygophora*, and also to *Egregia*. Its stalk is short and is continued as the midrib of the long, wavy-edged blade, which may be 2 or 3 m long. On either side of the stalk are a number of small, oval blades which are specialized for the production of spores.

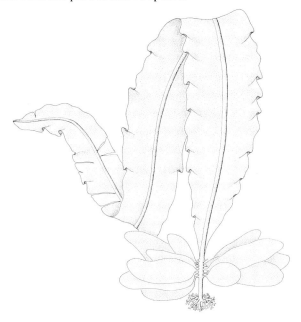

106. *Alaria marginata*

Desmarestia ligulata (figs. 107 and 108) grows to a fairly good size—up to about 3 m long—but it is comparatively delicate for a kelp as large as this. The growth form shown in Figure 107 has a broad main axis, generally 2 or 3 cm wide, from the edges of which arise numerous pairs of almost perfectly opposite branches that resemble elongated leaves; these usually branch again. The main axis and branches have slender marginal teeth. This is a variable species, and younger stages and certain growth forms have in the past been accorded separate names. Desmarestias that fit the de-

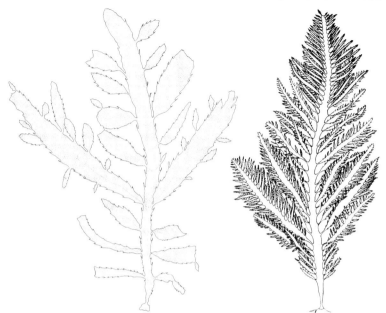

107. *Desmarestia ligulata* (the growth
form that has generally been called
D. munda)

108. *Desmarestia ligulata*
(younger stage)

scription just given were called *D. munda* and *D. herbacea*. The
type of plant shown in Figure 108, with a more delicate and nearly
featherlike pattern of branching, is what algologists have identified
as *D. ligulata*. It is apparently just a younger stage of *D. "munda"*
and *D. "herbacea,"* but its name has priority and now serves for
the whole complex.

D. *viridis* (fig. 58) is not at all like *D. ligulata*, for its branches
are wirelike and generally cylindrical or only slightly flattened. It
grows up to about 50 cm long.

Species of *Desmarestia,* as a group, have a very acid cell sap.
After they have been bruised, the sap that oozes out of them is a
menace to other organisms. Therefore, members of this genus must
not be used as packing material to keep animals and delicate algae
wet during the trip home.

The most talked-about kelp occurring in our region is *Nereocystis luetkeana* (figs. 109 and 110). It is both large and curiously

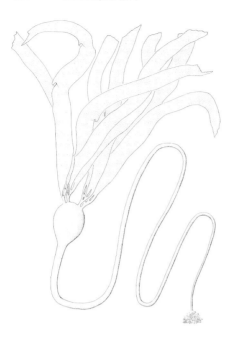

109. *Nereocystis luetkeana,* the bladder kelp

110. *Nereocystis luetkeana,* forming a kelp bed
just offshore

wrought. From a branching holdfast much like that of laminarians, a long stalk leads to a bulbous float, from which four groups of broad, flat blades arise. The stalk of a large specimen may be 20 m long, the float may be over 12 cm in diameter, and the blades may attain a length of 3 m. The gas in the cavity of the float, which is continuous with a cavity in the thicker upper portion of the stalk, contains a considerable proportion of carbon monoxide. But perhaps the most astonishing fact about this huge kelp is that it is an annual and makes all of its growth during part of one year. Plants that develop in the spring and summer die off the next winter and accumulate on the beaches. They are tough, however, and the stalks are especially durable, resisting decay and fragmentation for weeks. Even during the growing season specimens come loose and wind up on the beach, providing temporary cover and food for scavenging amphipods and other organisms. On almost any rocky shore, great beds of *Nereocystis* can usually be seen, but the holdfasts are below the level reached by low tides.

The kelp phase of *Nereocystis* reproduces asexually by microscopic motile spores. The sexual generation that develops from these spores is very small and filamentous. It lives through the winter to produce the next kelp generation. This same general type of life history is followed by laminarians and some other brown algae.

Sargassum muticum (fig. 111) is a newcomer, having been introduced to our West Coast from Japan, and has become well established in some places. Large plants are over 1 m long, and the color is usually yellowish brown. There is typically a short stalk, from which arise some flat outgrowths that look like long leaves and a number of branches that divide again several times. The younger portions of the branches develop either into flattened, irregularly toothed structures that look like leaves; into swollen, club-shaped bodies in which the reproductive organs are concentrated; or into almost spherical floats.

Cystoseira geminata (fig. 112) is much like *Sargassum,* but grows larger—up to 4 or 5 m long. Also, its floats usually consist of two to several vesicles in a series, the terminal one being sharply pointed. The species frequently serves as host to another brown alga, *Coilodesme californica,* which forms delicate, easily collapsible sacs up to about 20 cm long.

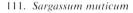

111. *Sargassum muticum*

112. Small portion of *Cystoseira geminata,* with *Coilodesme californica* attached

For a green alga, *Codium fragile* (pl. XXVIII) is decidedly un-usual in texture and habit of growth. The branches, which fork di-chotomously, are solid and cylindrical, almost as thick as a pencil. The tips are blunt and the surface is velvety and soft, so *Codium* is often mistaken for a sponge. The plant is actually composed of separate filaments all woven together. The color is such a dark green as to be nearly black. Young specimens of *Codium* may stand almost upright, but as they get longer they start to droop. In large plants, the length of the fronds may exceed 30 cm. The hold-fast disk is thin, but it may spread out irregularly over the rock to cover an area perhaps 5 cm in diameter.

Among the red algae that stand out in this zone, the coralline species just about have to be mentioned first, since they are so abundant and so distinctive. Like *Phyllospadix,* the coralline red algae may occur at tide levels well above 0.0, but then they are mostly in pools, gullies, or at the edges of cracks that hold water. In the infralittoral fringe, they are just about everywhere.

The coralline red algae are rendered hard and gritty by large amounts of calcium carbonate. In color, they range from reddish pink to purplish pink, but as they die they turn white. One genus, *Lithothamnion* (fig. 131; pl. VI), forms strictly encrusting growths resembling lichens. Other genera in our area produce tufts of articulated, branching stems, although a part of the thallus may have the encrusting habit; some that are reluctant to develop articulated growths are difficult to distinguish from *Lithothamnion*. The technical differences between them are not easy to explain simply. However, on the basis of superficial features, a partial differentiation of the three more common genera in our area can be provided. In *Corallina* (fig. 113), the branching produces, in general, nearly featherlike growths, and the segments are usually decidedly longer than wide; in the upper part, the segments are cylindrical or only somewhat flattened. More importantly, the reproductive structures are concentrated only at the tips of the branches, and these tips become swollen. In *Calliarthron* (fig. 114) and *Bossiella* (fig. 115;

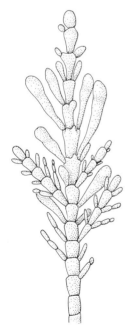

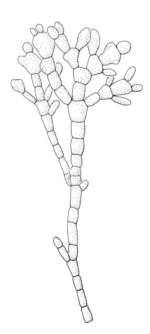

113. *Corallina*   114. *Calliarthron*

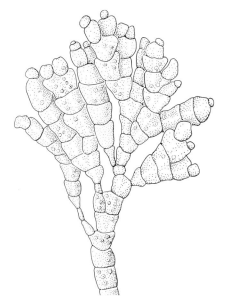

115. *Bossiella*

pl. XXVI), the reproductive structures are located in little elevations on the surfaces of some of the segments. It is almost impossible to distinguish between these two genera without recourse to
microscopic characters. In *Bossiella,* the segments are regularly
flattened, as they are in the species illustrated, whereas in *Calliarthron* they may be flattened or cylindrical. Thus a *Calliarthron* with
cylindrical segments can be distinguished from a *Corallina* on the
basis of the arrangement of its reproductive structures, but one
with flattened segments will be difficult to tell apart from a *Bossiella.*

Many of the noncoralline red algae of the infralittoral fringe are
relatively small. Delicate types such as *Antithamnion* (pl. XXVI),
mentioned in the chapter on floating docks, are abundant on rocks
and on the stipes and fronds of other algae. However, there is a
large assortment of medium-sized species and a few larger ones;
those described here will include a selected few that are more or
less unmistakable.

A real oddity is *Constantinea simplex* (fig. 116), which looks a
bit like certain terrestrial cup fungi. It has a short stalk which ordi-

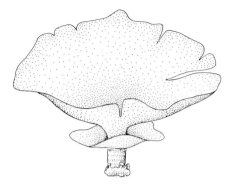

116. *Constantinea simplex*

narily does not branch but expands into a saucerlike blade. Sometimes there are additional blades encircling the stalk below the
primary one. Any or all of the blades may be frayed or split. The
color is usually a dark purplish red. The stalks are not often more

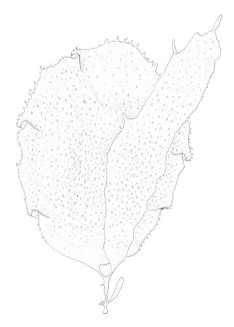

117. *Gigartina exasperata*

than 2 or 3 cm long, and the primary blade is generally under 5 or 6 cm in diameter; but larger specimens are occasionally found. The closely related *C. subulifera* may branch several times, and each branch may have a terminal blade as well as subsidiary ones below it. The most distinctive feature of this species is a fingerlike extension of the stalk coming up through each primary blade.

Gigartina exasperata (fig. 117) forms one or more broad, thick blades up to about 30 or 40 cm long, and the edges and flat surfaces of these are roughened by hundreds of tall, stiff outgrowths. The specific name is fully appropriate, as it refers to the rasplike character of the blades. The color of *G. exasperata* is usually a purplish brick-red, and the surface is often somewhat iridescent when it is wet.

Iridaea cordata (fig. 118) is much like *G. exasperata* in overall form, thickness, and color. However, its blades are on the whole darker and much more iridescent, portions of them appearing purple or blue; they are also very slick, for they lack the outgrowths that roughen the blades of *Gigartina*.

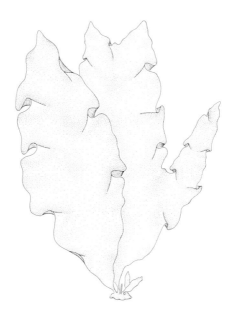

118. *Iridaea cordata*

G. exasperata and *I. cordata* are perennials, but they die back in winter to a sort of crust. The little blades that start to grow out in early spring enlarge quickly. Both of these seaweeds are good sources of carrageenin (or carrageenan), a substance used as a stabilizer in many products ranging from cottage cheese to printer's ink. They have been "farmed" in an experimental way by attaching young plants to racks or lines of nylon rope kept submerged below the low-tide mark. The crops have been good enough to encourage exploration of prospects for commercial production of carrageenin in our waters.

Odonthalia floccosa (fig. 119) and *Rhodomela larix* (fig. 120) are common in zone 4 and are also abundant in tide pools at appreciably higher levels. Neither is easily recognized as a red alga, for both are dark blackish brown. *Odonthalia* grows about 30 or 40 cm long and is much branched. As the branching tends to be in the same plane, the plant has a decidedly flattened look. The final branches are nearly awllike and usually sharply pointed.

119. *Odonthalia floccosa*

Rhodomela is a firm, crisp alga which reaches a length of about 20 cm. The generic name of larches, *Larix,* was adopted as its specific name because its clustered short branches are arranged after the fashion of the needles of this tree. Both *Rhodomela* and *Odonthalia* provide shelter for a variety of small animal organisms,

120. *Rhodomela larix*

especially amphipod crustaceans. Both—but especially *Rhodomela* —may have an interesting brown alga, *Soranthera ulvoidea* (fig. 121), attached to them. *Soranthera* develops from a solid mass into a more or less egg-shaped hollow sac about 5 cm long. The darker bumps all over the sac mark the location of reproductive structures and some accessory hairlike outgrowths.

Sponges

In the intertidal region, sponges tend to be found only at lower tide levels. Both *Haliclona* (fig. 5) and *Halichondria* (fig. 4) are found in zone 4, but these have been described at some length al-

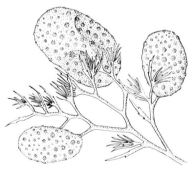

121. *Soranthera ulvoidea* growing on *Odonthalia floccosa*

ready, in Chapter 3. Bright red or orange-red patches, much thinner than typical growths of *Haliclona* or *Halichondria,* belong mostly to *Ophlitaspongia pennata* (pl. I); but some other red sponges look much like it. Microscopic analysis of the spicule complements is necessary before positive identification is possible.

Ophlitaspongia is pretty enough by itself, but it will often provide the more observant student with a delightful surprise. A small, orange-red sea slug, *Rostanga pulchra* (pl. I), generally only about 1 cm long, grazes on this sponge. This sea slug not only matches the color of the sponge it eats, but it also lays coiled egg masses of the same color. *Rostanga* is not often found far from *Ophlitaspongia* and can distinguish between it and other sponges if given a choice.

Hydroids

Hydroids are usually abundant in the lower part of the intertidal region, where they are attached to rocks, kelps, carapaces of certain crabs, worm tubes, and other firm substrates. Unfortunately, the very small species are likely to escape notice in the field, and the delicate beauty of larger hydroids cannot be appreciated when they are out of water. If you can get a few pieces back to the laboratory in plenty of cold sea water, then set them in a dish under a dissecting microscope, you will probably be able to observe the polyps in an expanded state.

Among the hydroids on fairly exposed rocky shores, some, as *Obelia, Coryne,* and *Tubularia,* are of the general types discussed in connection with the fauna colonizing floats. However, some others are not likely to be found on floats or anywhere else except on rocks where there is wave action, or in certain subtidal situations. Most of these have a stiff texture because the perisarc is thick. One of the more distinctive genera in this category of hydroids is *Aglaophenia* (pl. II), in which the main stem and branches collectively form a featherlike pattern. The individual feeding polyps are arranged in a row on just one side of each branch, and on some branches there may be basketlike structures, called corbulae, which contain the reproductive polyps comparable to those of *Obelia*. The medusa stage produced by these structures is not readily recognizable as such and never leaves the tissue in which it is formed. The abortive medusae do produce eggs and sperm, however, and the fertilized eggs develop into planulae which escape, settle, and start new colonies. Another firm-textured hydroid likely to be encountered at very low tide is *Abietinaria* (pl. II). Its polyps are arranged on both sides of the branches, which, as in *Aglaophenia,* come off the main stems in a featherlike pattern.

Sea Anemones and Their Allies

In this lowermost part of the intertidal zone, several species of anemones stand out. *Anthopleura xanthogrammica* (pl. IV), the green anemone, is characterized by a broad, flat oral disk; the color of the disk and tentacles is typically a beautiful muted emerald green. The diameter of the tentacular crown in a fully expanded specimen may reach 15 cm. The column is nothing special to look at, being a rather drab olive or brownish color. If a finger is placed on the tentacles of this or most other anemones of reasonable size, the tentacles will cling weakly to the skin, in part because of the discharge of nematocysts whose extruded microscopic threads engage the skin. However, a kind of suction seems largely to be involved in conferring this adhesive property upon the tentacles. In any case, the tentacles function effectively in trapping prey— probably mostly crustaceans and small fishes—and pushing the prey into the mouth.

Although *A. xanthogrammica* is a carnivore, it normally supports a large population of microscopic algae, which are responsible for much of the green color. *A. elegantissima* (already discussed under zone 3) also has symbiotic algae, though its tentacles are not often really green. Two distinctly different types of algal cells are known to occur in both of these anemones. Zooxanthellae, characteristically yellow-brown because of the presence of pigments that partially mask the chlorophyll, are dinoflagellates which have no flagella in the symbiotic phase. The other algae, called zoochlorellae, are bright green. The two types may be mixed in one specimen— even in the same tissue—or separate anemones may have only one type or the other. The algae are concentrated in the gastrodermal layer, that is, in the tissue that lines the digestive tract. Since the core of each tentacle is a branch of the digestive tract, the green color shows through the overlying tissue.

The biological relationship of the algae to their anemone hosts has been studied to some extent. It appears that the value of the association to the anemone is at least partially a nutritional one. Organic compounds synthesized by the algae move into the tissues of the anemone. When starved, anemones without algae lose weight more rapidly than anemones of the same species that have a normal complement of algae.

Two other large anemones need to be mentioned here. *Tealia crassicornis* (pl. III) is about the same size as *A. xanthogrammica* (the disk of a large specimen is about 15 cm in diameter), but its tentacles are proportionately longer and thicker. The prevailing color of the disk and tentacles is usually greenish gray or olive gray, but the tentacles typically have lighter cross bands and may also have a reddish suffusion. The column, not the prettiest part of most anemones, is very striking because of the way the light olive green ground color is streaked with red. (In Puget Sound, the column of most specimens is entirely red.) *T. crassicornis* is commonly found on the undersides of ledges, and the way it hangs down limply when the tide is out is fascinatingly obscene.

T. coriacea (pl. III) is a less common species, except in certain places. It favors situations where its column can be partially covered by fine gravel or bits of shell. The upper part of the column, which is bright red, regularly has particles from the substrate sticking to it. The prevailing coloration of the disk and tentacles is a mixture of red and gray; the tentacles, which are stubbier than those of *T. crassicornis,* have some ill-defined lighter bands.

Metridium senile (fig. 18; pl. II) may be abundant, especially in relatively protected situations where there is not much wave action. Intertidally, however, it does not often make a showing as impressive as it does subtidally or on floats (see Chap. 3). It is usually hidden away under ledges and in caves, and large specimens are uncommon.

Epiactis prolifera, the brooding anemone (fig. 207; pl. III), is a small species. The height of an expanded specimen does not often exceed about 3 cm. The basic color is ordinarily brown to greenish brown, but it is sometimes red, pinkish red, or dull green. The oral disk is generally marked with radially arranged white lines; the pedal disk and column have similar lines, though they may not be as sharp. The numerous young regularly found on the pedal disk do not originate there by asexual budding, but are derived from eggs fertilized in the digestive cavity. The motile larvae, after swimming out of the mouth, migrate down to the disk and become installed there until they become little anemones ready to move off. *Epiactis* is so abundant on eelgrass in quiet bays that it will be considered again in Chapter 5.

One of the real gems of this lowest zone is the cup coral, *Balanophyllia elegans* (pl. V). Its disk and column are bright orange; the tentacles are barely tinged with orange and almost transparent. Though it looks like a squat little sea anemone, about 1 cm in height and in diameter, the cup coral has a strong calcareous skeleton; this not only supports the body wall but also the partitions in the digestive cavity. Dead specimens, of which only the skeleton remains, look something like short lengths of dry bone, though the inner portion, on account of the centripetal partitions, does not really resemble a marrow cavity. *Balanophyllia* is not often found in really exposed situations. It seems to prefer dark places, and in the intertidal region it is generally restricted to caves and the undersides of ledges.

Usually rarer than *Balanophyllia* in the intertidal region is *Epizoanthus scotinus* (pl. III), our only representative of a group of anemonelike anthozoans called the zoanthids. There is no calcareous skeleton in *Epizoanthus,* but sand grains, bits of shell, and diatoms become incorporated into the body wall. Foreign material of this sort is also embedded in the surface of the tan or flesh-colored column, so that the animal has a gritty texture. The tentacles are much paler than the column. If they are caused to contract, it may take them several hours to become extended again, especially if the animal has been detached from the rock on which it has been living. *Epizoanthus* can reproduce asexually by budding and thus may form clumps of several to many individuals. Large polyps reach a height of about 7 cm, but most specimens are not over 3 cm tall. Although the coloration of *Epizoanthus* is undistinguished, a colony of expanded animals is a beautiful sight.

Flatworms

In our area, the only free-living flatworms large enough to see without the help of a microscope are the polyclads, so-called because of their much-branched digestive tracts. Most are about 1 to 3 cm long. *Kaburakia excelsa* is about the only common large species, reaching a length of 5 cm or even more, and has already been mentioned in connection with the fauna of floating docks. It is occasionally seen clinging to the undersides of rocks, to rocks exposed when other rocks are lifted off, or under clumps of mussels. The medium-sized polyclads (a typical species is shown in Figure 21) fall into a variety of genera. Unfortunately, the classification is based largely on details of the reproductive system, and cannot be understood without a lot of microscopic work and preparation of sections. Patterns of eyespot arrangement, coloration, and general shape are helpful, but it would be misleading to attempt to help the user of this book to identify even a few species on the basis of superficial characteristics alone. Our more common polyclads seem to be *Freemania litoricola* and several species of *Notoplana*. One of the latter, *N. sanguinea,* is distinctive enough to be recognized in the field because of a dark red saddlelike blotch on the central part of its dorsal surface.

Nemerteans

Members of the phylum Nemertea are represented by several easily recognized species and by some others better omitted here, as they cannot be identified without recourse to microscopic characters. *Tubulanus polymorphus* (pl. V) is large, up to about 1 m long when fully extended; however, when it is uncovered by lifting up seaweed or turning a rock, it is usually at least partially contracted, and then parts of it may be nearly as thick as a pencil. *Emplectonema gracile* is as slender as a thin rubber band, dark green above and whitish or yellowish below; it reaches a length of about 7 or 8 cm, and is sometimes abundant higher up in beds of the California mussel.

The most beautiful of our nemerteans is *Micrura verrilli*. It secretes almost papery tubes on the undersides of rocks and thus may be overlooked. The undersurface of *M. verrilli* is nothing special, being just more or less uniformly ivory-white. The upper surface, however, is a dark purplish brown, crossed transversely by regularly spaced white lines, and the head is bright orange.

All typical nemerteans are predators on worms (especially polychaete annelids), small molluscs, crustaceans (including barnacles), and other animals. They use their eversible proboscis, which may be sticky or armed with stylets that operate in conjunction with a venom gland, to capture and quiet the prey. Some nemerteans swallow their prey whole; others suck out their juices.

Polychaetes

Most of the many polychaete annelids are hidden away in crevices, in holdfasts of large seaweeds, and in the sediment that accumulates between and under rocks. Those in the open secrete tubes as personal hiding places. Among these the serpulids stand out because they are so abundant and because their tubes, even when tiny, are white and calcareous. The common species found in the lowermost reaches of the intertidal region are the ones whose characteristics and life styles have been discussed in connection with the fauna of floats. *Serpula vermicularis* (pl. VI) can be a gorgeous sight when all of the specimens in a group have their bright red tentacular crowns extended. They are likely to be seen this way only in a tide pool, of course. The various species of *Spirorbis* (fig. 24), with their tubes generally coiled like snail shells, are so small and so ubiquitous that study with a low-power microscope is necessary to make one appreciate that they are as beautiful as *Serpula* in form if not in coloring.

The principal sabellid in rocky situations is generally *Eudistylia vancouveri* (pl. VI), which builds leathery tubes about 1 cm wide and sometimes 20 or 25 cm long, and is characteristically aggregated in large clumps. The crown of featherlike tentacles at the anterior end is deep maroon, banded with green, and may be 5 cm in diameter when expanded. Occasionally *Eudistylia* is found in zone 3, especially if it can establish itself in a deep fissure.

In crevices, between rocks that fit tightly together, and under rocks lying on sand or gravel, there will probably be a variety of polychaete annelids. Some of these may seem nondescript unless they are examined carefully with a low-power microscope. However, be on the lookout for the larger terebellids, which are quite distinctive. The terebellids are characterized by numerous, very extensile tentacles arising from the extreme anterior end of the body, and two or three pairs of gills arising from the dorsal surface of certain of the segments just a little farther back. These gills may be bushy or they may consist of clusters of unbranched filaments. The bodies of terebellids tend to be pudgy, especially when they are contracted, and often have a flabby look. The anterior portion is usually somewhat swollen, and the bristles on the segments of this region are specialized as short, thickened hooks. These hooks are often arranged in such a way that they resemble one row or both rows of teeth in a zipper.

Most terebellids form parchmentlike tubes or thin muddy tubes around themselves. From the mouth of the tube, their tentacles range widely over and through the substrate, trapping microscopic food and passing it, in a film of mucus, down a ciliated groove toward the mouth. As food accumulates near the base of a tentacle, it is rubbed off onto a sort of lip near the mouth, from which food is driven by cilia into the mouth itself.

In rocky intertidal areas, *Thelepus crispus* (fig. 122) is usually the prevailing terebellid. A large specimen, fully extended, is about the diameter of a pencil and about 10 cm long. Its gills, in three pairs, consist of clusters of unbranched filaments. The body color is a sort of brownish pink, and the tentacles are whitish and translucent. When broken-off tentacles of *Thelepus* and its relatives are found crawling around by themselves, they are apt to be taken for delicate little nemerteans. Along with some other things seen out of context, like chopped-off clam siphons, they provide some embarrassing levity to laboratory sessions devoted to identification of the morning's catch.

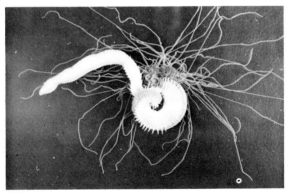

122. *Thelepus crispus*

Sipunculans

Under rocks and in tight crevices between rocks, especially where some muddy sand or gravel has accumulated, one may frequently find a rubbery worm so firm when it is contracted that it

123. *Phascolosoma agassizii,* a peanut worm

resists being squeezed. This is *Phascolosoma agassizii* (fig. 123), a member of the small phylum Sipuncula. Its firmness is due in part to its strong, muscular, and rather inelastic body wall, and in part to a high hydrostatic pressure within its body cavity. If put back into sea water, it will soon extend its more slender anterior portion by turning it inside out; it will then probably alternately withdraw and extend this part more or less indefinitely. There are a few very short tentacles around the mouth, which are used for feeding on detritus at the surface of the substrate where the worms peek out from under or between rocks. The digestive tracts of sipunculans are almost U-shaped, so the anus is not at the posterior tip of the body, but on the dorsal side, and is rather far forward. The length of a large *Phascolosoma,* when stretched out, is about 6 or 7 cm. The plump posterior part of the body is tan or greenish tan; the introvertible anterior portion is basically paler, but it has a number of black lines and blotches.

Some of our intertidal animals, while in the larval stage, settle in small holes or in burrows made in rock by other animals, and then just stay there for the rest of their lives. Many of these animals, called nestlers, grow to a point where they fit tightly in their little abodes. Chief among them are certain clams and sipunculans. One of the sipunculans, *Phascolosoma agassizii,* has just been mentioned; it is not at all limited to holes, for it is fairly abundant between or under rocks, but it does often qualify as a nestler. A different sipunculan, *Themiste pyroides,* is almost strictly a nestler. It is more plump than *P. agassizii,* lacks the dark markings on the introvertible anterior portion, and has bushy tentacles. *Themiste* favors burrows excavated by rock-boring bivalve molluscs, and it fits these about as snugly as possible. It is only occasionally found within the region of the San Juan Archipelago, but is fairly common on the open coast.

Sea Stars

Pisaster (fig. 95; pl. XIII) has already been discussed because of its prevalence in zone 3, into which it ascends to feed. Somewhat similar to *Pisaster* and often needlessly confused with it is *Evasterias troschelii* (pl. XIII). Its diameter may reach 50 cm, but most specimens fall into the range of 25 or 30 cm. The arms are long in proportion to the size of the disk, so *Evasterias* is more graceful than *Pisaster.* Its pattern of white spines is much like that of *Pisaster;* but its ground color is never really purple nor often as close to orange as is characteristic of some specimens of the latter. The color nevertheless varies greatly, ranging from gray or gray-green to brown and nearly red.

The leather star, *Dermasterias imbricata* (pl. XV), has short, thick arms, and the texture of its upper surface is soft and slippery. This species, which reaches a diameter in excess of 20 cm, smells much like exploded gunpowder. The coloration of the upper surface is blotchy, but is predominantly reddish brown, mixed with a sort of leaden gray; nearly purple patches are mixed into the coloration of some specimens.

Perhaps our most beautiful intertidal sea star is the sun star, *Solaster stimpsoni* (pl. XIV). Typically, it has ten graceful even if somewhat gritty rays, and it attains a diameter of about 25 cm. The background color of the upper surface of most specimens is usually either orange or rose, and wide streaks of grayish blue or grayish purple run from the center of the disk to the tip of each arm.

The most common of the sea stars of the intertidal zone is, with respect to size and color, the least conspicuous. *Leptasterias hexactis* (fig. 124) is especially abundant on beaches where there are a lot of loose rocks resting on one another. It is a six-rayed species with a maximum diameter of around 8 or 9 cm. The color is char-

124. *Leptasterias hexactis,* the six-rayed, or brooding, sea star

acteristically drab—leaden, gray, greenish gray, or occasionally nearly black. Once in a rare while a brightly colored specimen with some orange or pink tones shows up. *Leptasterias* compensates for its lack of physical attractiveness by some interesting habits connected with reproduction. Between about December and March, mature individuals congregate, in groups of a dozen or more, under rocks. Both sexes spawn more or less simultaneously. As each female liberates her eggs from pores on the upper surface, she collects those that do not slip away into a cluster, which she holds with her tube feet and over which she humps her body, remaining attached to the rock only by the tips of her arms. When the tube feet of the young have developed to the point where they can cling to the rock—after a period of about forty days—the mother finally can flatten out. The brooding period continues for approximately twenty days more. By this time the young are a little more than 1 mm in diameter, but they are essentially fully formed and the female leaves them.

During the period she is looking after her young, the female evidently does not eat. She pays close attention to her brood, cleaning the eggs as they develop and in some way helping them to escape from the thin membrane that surrounds them for the first three weeks or so.

The most brightly colored sea star in the intertidal zone is *Henricia leviuscula* (pl. XV), the blood star. The upper surface is typically a brilliant orange-red, but the color may range from tan to nearly purple, and some specimens are mottled. This species is relatively small, its diameter rarely exceeding 12 cm. The graceful appearance and smooth texture of *Henricia* are due to the absence of pedicellariae and spines from the upper surface.

A thoroughly astonishing sea star is the sunflower star, *Pycnopodia helianthoides* (pl. XIV). It is common in certain situations on rocky shores, but is probably even more abundant on sandy or gravelly substrates in deeper water. A large specimen may attain a diameter of nearly 1 m. The number of rays varies, as do their lengths, because some may be regenerating in the place of rays that have been lost. The color also varies extensively, but *Pycnopodia* is characteristically more or less orange, with violet or purple tufts where the pedicellariae and dermal branchiae are concentrated. Some specimens are a purplish color almost throughout. Although *Pycnopodia* is spiny, its rays are rather soft and flabby. They are also quite fragile, and specimens clinging tightly to rocks may part with a ray or two if they are pulled too roughly from the substrate. The helpless appearance of a sunflower star draped over the palm of one's hand is misleading. For a sea star, this species moves rapidly, especially when submerged, and it is a powerful predator. It feeds on a wide variety of organisms, but concentrates on bivalve molluscs; it will also scavenge on dead fish. *Pycnopodia* is definitely feared by other invertebrates. The large sea cucumber, *Parastichopus californicus,* which is about as lethargic as any of our animals, will work itself into a writhing gallop if the tube feet of a *Pycnopodia* make contact with its skin. Some bivalves, stimulated by the prospect of being eaten, go into violent activity in order to escape. Scallops, for instance, clap their valves together to swim out of danger, and the common cockle extends its foot and pushes it against the substrate to get away. Sea urchins respond to *Pycnopodia* by extending their pedicellariae.

Brittle Stars

On really rocky shores (as opposed to situations where rocks are scattered over muddy sand or gravel), only one brittle star, *Ophiopholis aculeata* (pl. XVI), is common. However, it is our most beautiful species. The coloration is generally a mixture of brown or buff and either bright red or dark red; on the upper side of the disk, the brown and red markings are often in bold juxtaposition.

On the whole, reddish tones seem to predominate. The prickly look of this species is due to the prominence of the arm spines. *Ophiopholis* can be very abundant in the lower part of the intertidal region, where it prefers crevices, especially those between rather tight-fitting rocks. The maximum diameter of this species is about 8 cm.

Sea Urchins

Of the several species of sea urchins occurring in our area, three may be found in the lower part of the intertidal region. One of them, the green sea urchin, *Strongylocentrotus droebachiensis* (pl. XVI), has a wide distribution in northern waters. (It was originally described from specimens collected at Drobak, Norway.) Its spines are crowded, short, and rather fine. The color of the animal as a whole is decidedly greenish, but there are reddish brown tones here and there, especially near the top. The test of a large specimen is about 8 cm in diameter.

The red sea urchin, *S. franciscanus* (pl. XVI), is one of the giants of the group. Its test may be more than 12 cm in diameter, and the spines may be more than 5 cm long. It is typically a kind of acid red, though the tube feet tend to be darker. This species, which has a range from Alaska to Lower California, inhabits relatively quiet shores as well as those where there is considerable wave action, and it is common subtidally.

The purple sea urchin, *S. purpuratus* (pl. XVI), has a geographic range comparable to that of *S. franciscanus,* but is decidedly partial to shores having strong wave action. It is therefore common on the open coast, but will not be found in Puget Sound, and only a few restricted populations of it are known in the San Juan Archipelago. It is apparently even more dependent than the California mussel on wave action. The test of the purple urchin may be up to about 8 cm in diameter. The spines are short, like those of the green urchin, but they are much stouter. The color of the spines is such a rich purple that one almost expects a dye to start dripping from the animal as soon as it is picked up. In situations on the open coast where this species is abundant and the substrate is of relatively soft rock, the urchins work themselves into hollows that may eventually become deep enough to enclose them completely. Just how they do this is not fully understood, but the abrasive action of the movable spines is suspected to be the primary cause. The spines are covered by living tissue which continues to deposit calcareous material. The rock, however, cannot restore itself, so the holes get deeper.

The food of all of our sea urchins consists largely of pieces of seaweed. Whatever lands on them or under them is passed to the mouth with the aid of the tube feet. The sharp tips of the five jaws that make up a structure called Aristotle's lantern chop the food into tiny fragments which can be swallowed and digested for whatever nutritional value they have. *S. franciscanus* is known to use its jaws to scrape off small barnacles.

If you have a strong hand lens or a microscope, you may wish to compare the pedicellariae of an urchin with those of a sea star. The former have three jaws, the latter have two.

The digestive tracts of most sea urchins, including all of ours, support an astonishing assortment of ciliated protozoa, most of which seem to be commensals feeding on bacteria in the gut. Then there is a pretty, reddish rhabdocoel turbellarian, about 4 or 5 mm long, called *Syndisyrinx franciscanus*. Just what it lives on is still uncertain. Mature worms usually contain a conspicuous golden egg capsule with a long, threadlike extension. After a capsule is laid and finally escapes with the feces of the urchin, the thread probably gets tangled up with a piece of seaweed and the capsule thus has a chance to enter another host. Sometimes as many as 30 or 40 worms will be found in one urchin. Rarely, another worm of the same general type, but brown rather than reddish, occurs along with *Syndisyrinx*. This other species seems to belong to the genus *Syndesmis*.

Sea Cucumbers

The largest of our sea cucumbers is *Parastichopus californicus* (pl. XVII). It regularly attains a length of about 40 cm, and may be even larger. It cannot be said to be beautiful, or even typical, but it is interesting. The body is limp when extended, but firm and fully packed when contracted. The coloration is dark reddish brown above, somewhat lighter below, and all over the upper surface and sides are pointed, fleshy warts. The tube feet are crowded together on the lower side, and only three of the five pairs of rows are distinct; the others have essentially abortive tube feet. The specialized tube feet around the mouth look something like mops, with the tips of the branches elaborated into little disks. As detritus is collected on the tube feet, they are inserted into the mouth and licked clean. Next in order of size is *Cucumaria miniata* (pl. XVII), which grows to a length of about 20 cm. It lives in crevices or between rocks piled one on top of the other, and normally only the crown of bright orange oral tentacles (pl. XVIII) is visible. Most of the rest of the body is reddish brown or pinkish brown. It is, on the whole, an attractive cucumber. The oral tentacles are much branched and trap particles of detritus suspended in the water. After a tentacle is "saturated" with food material, it is pushed into the mouth and cleaned off.

Eupentacta quinquesemita (fig. 44) has already been dealt with in connection with the fauna on floating docks, where it is the predominant cucumber. In rocky habitats it occupies the same general situations as *Cucumaria,* living in crevices and between rocks. Its color ranges from nearly white to very pale orange, and its maximum length is usually about 8 or 9 cm. The five sets of tube feet are almost evenly spaced around the body, and the individual tube feet are distinctive because when they contract to the fullest extent possible, they are still obvious. In most sea cucumbers, they practically disappear.

The only other sea cucumber occurring here—there are indeed more species, but they are almost strictly subtidal—is perhaps the most astonishing. *Psolus chitonoides* (the species name means "resembling a chiton") is odd enough not to be even recognized as a holothurian by many who encounter it for the first time. *Psolus* (pl. XVIII) has the shape of a short cucumber sliced lengthwise, for one side of it—the side with the tube feet—is almost perfectly flat. It clings tightly to rock and is essentially sedentary. The upper surface is covered with overlapping calcareous plates, and the mouth is situated on this surface some distance from the anterior end. When the bright red oral tentacles are extended, *Psolus* is a gorgeous sight. Unfortunately, it is not often encountered in shore collecting. It is abundant in deeper water, however, and it is joined there by a smaller species, more or less purplish pink in color, called *Psolidium bullatum. Psolus* reaches a length of about 5 cm, and *Psolidium* a length of about 3 cm.

Brachiopods

There are several species of brachiopods in our area, but only one of them, *Terebratalia transversa* (figs. 125 and 126), is regularly seen intertidally. On the open coast *T. transversa* is not often observed except at very low tide levels, and even then it is rare. In the San Juan Archipelago, however, it may be quite abundant at − 2.0, and sometimes occurs as high as 0.0. Its variability partially accounts for the number of invalid species names applied to it. Most individuals look like those shown in Figure 125—tumid, a little broader than long, and without much ribbing. The width is usually about 2 or 3 cm. A particularly attractive variant (fig. 126)

125. *Terebratalia transversa* (usual form)

126. A strongly ribbed variant of *Terebratalia transversa*

seems to be quite common on Saltspring Island, in the Canadian San Juans, and perhaps elsewhere in the same general region. The shell is strongly ribbed, and the width is much greater than the length.

Chitons

The chiton *Katharina* (fig. 91), characteristic of zone 3, also occurs in zone 4; but it is overshadowed here by several other distinctive species. One of them, *Cryptochiton stelleri* (pl. VII), is the largest chiton in the world, frequently reaching a length of 20 cm. *Cryptochiton* may not be recognized for what it is because all eight of its shells are completely covered by the thick, gritty girdle. The genus name alludes to this feature; the species name, as in *Cyanocitta stelleri*—Steller's jay—commemorates Georg Wilhelm Steller, a naturalist on an early Russian expedition to Alaska.

Our most beautiful chiton is the lined chiton, *Tonicella lineata* (pl. VII). It is brightly colored, with dark brown lines zigzagging over a lighter background in which yellow, orange, pink, orchid, and lavender predominate. It attains a length of about 5 cm. *Tonicella* will generally be found close to the encrusting coralline alga *Lithothamnion,* on whose surface it grazes. It seems to eat the more superficial layers of the encrustations, and in doing so it also takes in the film of diatoms and other small organisms that happen to be in the way.

A smaller chiton most frequently found on the underside of rocks is *Ischnochiton mertensii* (fig. 127). Its color, as the animal is seen from above, tends to be nearly uniformly brick red or reddish brown, but sometimes there are conspicuous blotches of white. Though the color varies, this species is unmistakable among intertidal chitons because the surface of its girdle is composed of tiny

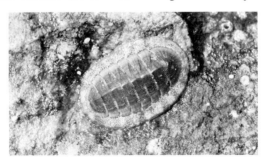

127. *Ischnochiton mertensii*

scales; other species of *Ischnochiton* with this same characteristic are essentially subtidal.

Three other chitons inhabiting this zone are the mopalias, which are characterized by hairs or bristles sticking out of the girdle. *Mopalia muscosa* (fig. 128) has the stiffest and thickest bristles,

128. *Mopalia muscosa,* the mossy chiton

and is the species most likely to have barnacles or other settlers growing on its back. The other two mopalias have rather soft hairs, but *M. ciliata* (fig. 129) has a distinct cleft at the posterior end, whereas *M. lignosa* (fig. 130) does not; the girdle hairs of *M. lignosa,* moreover, generally originate in the center of light spots.

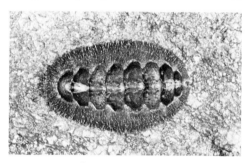

129. *Mopalia ciliata*

Snails and Limpets

Acmaea mitra, the whitecap limpet (fig. 131), is unusual for a member of its clan in having such a thick and conical shell. The height sometimes equals the length, which in exceptionally large specimens is a little more than 3 cm. *A. mitra,* like the lined chiton, *Tonicella,* is closely tied to the encrusting coralline red alga, *Lith-*

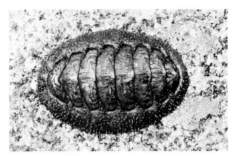

130. *Mopalia lignosa*

131. *Acmaea mitra,* the whitecap limpet, covered with *Lithothamnion,* the coralline red alga on which it feeds

othamnion; it not only eats this alga, but its shell is almost always overgrown by it.

The keyhole limpets are rather close relatives of true limpets. In the latter group, however, water enters the mantle cavity on the left side, passes over the single gill, picks up wastes from the kidney and digestive tract, and then flows out on the right side. In keyhole limpets, which are considered to be more primitive, there are two gills, one on each side of the mantle cavity. Water enters the mantle cavity on both sides of the head, passes over the gills, and flows out through the opening at the apex of the shell. The kidneys and digestive tract discharge their wastes not far from the exhalant aperture.

The only keyhole limpet likely to be found in the intertidal region—and then only in the lowermost zone—is *Diodora aspera* (fig. 132). Its shell reaches a length of about 5 cm. Like true limpets, it is a grazing herbivore.

132. *Diodora aspera,* the keyhole limpet

Almost every keyhole limpet will have a scaleworm, *Arctonoë vittata* (fig. 133), tucked away between the foot and mantle. The coloration of this polychaete—ivory, with a few dark transverse stripes—almost perfectly matches that of the mantle of its host.

133. A scale worm, *Arctonoë vittata,* in the mantle cavity of *Diodora*

Arctonoë is associated with some other animals, including *Cryptochiton,* and its behavior with respect to its several hosts has been the subject of numerous investigations. Specimens taken from *Diodora,* if placed in an apparatus designed to test host preference, will tend to select *Diodora* over other molluscs; those from *Cryptochiton* will usually go back to *Cryptochiton.* Just what *Arctonoë* feeds on is still uncertain. It has been observed to bite at the tube feet of a sea star about to touch *Diodora,* but it is not known whether this behavior helps to protect its host or whether it merely represents a more or less fortuitous nipping at what could be something to eat.

The northern abalone, *Haliotis kamtschatkana* (fig. 134), is sometimes found intertidally, but it becomes more abundant in the domain of divers. Its shell, which reaches a length of about 12 cm,

134. *Haliotis kamtschatkana*, the northern abalone (a small specimen)

is thinner than that of some species found on the coast of California, and much of the surface is wavy. The series of holes—the more recent ones, that is, which are still functional—serves in the same way as the single apical aperture of *Diodora*, to permit water that has passed over the gills to exit from the mantle cavity, taking with it the wastes from the excretory organs and digestive tract.

Two kinds of snails with shells shaped like tops are abundant in our waters. Superficially they look much alike, except for size, for the whorls are spirally sculptured with alternating light ridges and pinkish brown furrows. In *Calliostoma ligatum* (fig. 135) the height (maximum slightly more than 2 cm) is a bit greater than the width. There is no opening near the center of the base of the shell. *Margarites pupillus* (fig. 136) is wider than it is tall and is smaller than *Calliostoma*, reaching a height of about 1.5 cm. It does have a distinct opening, called the umbilicus, near the center of the base of the shell; this opening goes into the column around which the whorls are organized. *Margarites*, when its shell is dry, is less likely than *Calliostoma* to show the alternating light and dark markings that follow the whorls, and it is more likely to show pearliness externally. Both *Calliostoma* and *Margarites* are grazers on coat-

135. *Calliostoma ligatum*

136. *Margarites pupillus*

ings of diatoms and other plant material, and both are closely related to limpets and keyhole limpets, though the form of the shell
does not suggest this.

A limpetlike shell turns up in gastropods of various unrelated
groups. The slipper shells of the genus *Crepidula,* for instance, are
not at all close to true limpets, though they resemble them superficially. *Crepidula adunca* (fig. 137) may as well be mentioned at
this point, because it is so commonly found on the shell of *Calliostoma.* (On the open coast, it is also on turban shells of the genus
Tegula.) It has a definite beak on its posterior slope (when there is
something of a beak in true limpets, as *Collisella digitalis,* it is on
the forward side), and the color of the outside is brown. Inside, the

137. *Crepidula adunca,* a slipper shell, on *Calliostoma ligatum*

shell has a well-developed white shelf. The largest specimens are only about 2 cm long.

The largest shelled gastropod commonly found in our region—other than the abalone—is *Fusitriton oregonensis* (fig. 138). It is more abundant subtidally than intertidally, but is nonetheless frequently seen in the infralittoral fringe. The shell has very distinct, rounded whorls, with spiral ridges as well as axial ribs. The copious brown periostracum is conspicuously hairy, and this gastropod is often referred to as the "hairy triton." Large specimens have shells about 10 cm long.

138. *Fusitriton oregonensis,* the hairy triton

Fusitriton is a predator, and evidently not a timid one. It attacks, among other animals, sea urchins, destroying the living tissue on the outside of the test, and sometimes even boring clear through the test. At least some of the urchins showing blackish, tar-like discolorations are survivors of skirmishes with *Fusitriton*. The egg masses of this snail are always amazing—big sheets of what look like sawed-off translucent grains of corn packed into a spiral pattern.

Amphissa columbiana (fig. 139), about 3 cm long, at first may seem nondescript, partly because of the uninteresting brown or pinkish brown color of the shell. However, when the shell is exam-

139. *Amphissa columbiana*

ined carefully, it turns out to be rather nicely wrought. The almost elliptical aperture is bordered on its inner side by a conspicuous enameled area, and there is a distinct notch—almost a canal—through which the snail sticks out its long siphon. Externally, the whorls are marked by very fine spiral lines, which are intersected in the upper half of the shell by prominent longitudinal ridges. *Amphissa* is primarily a scavenger on dead animal tissue, and has good olfactory equipment for locating food.

Bittium eschrichtii (fig. 140) is the only really abundant snail with a slender, drill-shaped shell. This species is small, just a little

140. *Bittium eschrichtii*

over 1 cm long when full-grown. The whorls are generally brown or gray and marked with closely spaced grooves. *Bittium* is usually found beneath rocks, and its shell is popular with very young hermit crabs.

The shell of *Ceratostoma foliatum,* the "leafy horn-mouth" (fig. 141), reaches a length of about 8 cm. It looks heavier than it is because of the extensive frills with which it is ornamented. These

141. *Ceratostoma foliatum*

vary greatly from specimen to specimen. The canal through which the siphon is extended is closed over, thus becoming a tube. A big tooth on the outer lip of the aperture of *Ceratostoma,* near the base of the canal, is thought to be handy for hooking onto the ridges of large barnacles on which this snail feeds.

Ocenebra lurida (fig. 142) is related to *Ceratostoma,* but lacks the leafy excrescences. It is only about 2 cm long. It might be confused with *Amphissa,* because its shell shows a similar mixture of

142. *Ocenebra lurida*

fine spiral lines and axial ribs. However, it is less slender than *Amphissa,* its canal is better developed, and its aperture is not at all the same shape, being oval rather than nearly elliptical. The yellow-brown or orange-brown coloration, and the fact that the axial ribs cross the body whorl, enable one to distinguish it from a small specimen of *Searlesia.*

A snail that almost never is found intertidally, but is so distinctive that it can hardly be neglected, is *Trichotropis cancellata* (fig. 143). It grows up to about 3 cm long, has a nearly round aperture,

143. *Trichotropis cancellata*

and is marked with both longitudinal and spiral lines, of which the latter are the stronger. The periostracum is light brown and elaborated into coarse hairs, as in *Fusitriton.* Specimens from deeper water, where *Trichotropis* is abundant, often have a tiny white-shelled snail, *Odostomia columbiana,* next to the aperture. This parasitizes *Trichotropis,* using its eversible proboscis provided with a puncturing stylet, to suck the juices of its host. *Trichotropis* itself is a filter-feeder, using mucus and ciliary pathways to trap microscopic food and move it to its mouth. It seems not to move around a great deal. Once situated on a stone or empty shell and out of the way of clogging mud, it may stay there indefinitely. This immobility probably explains why *Trichotropis* is often overgrown by solitary ascidians and other sessile animals.

Sea Slugs

The beauty of most of our sea slugs is usually apparent at first sight. However, some of the smaller species may escape notice because their coloration blends into that of the animals on which they live. *Doridella* (fig. 28) and *Corambe,* for instance, are not easily seen unless colonies of the bryozoan *Membranipora* on kelp are examined with the aid of a magnifier. *Eubranchus* (fig. 6), regularly associated with *Obelia,* likewise may be overlooked, although it is one of our more common species. All three of these sea slugs occur on rocky shores, but they have been discussed already in connection with the fauna of floating docks. *Rostanga* (pl. I), whose color matches that of the red sponges on which it grazes, was considered earlier in this chapter.

The majority of the conspicuous sea slugs on floating docks may be expected in rocky intertidal situations. *Hermissenda crassicornis* (pl. VIII), *Aeolidia papillosa* (fig. 39), *Archidoris montereyensis* (pl. IX), and *Diaulula sandiegensis* (pl. X) are probably the ones found with greatest regularity. *Archidoris odhneri* (pl. IX) and *Acanthodoris brunnea* seem to be less common.

A dorid that is sometimes very abundant intertidally is *Onchidoris bilamellata.* It is similar to *A. brunnea,* but has more gills around the anus—at least sixteen, instead of just seven—and the brown coloration of the upper surface is concentrated in a few bands instead of being more or less uniform. *Onchidoris* preys on barnacles, and sometimes is common in zone 3.

Among the more stunning dorids are *Triopha carpenteri* and *Laila cockerelli.* Both of these sea slugs are so brilliantly decorated that they seem almost unreal. In *Triopha* (pl. XI) the dorsal papillae, as well as the rhinophores and the gills, are tipped with orange; there are also spots of this color scattered over the otherwise white or yellowish white upper surface. *Triopha* reaches a length of about 6 or 7 cm. It eats bryozoans.

Laila (pl. XI) has an unusual feature for a dorid, namely, numerous long, fleshy processes that superficially resemble the cerata found on eolid nudibranchs such as *Hermissenda.* These, and the rhinophores also, are tipped with orange, but there are no spots on the body surface and the gills are not colored. *Laila* is only 2 or 3 cm long, and not common.

Another dorid that was not mentioned in connection with floating docks, for it is only rarely found on them, is *Cadlina luteomarginata* (pl. X). It is a relatively broad, flat species that does not often exceed a length of about 4 cm. The ground color is almost white, but all the way around the edge of the foot and the edge of the mantle there is a band of lemon yellow, and the low tubercles on the dorsal surface are tipped with this same color. *Cadlina* subsists on sponges.

Among larger eolid nudibranchs found in this zone and not previously described in Chapter 3 are two members of the genus *Dirona* that are characterized by numerous strongly flattened and pointed cerata. *D. albolineata* (fig. 144) is nearly translucent and usually almost colorless (or only faintly pinkish or purplish), except for the internal organs that may show through the body wall. The cerata are edged with brilliant white lines. *D. albolineata* eats small snails, whose shells it can crack with its jaws, and also consumes ascidians and bryozoans. Large specimens are 5 or 6 cm long.

144. *Dirona albolineata*

D. aurantia is similar, but it may grow a little larger than *D. albolineata*. It is a dirty orange color, with white edges on the cerata and white spots scattered over the dorsal surface. It feeds on bryozoans and occasionally turns up in fair numbers around floating docks.

Bivalves

Our scallops are basically subtidal animals. Of the several species reported in this area, one—*Pecten caurinus,* the weather vane scallop—is huge, up to more than 15 cm in diameter. Although it will never be found intertidally, two of its relatives occasionally turn up in the course of shore collecting; they are extremely abundant on gravelly and shelly bottoms in deeper water. *Chlamys hastata hericia* (fig. 145) and *Chlamys rubida* (fig. 146)

145. Left valve of *Chlamys hastata hericia*, the pink scallop

146. Left valve of *Chlamys rubida*

are similar to one another, but the ribs of the former are rendered rasplike by the presence of little curved spines, whereas those of the latter are practically smooth. The shells of both reach a height of about 6 cm. Scallops normally lie with their right valves against the substrate, and they may be attached periodically, especially when they are younger, by means of a byssus, something like that secreted by mussels. Their valves are normally agape, so that they can process water for extraction of microscopic food. When they are in an aquarium and in their typical posture, the beautiful green eyes—which are iridescent and almost luminous—can be seen around the edge of the mantle in both valves. Sometimes spontaneously, and just about always when menaced by a predator, such as certain sea stars, they swim by a sort of jet propulsion, clapping the valves tightly together and forcing water out through a canal-like opening on either side of the hinge.

Both *C. hastata hericia* and *C. rubida* are regularly colonized—mostly on the left valve—by sponges. These form rather thick growths, generally grayish, brownish, or yellowish in color. *Myxilla incrustans* has relatively few and rather large oscular openings; *Mycale adhaerens* (fig. 147) has more numerous, very small oscula.

The purple-hinged rock scallop, *Hinnites multirugosus* (fig. 148), is attached firmly to rocks by the right valve of its heavy shell. The left valve is generally somewhat irregular, and may be

147. *Chlamys hastata hericia*, with its left valve overgrown by a sponge, *Mycale adhaerens*

148. *Hinnites multirugosus*, the rock scallop

grotesquely misshapen. It is rather coarsely ribbed, and the ribs show some spinous or membranous excrescences. Both valves are white internally, except close to the hinge, where there is a large blotch of rich purple. The purple color penetrates deep into the shell, and as the area next to the hinge is the thickest part, it is the last to be worn away completely by erosion. Many of the purple bits of shell found on the beach can be traced to this species. The outside of the free valve is on the whole brownish, but when it becomes colonized by sponges, the coralline red alga *Lithothamnion*, and other encrusting organisms, it becomes varicolored.

The valves of the rock scallop are frequently partially eaten away by the boring sponge, *Cliona celata* (pl. I). The presence of this sponge is evident at the surface as little yellow patches, but below the surface the shell may look something like a honeycomb. Evidently, certain amoeboid cells of *Cliona* are able to erode the calcareous substrate by etching out small portions until they are finally undercut and break off. The process of burrowing thus seems to be accomplished partly by mechanical means and partly by chemical means.

When *Hinnites* is young, it is free-swimming, after the fashion of real scallops, and the shell has the shape characteristic of a scallop. Even after the shell becomes thick, heavy, and irregular, the telltale "ears" remain as reminders of its relationship to scallops. The diameter of large specimens sometimes exceeds 15 cm.

Octopuses

We have two species of *Octopus* in shallow water. One of these, *O. dofleini* (pl. XII), is probably the largest anywhere, with an arm spread of perhaps more than 3 meters and a weight of about 100 pounds. Divers encounter it frequently, and once in awhile a little one is found under a ledge, between rocks, or in a pool in the lowest part of the intertidal region. When a larger individual climbs part way out of the water, as if to menace intruders coming too close to its lair, it is probably protecting eggs or a brood of young. On the whole, octopuses do not seek the company of people.

Baby octopuses found swimming at the surface, as around floating docks, are probably the young of a different species, evidently still not named, that is occasionally collected intertidally as well as subtidally. The adults have a body length, exclusive of the arms, of only about 5 cm and a skin that is roughened by small papillae.

Octopuses feed to a large extent on crabs and generally eat heartily in captivity. In other respects, unfortunately, they are difficult to keep, as they require cold water and plenty of dissolved oxygen. Large tanks that have sea water running into them continuously are just about essential. Octopuses also have to be protected from their own bad judgment, for they will try to climb out of almost anything they are put into and will in the course of other acrobatics pull out standpipes that maintain the water level in their tanks. The moral of all this is that if you find a little octopus, it would be best to leave it in nature's care.

Shrimps

Broken-back shrimps of the genus *Heptacarpus* (fig. 37) are common in tide pools, where they are usually hidden away in growths of algae. Occasionally they are shaken out of a mass of kelp that is lifted from rock for examination. The broken-backed look of these shrimps is due to a sharp bend in the body in the region of the third abdominal segment. They are sometimes so nearly transparent that the beating of the heart can be observed in the dorsal region. We have a number of species of *Heptacarpus* in our area, mostly ranging in length from around 2 to 3 cm; some of them are not found intertidally. (The closely related genera, *Spirontocaris, Eualus,* and *Lebbeus,* superficially indistinguishable from *Heptacarpus,* seem to be represented almost entirely by subtidal species.) The coloration varies greatly—from green through olive and brown to pink or red, sometimes complicated by opaque white bars or darker streaks—and frequently matches that of algae to which they cling. The coloration must depend to some extent on acquiring pigments of the seaweeds, either by eating them or the small animals that subsist on them. The few published observations on feeding by *Heptacarpus* and its relatives indicate that these shrimps are largely carnivores.

Crabs and Hermit Crabs

In zone 4 the predominant hermit crab is *Pagurus granosimanus,* a carry-over from zone 3. However, *P. hirsutiusculus* (fig. 84) is generally present in fair numbers, and *P. beringanus,* which is principally subtidal, is also found here. In large specimens of *P. beringanus*—those around 4 cm long—the coloration of the claw of the second and third legs is distinctive: two orange bands separated by a white band. Younger individuals do not show this, but can be recognized by a red band at the joint below the claw. Iridescent green eyes are characteristic of all ages. In the intertidal region, *P. beringanus* mostly uses shells of *Thais lamellosa, Thais canaliculata,* and *Searlesia dira.* Shells of *Amphissa columbiana, Calliostoma ligatum,* and *Bittium eschrichtii* commonly house smaller hermit crabs of this species.

Clinging to kelp or hiding under it are two very common spider crabs. The larger of these is the kelp crab, *Pugettia producta* (fig. 149), which may have a carapace length of up to almost 10 cm.

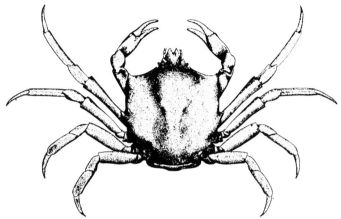

149. *Pugettia producta,* the kelp crab

This crab is difficult to see, especially when the color of its slick carapace is an olive green that almost exactly matches that of *Egregia* and some of the other kelps on which it is found. Sometimes a bit of red or orange is worked into the coloration, especially underneath. *Pugettia gracilis* (fig. 215) is a smaller species, with a carapace length rarely exceeding 3 cm. Its color is mostly reddish brown, but there are various subdued mottlings. The upper side of the carapace, unlike that of *P. producta,* has a few sharp spines. *P. gracilis* encourages the growth of small algae and other organisms on its carapace. Both *P. gracilis* and *P. producta* are also found on eelgrass, so they will be mentioned again in Chapter 5.

Oregonia gracilis, the decorator crab (fig. 150), is the most spidery of our intertidal spider crabs and the one most likely to have a really luxuriant growth of small seaweeds, hydroids, bryozoans, and other colonists. The carapace, broadest near the posterior end, is almost triangular and narrows anteriorly into two slender and nearly parallel rostral horns. The legs are very long and slender in proportion to the size of the body as a whole. The length of the carapace, including the rostrum, occasionally reaches 5 cm. The roughened surfaces of the carapace and legs probably encourage the settlement of foreign organisms, but *Oregonia* is an active decorator: some of the pieces of plant and animal material stuck to it are not permanently fixed to the exoskeleton, but are merely pressed into the matrix of other growths. The delicate pincers of

150. *Oregonia gracilis,* the decorator crab

the first legs are admirably constructed for handling the sort of decorations *Oregonia* likes. This crab is sometimes so heavily over-grown that the camouflage is perfect.

In *Scyra acutifrons,* the sharp-nosed crab (fig. 151), the shape of the carapace is about the same as that of *Oregonia.* The rostral horns, however, are relatively short and strongly flattened, and the legs are less spidery than they are in *Oregonia.* The roughened surfaces of the carapace and legs probably help colonizing organisms

151. *Scyra acutifrons,* the sharp-nosed crab

become well entrenched. In larger specimens, the carapace is about 3.5 cm long.

The red crab, *Cancer productus* (fig. 214), is frequently taken on rocky shores, although it is more typically found in quiet bays, particularly where there are well-developed beds of eelgrass (see Chap. 5). It is, in any case, a versatile animal. The carapace width of a large *C. productus* is about 15 cm. The coloration of the upper side of the body is on the whole a dark brownish red. The pincers are distinctive in being tipped with black. It is probably more common on shores strewn with rocks and boulders than on massive rock formations and reefs.

Cancer oregonensis (pl. XXI) likes neat holes into which it can fit without much room to spare. This little crab is mostly dull red, but the tips of its pincers are nearly black; in both these respects it is similar to *Cancer productus*. However, it is much smaller, being at most only about 4 cm across, and the outline of the carapace is nearly circular. Below the intertidal zone, where the giant barnacle *(Balanus nubilus)* is abundant, it must be in seventh heaven, as many of the empty shells of this barnacle dredged from deep water are occupied by *C. oregonensis*.

The helmet crab, *Telmessus cheiragonus* (pl. XXI), is a bristly, hairy species with a distinctly greenish look, especially when it is younger. Older specimens generally have considerable red, orange, or brown worked into the coloration, but some of the greenish cast usually persists. The carapace, which in larger individuals may reach a width of about 6 cm, has six coarse teeth on either side; most of these have small secondary serrations.

The strangest crabs found in the intertidal region look little alike, but they belong to the same family (Lithodidae). Moreover, they are more closely related to hermit crabs and porcelain crabs than to true crabs.

Hapalogaster mertensii (pl. XXII) is basically brown or red and brown, but the body is so thoroughly covered with golden brown bristles and hairs that the ground color may be mostly obscured. The fifth pair of legs is small and tucked out of the way in the gill chamber under the carapace. The abdomen is soft and cannot be folded up under the carapace. The carapace of this species may attain a length of about 3 cm.

The other crab in this odd series, *Cryptolithodes sitchensis* (the "hidden lithode from Sitka") (pl. XXII), is quite weird-looking. Its carapace extends outward after the fashion of an oblong saucer to cover the animal so completely that its legs cannot be seen from above. "Turtle crab" is a good common name for this species. In a large individual, the width of the carapace may exceed 5 cm. The rostrum is broad and abruptly truncate. As in *Hapalogaster,* the fifth pair of legs is out of sight, but the abdomen is more nearly like that of porcelain crabs and true crabs in being flat, bent under the carapace, and covered with several distinct, hard plates. The underside is generally almost white. The coloration of the upper side of the carapace varies extensively: sometimes it is almost completely red or purplish red (much the color of the coralline alga *Lithothamnion,* though duskier), but it often has considerable gray or brown and may be blotched and streaked.

Ascidians

The solitary ascidians found in the lower intertidal include some of those that colonize floats. *Pyura haustor* (fig. 49), with an ugly, wrinkled lower portion and gorgeous, nearly carmine red siphons, is almost always present, especially in holes and at their edges. The wrinkled part of the tunic, which ranges from orange-brown to reddish brown in color, may be studded with bits of shell and other foreign material, and may have various small animals using it as a substrate. When the siphons of a large *Pyura* are extended, its height may be close to 5 cm.

Boltenia villosa (fig. 50) is not as common as *Pyura,* but it is easier to see and recognize because it is distinctly stalked, and its light orange-brown color and hairy tunic keep it from blending so easily into the background.

Cnemidocarpa finmarkiensis (fig. 150) may be hard to find because of its habit of living in holes, into which it sometimes fits so neatly that it will be unnoticed unless its siphons are extended. In spite of the fact that it looks as if it had just been skinned, it is a beautiful animal, with an almost pearly pinkish-red look. The apertures of both its siphons are round when functioning, but they close down into the form of little crosses when the animal is disturbed. A large *Cnemidocarpa* is about 2.5 cm high.

Styela gibbsii (fig. 153) is not common intertidally, but it is abundant in deeper water, where it is attached to stones and shells,

152. *Cnemidocarpa finmarkiensis*

153. *Styela gibbsii*

especially those of the snail *Trichotropis*. It frequently forms clumps and is often mixed with *Pyura, Boltenia*, and other ascidians. The tunic of *Styela* is wrinkled, like that of *Pyura*, but the body is rather slender and shaped like a cucumber. The color, on the whole, is tan or brown; the short siphons generally have a faint tinge of orange when they are expanded. The height of large specimens is about 4 cm.

Metandrocarpa taylori (pl. X) is another species that is only occasionally seen at low tide. It is usually hidden away under ledges. *Metandrocarpa* is approximately hemispherical, and the largest specimens are not quite 7 mm in diameter. The color is typically orange-red. This ascidian proliferates asexually to form groups of several to many nearly contiguous individuals. The young develop from short runners that are budded from the bases of adults. The connections between individuals are not permanent, but a few can usually be found in any large aggregation of *Metandrocarpa*.

Intertidally, only a few compound ascidians are reasonably abundant in our region. *Distaplia occidentalis* (fig. 48; pl. XIX), so common on floats and pilings, also grows on rocks. Its colonies range from club-shaped or mushroomlike masses, just 1 or 2 cm in diameter, to broad mounds several times as large as this. Characteristically, a number of colonies of various sizes and shapes form tight aggregations. The color varies greatly, from pale orange or tan to dark purplish red.

Aplidium californicum (pl. XIX) is frequent on the outer coast, especially where large rocks and reefs are exposed to heavy wave action, but it occurs only sparingly in the San Juan Archipelago. This species of *Aplidium* forms irregular slabs and cakes about 1 cm or more in thickness and perhaps 20 cm in diameter. When it grows over something else that happens to be stuck to the rock, as the shell of a barnacle or the base of a dead seaweed, it may look considerably thicker than it really is. It is commonly called "sea pork" because of its form and consistency. The color ranges from almost white to reddish brown, but most colonies are brownish yellow.

A rather different type of compound ascidian is one resembling white glove leather—the kind that shows little grayish pits in it. Ascidians of this type are sometimes mistaken for sponges, not only because of their appearance but because when they are teased apart and examined with a microscope, they show an abundance of calcareous spicules. The spicules, however, are globular and unlike those of any calcareous or siliceous sponges likely to be found here. Moreover, close examination of a colony will reveal the numerous tiny zooids characteristic of compound ascidians. There are apparently two genera in the San Juan Archipelago: *Didemnum* (pl. V) and *Trididemnum*. They cannot be differentiated in the field, as the characters involved in identification require close attention to microscopic details.

Fishes

The small fishes of intertidal habitats fall largely into four groups: clingfishes, sculpins, pricklebacks, and gunnels. The pricklebacks and gunnels, taken together, are what most people call blenny eels, but they belong to separate families.

The tidepool sculpin has already been discussed in connection with higher levels of the intertidal region. It may be found in zone 4, but a related species, *Oligocottus snyderi,* is more characteristic here. It is called the fluffy sculpin because it has tufts of little fingerlike projections along both sides of the base of the dorsal fin. The color of *O. snyderi,* like that of other small sculpins, varies a great deal, but green tones seem to prevail, at least in some populations.

The flathead clingfish, *Gobiesox meandricus* (fig. 154), is the only representative of its group that one is apt to find in the intertidal region. It is common, however, especially beneath rocks that

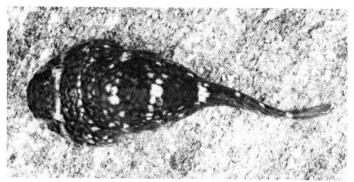

154. *Gobiesox meandricus,* the clingfish, attached to the underside of a rock

have smoothly rounded undersides. The basal portions of the pectoral and pelvic fins of the clingfish contribute to the formation of a surprisingly powerful sucker, by which the fish attaches itself.

The blenny eels—that is, the pricklebacks and gunnels—are also plentiful under rocks, slithering around like snakes when exposed. In gunnels, the soft extensions of the lower portions of the right and left gills are connected to one another across the ventral surface; in pricklebacks, on the other hand, there are no such connections. The cockscomb prickleback, *Anoplarchus purpurescens* (pl. XXIII), with a fleshy crest on the top of its head, is the most common species through much of our area, although in Puget Sound proper the penpoint gunnel, *Apodichthys flavidus,* may be more numerous in many situations; it is often bright green or orange-yellow.

5. SANDY BEACHES AND QUIET BAYS

MUCH of the shoreline of our area, especially in protected bays, inlets, and coves, is characterized by substrates of mud, sand, and gravel. The assemblages of animals and plants found in these situations are very different from those associated with rocky shores. This chapter is concerned primarily with organisms that live in sand and mud. Relatively clean, coarse gravel usually has almost no conspicuous animals and plants. However, it must be pointed out that in many bays where the substrate appears at first glance to consist largely of mud or muddy sand, the amount of gravel and pebbles may constitute more than half the total volume. The coarse material contributes in an important way to the character of the substrate, and many organisms are typically found in gravelly muds. Nevertheless, the proportions of various sizes of small particles and the amount of organic detritus essentially determine which kinds of organisms can live in sandy and muddy habitats.

The finer the hard particles, the more water the substrate can hold by capillary action. The type and amount of organic matter also influence the water-retaining capacity of the substrate, as well as the extent to which the particles cohere to one another. On exposed sandy beaches, most of the hard particles—generally of quartz or its variants, as found in granitic rocks—have a diameter larger than 0.1 mm, and the amount of organic detritus is low. Water percolates rather freely through the sand, but the sand is not especially effective in retaining water in its interstices. In mud flats, the substrate contains high proportions of silt and clay. In silt, the particle size ranges from about 0.06 mm down to 0.004 mm; in clay, it is below 0.004 mm. The fine grain size and corresponding capillary force of the surface sediments, and the cohesive property of organic matter and microorganisms, encourage the persistence of shallow pools. They are typical not only of mud flats, but also of many situations in which very fine sand predominates.

When the substrate retains considerable water, at least near the surface, it tends to liquefy when walked upon. This is an entertaining property of many of our gooey mud flats, which makes mushing through them quite strenuous. On sandy beaches, the substrate simply packs down when it is stepped upon.

In mud, the microbial flora concerned with decomposition of organic matter is apt to be rich, and the rotten-eggs smell of hydrogen sulfide may be quite strong. Digging down into mud, one will generally encounter a black layer just a few centimeters below the surface. This marks the zone at which compounds of iron, especially iron oxide, react with hydrogen sulfide and become converted into sulfides. Conditions in the mud above this black layer are aerobic; that is, most of the organisms conduct their biological activities in the presence of oxygen. Below the black layer, conditions are anaerobic, and energy-releasing life processes involve various chemical pathways that do not require free oxygen. On exposed sandy beaches, and even in protected bays where the particle size is coarse enough to facilitate circulation of water and oxygen dissolved in it, a black layer may not be encountered anywhere near the surface. It will almost certainly be there, however, if one digs deep enough.

In muddy and sandy substrates, the food habits of the animals are diversified, just as they would be in any other ecological situation. There are suspension feeders, which process the water flowing over the substrate, utilizing diatoms, other microscopic organisms, and fine detritus. A number of pelecypod molluscs, as cockles and littleneck clams, are in this category, in addition to certain polychaete annelids. Another type, deposit feeders, is either somewhat selective or almost completely unselective. The former includes certain macomas, which sweep the surface with the incurrent siphon to pick up lighter particles, and terebellid polychaetes, which utilize ciliary tracts along their extensile tentacles to bring microscopic food to the mouth. A good example of an unselective deposit feeder is the lugworm, which extracts what nourishment it can from mud in its burrow. Deposit feeders are generally restricted to muddy habitats, whereas suspension feeders are present in both sandy and muddy areas.

Scavengers on animal or plant material include many of the crabs, isopods, amphipods, and polychaetes. Finally, there are out-and-out carnivores, such as the nemertean *Cerebratulus*, certain polychaetes (including *Nephtys*), the moon snail, and most of the fishes and birds.

For a systematic discussion of the fauna and flora associated with sand and mud, these substrates will be considered in terms of the topography of places where they are found, the extent that these places are exposed to wave action, and conditions that influence the accumulation of organic detritus. This format leads to three general situations: exposed or moderately exposed sandy beaches of the open coast; relatively protected sandy beaches and coves; and quiet bays where sand and mud are present in varying amounts. However, the user of this book must realize that the distributions of animals and plants depend on many factors, and that one type of habitat may pass so gradually into another that one cannot draw up hard and fast rules to which the animals and plants invariably adhere.

Exposed Sandy Beaches of the Open Coast

The extensive sandy beaches found in certain areas of the outer coast provide, in terms of substrate, an unstable habitat. Depending on tides, currents, and weather, the sand shifts a great deal from season to season and from year to year. Moreover, at any given time the sand is stirred by the beating of breaking waves and by the subsequent rush of receding water. Thus the only large animals able to live on the portion of a beach that sustains heavy wave action burrow at least a few inches into the sand, or move up and down the beach as the tide level fluctuates. Sand is not at all suitable as a substrate for attachment of seaweeds, so the only plants likely to be found in this kind of environment are diatoms and other microscopic forms that live attached to sand grains or between them. The sand grains tend to adsorb at least a little organic material, which is populated by a variety of bacteria.

The microscopic plants and bacteria provide food for some of the very small animals that live in this situation. These animals consist predominantly of ciliated protozoa, turbellarians, nematodes, annelids, and copepod crustacea. However, representatives of other groups are known to occur, and of the more remarkable and previously unsuspected organisms discovered in recent years, a large proportion have been found in sandy beaches. The small animals and plants living on and between sand grains are referred to as the interstitial fauna and flora. On the Pacific Coast, studies on these interstitial organisms have hardly begun, so some rewarding opportunities await those who may wish to investigate them.

Although this guide concentrates on the area of Puget Sound and adjacent inland waters, the sandy beaches of the open coast are so important that a brief discussion of some of the more common larger animals living in them will undoubtedly be appreciated. In discussing the more obvious elements of the fauna of sandy beaches, it seems easier to begin at a low tide level and to work gradually up the slope to the fringes of the marine environment, dealing primarily with the animals that actually live in or on the sand, rather than with jellyfishes or other pelagic organisms that just happen to be washed up on the beach.

The animal most people associate with wave-swept sandy beaches of the unprotected outer coast is the razor clam, *Siliqua patula* (fig. 155). It is an important article of food, and the sport of

155. *Siliqua patula,* the razor clam

digging it provides pleasant recreation for many who live in the Northwest. Normally, the razor clam is found only on the lowermost part of the beach—the region exposed by tides of about −1.0 foot and lower. It is usually rather close to the surface and is sometimes washed out of the sand by the action of the surf. Most clam diggers look for little dimples in the sand or for a shimmering, which indicates some activity beneath the surface. A quick thrust with the spade may bring instant reward, or it may lead to frantic digging to keep from losing the rapidly retreating clam. Too often, however, a little olive snail or some kind of polychaete worm just beneath the surface is all he gets for his trouble.

The astonishing capacity of the razor clam to burrow is due to intense muscular effort which is linked to changes in the shape of the foot caused by displacement of body fluids. As the foot is extended and fluid is squeezed out of it, it pushes into the sand. Its tip then swells up, the foot as a whole contracts, and the animal is pulled deeper into the substrate.

On cleaning his day's catch, the happy digger may find what looks like a leech, up to about 2 or 3 cm long, in the mantle cavity. This is *Malacobdella,* a short-bodied, highly specialized nemertean. It is attached to the wall of the mantle cavity, usually close to the siphon, by its posterior disklike sucker. It feeds upon microscopic and nearly microscopic organisms, especially small crustacea, which the clam brings into the mantle cavity through its incurrent siphon. *Malacobdella* is indeed an unusual nemertean; almost all of its relatives are slender, free-living worms that subdue relatively large prey, especially polychaete annelids.

Olivella biplicata, the purple olive snail (fig. 156), is a beautiful little snail that plows through the sand, searching for animal matter upon which to scavenge. It is one of the few snails in our area that

156. *Olivella biplicata,* the purple olive

has a highly polished shell and such a proportionately long aperture. The length of the shell of a large specimen is about 2 cm. The coloration is primarily a mixture of gray and purple, with some dark lines defining the edges of the whorls or crossing them lengthwise. The trail of *Olivella* is generally right at the surface, so that the shell is at least partially exposed. Sometimes, however, *Olivella* is completely buried, and creates a little dimple or shimmering of the sand that may bring false hope to a clam digger. The olive snail occupies a rather wide band on the beach and thus is commonly found at levels considerably higher than those to which the razor clam is restricted.

Digging in the sand of an exposed beach, at around the level of mid-tide or lower, will turn up several kinds of worms. Among the larger species, two types will probably be most frequently noticed. One is a nemertean, *Cerebratulus* (fig. 157), which is smooth, much flattened, very extensile, and very fragile. Large specimens may be

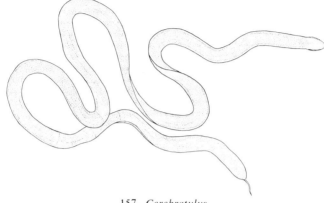

157. *Cerebratulus*

about 1 cm wide and 30 cm long, but they tend to break up into pieces when handled. We have a number of species of *Cerebratulus* in our area. They show conspicuous slits on either side of the head and have a little cirrus at the tail end, but this falls off altogether too easily. *Cerebratulus* feeds largely on polychaetes that burrow in the sand. It has a huge proboscis which, when called into action, emerges from a pore at the front end. This proboscis is not armed with piercing stylets, characteristic of nemerteans such as *Paranemertes* and *Emplectonema*; instead, it is extremely sticky, and apparently the glairy mucus secretion is all it needs to subdue its prey. The way in which the proboscis of a large *Cerebratulus* can wrap itself in a spiral around one's finger, by turning itself inside out until it is completely everted, is most impressive. The sticky secretion holds so firmly that the proboscis may have to be peeled away like a strip of tape.

The other worm frequently found in the same general habitat is *Nephtys* (fig. 158), a predaceous polychaete. It may at first look something like a *Nereis,* but its eversible pharyngeal equipment is altogether different, and there are no long tentacles on the head.

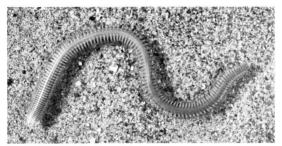

158. *Nephtys*

More or less following the tide is a little isopod, *Cirolana kincaidi* (fig. 159). This species, tending to congregate on dead fish and other animal matter, is an efficient scavenger. The speed with which a few dozen *Cirolana* can pick a fish skeleton clean makes this isopod a sort of marine counterpart of the terrestrial carrion beetles.

159. *Cirolana kincaidi*

Shrimps belonging to any one of the several species of *Crago* (fig. 160) are often abundant in shallow water. They are usually seen swimming after being dislodged by a wave, then settling back into the sand again. Like *Cirolana,* they move up and down with the tide to some extent.

Most common of all of the animals visible to the unaided eye, however, are small crustacea of a group called mysids (or opossum shrimps, because the females carry the young in a brood pouch under the thorax). *Archaeomysis grebnitzkii* (fig. 161) seems to be the prevailing species in our area. Mysids can be caught in large numbers by running a fine-mesh net through the water in the surf

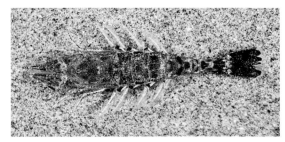

160. *Crago*

zone or by digging a hole that will fill with water. If there is sunshine, the shadows of the mysids will probably be seen before the animals themselves, because they are nearly transparent. They soon settle down into the sand again.

If the sand is disturbed while water is sloshing over it, some plump little amphipods may momentarily be dislodged. In almost no time, they manage to disappear under the surface. These amphipods belong to a rather unusual family of gammarids called the Haustoriidae, which is restricted to sandy beaches. Their appendages are fringed by abundant long hairs, some of which are featherlike, so haustoriids have a furry appearance. *Eohaustorius washingtonianus* (fig. 162), up to about 8 mm long, is known to occur in our area, but perhaps other species should also be expected.

Not far above mid-tide level there will probably be a large population of the bloodworm, *Euzonus mucronata*. Sometimes a strip of crowded, small holes is an indication that bloodworms are present,

161. *Archaeomysis grebnitzkii*

162. *Eohaustorius washingtonianus*

but the only sure way to find them is to dig a trench up the beach to intersect the narrow band in which *Euzonus* is concentrated. The band is generally less than a meter in width, but there may be more than a hundred worms in an area 10 by 10 cm. *Euzonus* is small— about 3 or 4 cm long—and of a purplish red color (the color is due to a rich supply of hemoglobin in the blood). It burrows through the sand, moving to a depth of 10 or 20 cm when the tide is out. It actually eats the sand grains, obtaining nourishment from the organic matter and microorganisms attached to them.

Having nothing directly to do with sandy beaches, the goose barnacles of the genus *Lepas* are sometimes washed up on them during storms. Unlike *Pollicipes polymerus* (see Chap. 4), which is fixed to rocks on wave-swept shores, the species of *Lepas* are pelagic. One of them, *L. fascicularis* (pl. XXIII), secretes material at the base of its stalk, contributing to a common float shared by several to many individuals. The other species, of which *L. anatifera* (fig. 163) is the most abundant, are attached to floating timbers or stalks of kelps. The colonies they form are sometimes massive, and various other kinds of sessile and semisessile organisms may be hidden away in them. Some of these goose barnacles must surely travel widely before they have the misfortune to get too close to shore. If the weather is cool, they may be very much alive even after a day or two out of water. The same timbers that are colonized by *Lepas* may also be riddled by the shipworm, *Bankia setacea* (see Chap. 3).

In, under, and around the decomposing seaweed on the upper reaches of a sandy beach, the more obvious animals are amphipod crustaceans, commonly called beach hoppers or sand fleas. (If you use the latter term, remember that they are not fleas, and not even insects.) When a mass of seaweed in which beach hoppers are scavenging is lifted, hundreds of them will usually start to jump in what looks like aimless behavior. It is nevertheless amazing how quickly they disappear back into the seaweed and wet sand.

Several kinds of beach hoppers are found in our region, but two are prominent. *Orchestoidea californiana,* our largest species, attains a length (exclusive of the antennae) of about 2.5 cm. The coloration of the body is basically grayish white or ivory, but the long antennae are a gorgeous pinkish orange. It is found only on exposed beaches, usually in decaying seaweed; but it also lives in

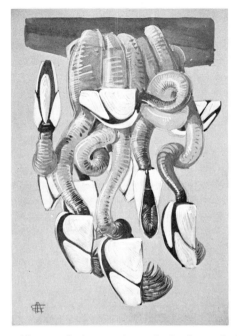

163. *Lepas anatifera,* a pelagic goose barnacle that is attached to floating timbers

burrows in the sand, from which it emerges after night falls. Where *O. californiana* is really common, the beach is a pretty lively place after dark, with many of the hoppers moving down the slope to scavenge closer to the water's edge. They are able to orient themselves with reference to the moon, and thus manage to find their way back to the upper part of the beach before daybreak.

Orchestia traskiana (fig. 164) is a smaller species, with a maximum length of about 2 cm. It is usually dark gray, and its antennae are not distinctively colored. *Orchestia* is the prevailing beach hopper in Puget Sound and the San Juan Archipelago, but it is occasionally observed on the outer coast in situations that are at least somewhat protected.

Still farther landward than the beach hoppers, in a zone where the driftwood is almost never disturbed except during the wildest storms, is a sandy beach counterpart of *Ligia,* the isopod that lives just above the high-tide line on rocky shores. *Alloniscus percon-*

164. *Orchestia traskiana*

vexus physically resembles its completely terrestrial relatives, the pill bugs. The maximum length of *Alloniscus* is slightly more than 1 cm. This isopod is most often found under pieces of wood resting on just slightly moist sand, but sometimes its presence out in the open is revealed by little telltale ridges in the sand.

Once this far up the beach, one starts running into insects that burrow in the sand or that like to hide beneath debris. The more obvious of these are beetles. Rove beetles (family Staphylinidae), characterized by rudimentary wings and wing covers, are especially abundant. Many of them are predators on other insects.

RELATIVELY PROTECTED SANDY BEACHES

Within the area for which this guide has primarily been written, there are a few sandy beaches and coves that bear some resemblance to beaches on the outer coast. However, they rarely sustain waves more than a couple of feet high, except during storms. The strip of shore exposed at low tide is frequently rather steep and therefore correspondingly narrow. Sometimes the substrate consists almost purely of rather fine sand, similar to that characteristic of broad, exposed beaches. Very often, however, there is coarse gravel mixed with it, so that some beaches consist almost entirely of gravel or cobblestones. These almost routinely have a steep slope and are relatively uninteresting biologically, though they may harbor a few organisms not found anywhere else.

Protected sandy beaches generally have a rich assortment of microscopic interstitial organisms, and some of the larger animals regularly associated with exposed shores may be present. However, the more distinctive animals of wave-swept beaches—the razor clam, the purple olive snail, and the large beach hopper with orange antennae—are missing. There is not likely to be an extensive or even a distinct backshore area with sand dunes and their characteristic vegetation.

On beaches of this sort, mysids (fig. 161) are usually about as abundant as they are on the open coast and can be scooped up in numbers from the surf zone or from hollows in the sand. The little scavenging isopod, *Cirolana kincaidi* (fig. 159), is, if anything, more common on somewhat protected sandy beaches. Shrimps of the genus *Crago* (fig. 160) may also be present; but since "swash" pools of the type found on less strongly sloped exposed beaches are not characteristic of relatively protected beaches, these shrimps may have to be hunted in shallow water of the surf zone. A little digging at various tide levels may turn up some large nemerteans of the genus *Cerebratulus* (fig. 157) and polychaetes of the genus *Nephtys* (fig. 158).

At about mid-tide level, or a little lower, there may be areas in which one of our three lugworms, *Abarenicola claparedii oceanica,* is abundant. Its cake-decorator fecal castings are similar to those of its relatives living in quiet bays, but are larger and usually appreciably sandier.

The zone of bloodworms is ordinarily lacking on relatively protected sandy beaches. The drift zone, where decaying seaweed accumulates, will have a joyful population of beach hoppers, but the predominating species will be *Orchestia traskiana* (fig. 164) instead of the more colorful and larger *Orchestoidea californiana. Orchestia* is smaller, with a body length under 2 cm long, and lacks the beautiful orange antennae of its open-coast cousin.

As previously mentioned, there is not likely to be any extensive backshore; and even when there is, looking under driftwood for the little isopod *Alloniscus perconvexus* is usually fruitless. It is another of those crustaceans whose requirements seem to be met only in a very narrow strip of the upper part of truly exposed beaches.

QUIET BAYS

The bays of our area are on the whole protected, so they have almost no wave action except during storms. Some of the bays in Puget Sound and Washington Sound are estuaries into which rivers or streams empty. In such situations, there is usually an abundance of fine silt brought down from the land, and the salinity at the surface of the substrate is apt to vary extensively from season to season and according to tidal fluctuations. However, within the muddy sand, mud, and clay, the salinity tends to remain rather stable in the face of fresh water flowing over the surface. This buffering capacity of fine-particled substrates thus protects burrowing animals against changes in salinity. This is not to say that the salinity of the substrate throughout a bay is always like that of sea water. Any estuary will show a gradient from sea water to fresh water, with daily or seasonal fluctuations all along the way. Nevertheless, in areas that are inundated by the sea daily, the substrate will tend to retain its salinity even when the tide is out and there are strong rains or runoff from a stream.

In the San Juan Archipelago, where there are few streams of any consequence, the fine silt that accumulates in quiet bays is largely a result of erosion around the margins. As wave action is so slight, this silt tends not to be stirred up and washed out to sea. Salinity generally remains remarkably constant, although there are places where seepage from the land reduces it somewhat.

The character of the substrate in bays ranges from fine sand, which is only slightly muddy, to real mud and finally to hard-packed clay. There may be gravel worked into the substrate, and rocks of moderate to large size may be scattered about, especially at higher tide levels. There are many variations on the theme, and any one bay may have several rather different but intergrading substrates within it. Thus the fauna and flora may be diversified, with many of the organisms being more or less restricted to certain areas.

A few of the principal ecological situations found in quiet bays will serve as the structure for discussing some of the animals and plants identified with each one. It must be remembered, however, that as long as there are intergradations in the size of the sand particles, the amount and nature of the organic matter, and other variables, it is neither possible nor desirable to make the classification of substrates rigid. And to complicate matters even further, in a particular bay one kind of substrate is apt to be at a different tide level than it would be in another.

Rather Clean Sand

What can definitely be called sand, as distinct from muddy sand, is likely to be found at lower tide levels (approximately 1.0 ft. and lower) and only near the mouths of bays. The particles will ordinarily be smaller, on the average, than those of more exposed sandy beaches and will be packed rather tightly. The sand will shift to some extent from season to season and from year to year as a result of currents, and sand bars may alternate with depressions. The bars will be free of any obvious vegetation; but the depressions—shallow pools at low tide—may have extensive growths of the eelgrass, *Zostera*. By forming thick colonies, with a system of creeping rhizomes and roots, *Zostera* helps to stabilize the substrate and to provide shelter for a variety of organisms. Eelgrass and the animals and plants commonly associated with it will be discussed in some depth later in this chapter.

The two most eye-catching animals found plowing through the surface of rather clean sand are sand dollars and moon snails. Sand dollars are echinoderms closely related to sea urchins, but their tests are flattened and their tube feet and spines are relatively small. The mouth is situated near the middle of the underside; but the anus, instead of being close to the middle of the upper side, is displaced to a position on the underside near the margin. The madreporite, by which water enters and leaves the water vascular system, is slightly off center on the upper side; and the five sets of tube feet radiating from this are of unequal size. The specific name of our local sand dollar, *Dendraster excentricus* (fig. 165), was given in

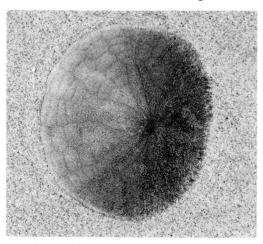

165. *Dendraster excentricus,* the sand dollar

allusion to this off-center look. *D. excentricus* reaches a diameter of about 8 cm, and its color ranges from gray to blackish red. As it pushes its way through the sand, generally partially exposed, fine particles of detritus that fall onto the surface between the spines are carried by tracts of cilia to the margins, and then other tracts on the underside convey them to the mouth. Sand dollars have an Aristotle's lantern similar to that of sea urchins, but it is modified for processing smaller particles of food that enter the mouth instead of for scraping and for chopping up larger pieces. Sand dollars release their eggs and sperms into the water, and the fertilized eggs develop into a bilaterally symmetrical, free-swimming larva which eventually, if it is lucky enough to find a suitable substrate, settles and metamorphoses into the adult, which is essentially radially symmetrical.

The moon snail, *Polinices lewisii* (figs. 166 and 167), is our most massive intertidal snail. Its shell, which may reach a height of about 12 cm, is composed almost entirely of the body whorl; the

166. *Polinices lewisii,* the moon snail (animal extended)

rest of the whorls (about five) form a low but distinct spire. The periostracum is very smooth, and the color is generally a soft brownish gray. The aperture is large and closed tightly by an operculum when the animal withdraws. While the animal is extended and working its way through the sand, its mantle is enormous and

167. *Polinices lewisii,* the moon snail (shell)

covers most of the shell; it is always something of a surprise to see that it can pull all of this soft tissue into the shell. (A lot of water is squeezed out in the process, of course.) The moon snail is a pure carnivore, feeding on clams by drilling a neat hole in one of the valves and then sucking out the tissue. Moon snails are less abundant intertidally during the winter months, when they seem to move out into deeper water, than they are during the spring and summer. After they appear in large numbers on the sand flats, they commence to lay their eggs in very characteristic collarlike configurations. The eggs are sandwiched between two layers of sand cemented together by mucous secretions. They hatch in midsummer, and the young go through a free-swimming stage before they settle down.

The relatively few holes seen at the surface in areas where there are sand dollars and moon snails belong principally to a burrowing sea cucumber, clams, and a variety of polychaete worms. Digging into the sand will expose a few other polychaetes that do not have a permanent burrow.

The burrowing sea cucumber, *Leptosynapta clarki* (fig. 168), lives within a few inches of the surface. It does not look much like a typical sea cucumber because it has no tube feet, except for the pinnately branched tentacles that encircle the mouth. These tentacles are used in processing the sand that the animal swallows to get the food value tied up in the organic coating on the grains and in the associated detritus. *Leptosynapta* is very pale, though it may have a faint orange cast, and a large specimen can be 6 or 7 cm

168. *Leptosynapta clarki,* a burrowing sea cucumber

long when extended. When handled, this cucumber may cling to the fingers, because numerous microscopic, anchorlike hooks projecting from the body wall engage the skin. The anchors undoubtedly serve the cucumber in its natural environment by preventing it from slipping as it contracts and elongates.

In the same general area as the sand dollar, moon snail, and *Leptosynapta,* there are apt to be several species of bivalve molluscs. Most of them—including the cockle and bent-nosed clam—

169. *Macoma secta,* the sand clam

are more abundant in a muddier habitat and will be considered in the following section. One species, however, seems to require quite clean sand. This is *Macoma secta,* the sand clam (fig. 169). When compared with other members of the genus found locally, it is large, sometimes reaching a length of 10 cm, and its hinge is very short. It is also much neater than most macomas, since its periostracum is light and thin. As in all species of *Macoma,* the incurrent and excurrent siphons are completely separate. The incurrent siphon is very mobile and is used much like a vacuum-sweeper hose to pick up detritus from the surface of the sand. *M. secta* is rarely found at depths more shallow than about 20 cm and it sometimes burrows to about 40 cm. However, the number of live specimens encountered by even intensive digging is much smaller than one might expect to find on the basis of the number of empty shells lying at the surface of the sand.

On sand flats, wherever there are pools or depressions that hold at least a little water at low tide, two fishes are usually encountered (excluding, of course, the fishes that move into the bay and out

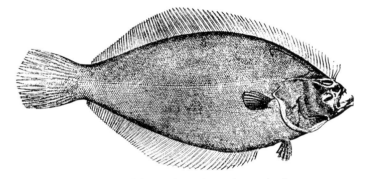

170. *Psettichthys melanostictus,* the sand sole

again during periods of high tide). Both of these are apt to surprise one when they dart off, as they may be difficult to see until they move. The sand sole, *Psettichthys melanostictus* (fig. 170), flattened like soles and flounders of our fish markets, reaches a length of about 60 cm, but most specimens one stirs up at low tide are smaller than 20 cm. Both eyes are normally on the right side, which is thus uppermost. The generally gray color of *Psettichthys* is complicated by some salt-and-pepper effects, and these, coupled with the transparency of the fins and the fact that the fish often is at least half buried, makes it difficult to see.

The other fish is the staghorn sculpin, *Leptocottus armatus* (fig. 171). It looks like sculpins in general, but is on the whole a rather slender species. It is also large compared to the species found intertidally on rocky shores, sometimes attaining a length of about 25 cm. Its coloration above consists mostly of grays of varying degrees

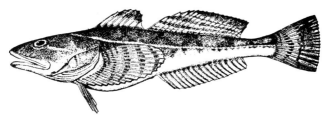

171. *Leptocottus armatus,* the staghorn sculpin

of darkness, but the underside is very light, with a weak yellow tint. *Leptocottus* is found also on mudflats and is one of the more common fishes of estuarine situations where the salinity is low on account of runoff from a river or stream. It is frequently taken with hook and line, though not intentionally.

Muddy Sand, Mud, and Gravel

As the amount of organic material increases, the fauna generally becomes richer. Mud and muddy sand support large populations of animals, and if you spread out a little of the surface sediment and sort through it with a low-power microscope, you will find an astonishing diversity of invertebrates, some of which are restricted to this type of situation. Diatoms and certain other small plants will also be abundant. When the microscopic organisms are discounted, the animals fall into three principal groups: polychaete annelids, bivalve molluscs, and crustaceans. The evidence, at the surface, that these are numerous can be seen as holes to burrows, as little piles of sand or mud around some of the openings, and as fecal castings. A person really familiar with the mudflat fauna can usually tell which clams, shrimps, and worms have made the various kinds of burrows, and which worms have deposited the several obvious types of fecal castings.

As the character of the substrate in most bays changes so gradually, and as the faunas considered typical of particular situations tend to overlap, it seems best to develop the discussion largely around groups of animals. This method will obviate considerable repetition, as well as prevent one from associating certain animals too definitely with very specific habitats.

172. Right side of *Macoma nasuta,*
the bent-nosed clam

173. Dorsal view of *Macoma
nasuta,* the bent-nosed clam

Bivalve Molluscs: Clams, Cockles, Mussels, and Oysters

Where the sand is rather muddy, two medium-sized clams reach their peak of abundance. The bent-nosed clam, *Macoma nasuta* (figs. 172 and 173), has a maximum length of about 5 cm and its valves are bent rather sharply to the right near the posterior end. This species is generally about 10 or 15 cm beneath the surface, lying with its left valve down. Its siphons, completely separate as in all macomas, are directed upward through the flexed portion. The orange coloration of its siphons is another distinguishing feature.

174. *Macoma irus*

The periostracum, usually most prominent near the lower edge and near the siphonal end of the valves, is dirty brown; the valves are otherwise white, and chalky where they have been eroded.

Macoma irus (fig. 174) is of about the same size and appearance as *M. nasuta,* but its valves are not bent and the shell is slightly more inflated. The siphons are barely yellowish, and definitely not orange. Both of these clams would be attractive as food if their mode of feeding did not bring considerable sand into the mantle cavity.

Another species of *Macoma,* whose shell rarely exceeds 1.5 cm in length, is also apt to be found in muddy sand, living close to the surface. This is *M. inconspicua,* which is the Pacific Coast counterpart of, or perhaps the same species as, the Atlantic *M. balthica.* Its shell is more nearly oval in outline than that of either *M. nasuta* or *M. irus,* and there is no appreciable amount of periostracum; moreover, it often shows—especially internally—a little pink, blue, yellow, or orange. It seems not to be as abundant in Puget

175. *Tresus capax,* the gaper clam

Sound or in the San Juan Archipelago as it is in San Francisco Bay and bays that front on the open coast of the Northwest.

The largest bivalve that a clam digger can depend on getting from tide flats of quiet bays is the gaper clam or horse clam, *Tresus capax* (fig. 175). It generally lives where the substrate is essentially mud with gravel and bits of shell worked into it, but it is sometimes found in rather stiff clay. The depth at which it lies depends to some extent on the character of the substrate: in clay, specimens are usually less than 30 cm below the surface; but in mud they may be deeper, down to nearly 50 cm. The valves of the shell may attain a length of about 20 cm. The periostracum, where it persists, is a dull brown color, and the rest of the shell is chalky white, unless blackened by sulfides. The siphon, though large, can be retracted almost completely into the shell. It is covered by wrinkled skin, and its tip has a couple of leatherlike flaps. These flaps are frequently colonized by one or two small barnacles, hydroids, an anemone *(Epiactis prolifera),* and delicate red algae such as *Polysiphonia.*

Almost every gaper clam will have a pair of small, soft-bodied crabs in its mantle cavity. Actually, two separate species of crabs are associated with gaper clams: *Pinnixa faba* (fig. 176) and *P. littoralis.* In both species, the female is larger than the male and is also less inclined to move around, generally staying put in one place. The mantle tissue may appear irritated or blistered in the area of her residence. Although several immature crabs of this sort

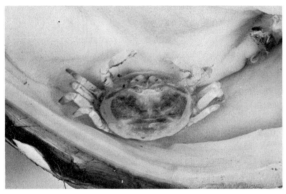

176. *Pinnixa faba* (female), a pinnotherid crab living in the mantle cavity of *Tresus capax*

may be found in a particular clam, no more than one female and one male are left after the crabs mature. The female seems to feed unselectively on the diatoms and other material brought in with the feeding currents produced by the clam, and also on strings of mucus. Just what the male lives on is not clear, as it has not been observed to feed actively.

Younger stages of both *P. faba* and *P. littoralis* are known to occur in various other species of clams, as *Mya arenaria, Clinocardium nuttallii,* and *Saxidomus giganteus.* Apparently they can later move from these hosts into gaper clams.

The geoduck (pronounced "gooey duck"), *Panope generosa* (fig. 177), is larger than the gaper clam: the shell of a really huge specimen may be 20 cm long, and its siphon, even after it has con-

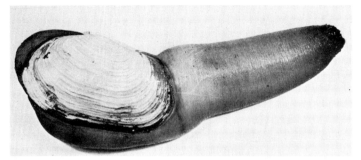

177. *Panope generosa*, the geoduck

tracted as much as it can, may hang out about 25 cm. The total weight occasionally exceeds 20 pounds. The geoduck is much prized but not often dug, for it is rather scarce intertidally and older individuals are generally at least 75 cm below the surface. The valves of the shell, as viewed from one side, are nearly rectan-

178. *Clinocardium nuttallii,* the heart cockle

gular and gape widely. The periostracum is yellowish, rather than brown as in *Tresus.* The siphon is less disagreeable looking than that of the gaper clam and has no leathery pads at the tip; moreover, it is light brown instead of dark brown.

The heart cockle, *Clinocardium nuttallii* (fig. 178), seems to prefer those portions of quiet bays in which the substrate consists of muddy fine sand. Beds of eelgrass growing on mud often support large populations. However, this cockle is versatile and is some-

times plentiful in rather clean sand. Its vertical distribution is likewise extensive, for it is found from rather high levels in the intertidal region to deep-water situations. As its siphon is very short,
the heart cockle lives with the posterior end of its shell just below
the surface of the substrate.

The shell of *Clinocardium* attains a length of about 10 cm.
Viewed from the right or left side, the valves have a shape something like a triangle with rounded corners; viewed from one end or
the other, they have a heart-shaped profile. There are about thirty-
five strong ribs radiating from the umbo. The coloration of young
specimens is characteristically a warm brown, with some mottling;
older specimens tend to be a monotonous darker brown. Although
appearing to be rather sedentary, cockles have a powerful and very
extensile foot, and specimens lying in a pan of water will sometimes push themselves around or even flip over. This activity will
become remarkably purposeful if the arm of a sunflower star, *Pyc-*

179. *Protothaca staminea,* the littleneck clam

nopodia, is applied to the edge of the mantle, so that the tube feet
actually touch the tissue: the cockle will flip itself violently to get
out of reach.

In protected situations where the substrate is composed largely
of gravel mixed with sand or mud, certain clams reach their peak
of abundance. First in order of importance, at least in the lower
reaches of the intertidal region, is the littleneck clam, *Protothaca
staminea* (fig. 179). The shell of this common species is moderately
heavy and reaches a length of about 6 cm. The valves are sculp-

tured with both radiating and concentric ridges. Younger specimens often have some brown markings that look like the outlines of teepees, or like squares in a checkerboard, but older individuals tend to be rather uniformly pale brown, sometimes with a pinkish cast. The interior of the valves is practically white. A distinguishing characteristic of this species is the filelike sculpturing of the valves just inside the ventral margins. The fused siphons of *Protothaca* are extremely short, so the posterior end of the clam is

180. *Venerupis japonica,* the Japanese littleneck clam

just at the surface. The population density of this species is sometimes so heavy that several specimens will be turned out in a single shovelful of gravel. Actually, it is hardly necessary to dig for this species, for it can be scratched out.

Venerupis japonica, the Japanese littleneck clam (or Manila clam) (fig. 180), is about the same size as *Protothaca,* but it is more graceful on account of its slightly more elongated shape. The radial ridges of the shell are decidedly more prominent than the concentric ridges, and they are proportionately better developed and more widely spaced than those of *Protothaca.* The color is usually grayish, greenish, or brownish, and very distinct darker or lighter markings regularly form designs resembling mountain ranges, maps, or graphs. Internally, the valves are typically yellowish, with a purple suffusion near the posterior margin. This species was originally imported with seed oysters coming from Japan and has become well established in our region, as well as in suitable situations in San Francisco Bay and elsewhere. It may be found together with

181. *Venerupis tenerrima*

Protothaca, but on the whole it tends to reside at slightly higher tide levels.

Venerupis tenerrima, the thin-shelled littleneck clam (fig. 181), is a native. As its common name suggests, its shell is proportionately thinner than those of the other two clams just discussed. The valves are also much more shallow than in these species. However, the shell may attain a length of nearly 10 cm. Externally, the valves are grayish white, without any dark markings, and the only prominent sculpturing consists of rather sharp concentric ridges; the lines radiating from the umbo are very fine. Internally, the valves are

182. *Saxidomus giganteus,* the butter clam

essentially white. *V. tenerrima* may be found in association with *P. staminea* or *V. japonica,* or with both at the same time; but it prefers beaches in which there is considerable sand in proportion to pebbles. In any case, it is never common.

A very thick-shelled clam that is found in gravelly beaches is the butter clam or Washington clam, *Saxidomus giganteus* (fig. 182). Its shell, commonly 10 cm long and sometimes even larger, is basically whitish, though it may have blackish discolorations due to the presence of iron sulfide. The surface is marked only by raised concentric growth lines and grooves. The more conspicuous grooves

183. *Mya arenaria,* the soft-shell clam

reflect the deceleration of growth in winter. The hinge is very heavy. When the valves are tightly closed, there is practically no gape at the siphonal end. This species may be as far as 30 cm from the surface, but it is frequently much closer. The flesh, on the whole, is rather rubbery, but it makes a superb chowder, and this species is extensively exploited commercially.

The soft-shell clam, *Mya arenaria* (fig. 183), is typically found in mixtures of sand and mud, or mud and gravel, where the salinity is reduced by influx of considerable fresh water, either from a stream or by seepage. It is usually about 20 cm below the surface. The shell may exceed a length of 10 cm. It is rather thin and fragile, hence often cracked when the clam is dug. In outline, it is rounded anteriorly and somewhat truncately pointed posteriorly. The color is basically whitish or chalky gray, and the brownish periostracum tends to be restricted to the edges of the shell. Internally, the left valve is characterized by a very large, shelflike excrescence, called

184. *Modiolus rectus,* the horse mussel

the chondrophore. The hinge ligament, being internal, cannot be seen from the outside of the shell. The soft-shell clam was almost certainly imported from the Atlantic coast, for it is not present in old Indian shell mounds. It is a common species in Europe, especially in areas with low salinity such as the Baltic Sea.

The horse mussel, *Modiolus rectus* (fig. 184), is primarily a subtidal species, being especially abundant on muddy bottoms that have a heavy accumulation of old shells. Horse mussels tend to form aggregates, being attached by their byssal threads to one another or to empty shells of the same or a different species. In younger specimens, the periostracum is a rather warm, shiny

185. *Crassostrea gigas,* the Japanese oyster

brown and is elaborated into soft, yellowish brown hairs at the broader end of the valves. Older specimens tend to be more nearly blackish brown and to lack the hairs. Once in awhile this species is encountered in quiet bays, where it is apt to be nearly buried, with the broader end of the shell protruding just enough to permit the inhalant and exhalant currents to operate.

The Japanese oyster, *Crassostrea gigas* (fig. 185), was introduced to many areas on the Pacific Coast long ago and is now so well established in some places that it looks like part of the natural fauna. It is, as oysters go, a giant: the length of very large specimens may exceed 25 cm. Normally, the left valve, which is deeper than the nearly flat right valve fitting into it, is partially or almost completely cemented to a hard substrate. As this species tends to settle on shells of its own kind, sizable clumps are sometimes built up. The shells are often grotesquely twisted and deformed, and no two specimens are quite alike. The fluting of the external surface is almost always prominent.

When summer water temperatures are favorable for spawning and normal development of larvae, the Japanese oyster reproduces naturally. Many commercial growers, however, periodically restock their beds in spring by importing young oysters ("spat") that have settled on empty shells ("cultch"). These shells, on arrival, are strung out from racks or floats in suitable situations, usually muddy tidal flats. In some places, conditions are not regularly favorable for both spawning and normal development of young, so annual importations of spat are essential to insure future crops. The Japanese oyster will tolerate a salinity considerably lower than that of normal sea water, so it grows well in estuaries.

To those who take oysters seriously, the Japanese oyster just about has to be fried, stewed, or worked into a casserole dish to make it acceptable. It is generally concluded, even by those who put on no airs, that it is far from being the equal of the European oyster or Atlantic oyster when eaten raw. Unfortunately, neither of these species has been coaxed into really successful cultivation on the Pacific Coast, though both have been introduced, and small colonies of the Atlantic oyster *(Crassostrea virginica)* seem to be reproducing in some estuarine situations in our area. The shell of the Atlantic oyster rarely exceeds a length of about 10 cm and is relatively smooth; it is marked by concentric lines, which do not become fluted. A distinctive characteristic of the species is a dark blue blotch found on both valves at the point where the adductor muscle is attached.

Our native oyster, or Olympia oyster, *Ostrea lurida,* fulfills most of the taste requirements of learned sophisticates. Unfortunately, although it is widely distributed in our region, and along the Pacific Coast in general, it is common nowhere. Moderately successful cultivation of this species is at the basis of a rather esoteric industry, and it yields an expensive delicacy. The native oyster lives on the undersides of rocks, except in muddy places, where it will usually be on the upper sides of rocks. It is small, the length rarely exceeding 5 cm. The shell may be gnarled and eroded, but it does not often show flutings like those on the Japanese oyster. Externally, it is grayish, and internally it is usually a shiny grayish green or grayish olive color, with a touch of mother-of-pearl.

Burrowing Crustaceans

The ghost shrimp, *Callianassa californiensis* (fig. 186), burrows in very muddy sand with enough clay and organic matter to make the substrate reasonably cohesive and to provide the animal with material for lining its tunnels. The appearance of *Callianassa* is indeed ghostly, but the delicate coloration—waxy pale pink and orange—is beautiful. Out of water, the animals are flabby and helpless, and it is unfortunately nearly impossible to dig for them without damaging some specimens in the process. Normally, however, they are rarely exposed to predators, and the largest specimens, with a body size of about 10 cm exclusive of the appendages, are probably at least ten years old.

186. *Callianassa californiensis,* the ghost shrimp

Callianassa burrows by means of the chelate first and second legs, which loosen the substrate and pull it backward. A pushing movement of the third legs, aided by a raking activity of the mouth parts, causes accumulation of the material in a sort of receptacle formed by the last pair of mouth parts (third maxillipeds). The animal then crawls backward, reverses itself in a special turn-around chamber, and moves to the mouth of the burrow to dump its load. Eventually the burrow will have a number of branches and turnaround chambers, with at least two openings to the surface, which provide for some circulation of sea water through the system of tunnels. The openings to *Callianassa* burrows are typically in the middle of little piles of sand or of sand mixed with small pebbles (fig. 187).

187. Opening of a burrow of *Callianassa* at the surface of muddy sand

The ghost shrimp obtains much of its food from detritus in the mud that it handles. It collects the very fine particles on the hairs on its legs, allowing the coarser material to fall through. The hairs on the third maxillipeds scrape the prospective food off the legs and pass it to the forward mouth parts, which then deliver it to the mouth. When the burrow is under water at high tide, *Callianassa* fans water through the tunnel it happens to be in by means of its leaflike abdominal appendages (pleopods). When the tide is out, the animal is believed to slow down all of its activities.

The burrows of *Callianassa* are populated by a wide variety of organisms that profit in one way or another by their association with the ghost shrimp. There are small pea crabs (mostly of one species, but as many as three species are reported); a scale worm,

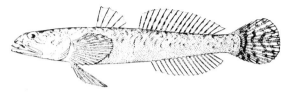

188. *Clevelandia ios*

Hesperonoë adventor; a small clam, *Cryptomya californica,* whose siphons open into the burrow instead of to the surface. Most interesting of all of the animals loosely associated with *Callianassa* is the little goby, *Clevelandia ios* (fig. 188). This fish is not restricted to burrows, and is occasionally observed in pools in the same general area, but it is nevertheless rather regularly linked with *Callianassa.*

Living under the carapace of *Callianassa* is a dark reddish copepod, *Clausidium vancouverense.* It is only about 2 mm long, but it can easily be seen through the translucent portion of the carapace that covers the gills. Occasionally parasitic isopods occur on *Callianassa,* forming bulges under the carapace on one side of the body. These normally live as pairs, the asymmetrical fat female being accompanied by a small, slender male.

The blue mud shrimp, *Upogebia pugettensis* (fig. 189), generally lives where the substrate is even muddier than that occupied by *Callianassa,* but the two species are often found together. *Upogebia*

189. *Upogebia pugettensis,* the mud shrimp

is much more hairy than *Callianassa,* and its coloration is a mixture of gray, brown, and bluish tones. It makes burrows similar to those of *Callianassa,* but usually does not heap up much sand around the openings. Like *Callianassa,* it uses its pleopods (swim-

190. *Pseudopythina rugifera,* a small clam sometimes found attached to the underside of the abdomen of *Upogebia*

merets) to fan water through its tunnels, feeding on detritus that it thus strains out. It is frequently parasitized by isopods of the same general type as are found on *Callianassa,* but it rarely has the co-pepod found on the gills of the latter. A very interesting commensal clam, *Pseudopythina rugifera* (fig. 190), is attached to the anterior part of the underside of the abdomen of some specimens; this secretes a byssus something like that of mussels to moor itself tightly to its host. Presumably it benefits from its relationship with *Upogebia* by enjoying the protection of a burrow while having access to currents of water containing the sort of microscopic food it requires. In our area, *P. rugifera* is found only on one other animal, *Aphrodita,* the sea mouse—a large, bristly polychaete that plows through surface sediment on sandy and muddy bottoms in deep water.

Polychaete Annelids

Where the substrate is of rather hard-packed, slightly muddy sand, without any appreciable algal cover, there will usually be some brittle, sandy tubes, about 3 mm in diameter, sticking up. If dug out carefully, down to a depth of at least 15 cm, and then picked away, the worms that make the tubes may still be intact. They will probably turn out to be bamboo worms, *Axiothella rubrocincta* (fig. 191), which are polychaete annelids belonging to the family Maldanidae. The maldanids as a group are characterized by having segments that are much longer than wide; moreover, the

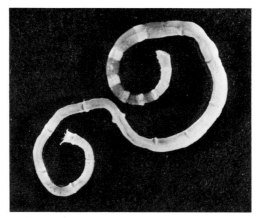

191. *Axiothella rubrocincta,* the bamboo worm

areas where segments join one another tend to be somewhat swollen. *Axiothella* does indeed resemble a cane of bamboo, prettily banded with dull red. The anterior end looks as if it had been sliced off obliquely, and the posterior end is elaborated into a sort of inverted funnel that is used to plug the lower end of the tube tightly when the animal contracts. Maldanids feed by ingesting sediment.

Almost every quiet bay has an extensive area, most likely near its inner margins and at a rather high tide level, that is ornamented by coiled sandy castings (fig. 192), which look as if they have been squeezed out of a cake decorator. These are produced by the lugworm, *Abarenicola pacifica* (fig. 193). If you observe a group of castings for awhile, you may see one of them almost suddenly grow

192. Fecal castings of a lugworm, *Abarenicola pacifica*

193. *Abarenicola pacifica,* a lugworm

by a loop or two. (This is more likely to happen if the area is covered by at least a little water.)

Lugworms belong to a family of polychaete annelids called the Arenicolidae. They excavate L-shaped or J-shaped burrows and are oriented with their posterior ends close to the surface, so that ejection of the fecal castings is simplified. Lugworms swallow sand and mud, which adhere to mucus secreted on the proboscis. When the proboscis is inverted, the material sticking to it is pulled into the digestive system. As the mud passes through the gut, at least much of the usable organic detritus is digested. Lugworms often reach a high population density—perhaps fifty per square meter—and play an important role in turnover of organic matter in mudflats.

When a lugworm is first dug out, it may not appear to be a particularly attractive animal. Its general coloration is a rather unpleasing mixture of yellow, green, and brown. However, after it has been washed off and placed in a dish of clean sea water for examination, it becomes more interesting. From its thicker anterior portion arise several pairs of branched gills. These are supplied with blood vessels, and the hemoglobin in the blood makes the expanded gills a very beautiful bright red. Lugworms irrigate their burrows, to bring in fresh sea water with sufficient oxygen for respiratory activities, by pulsating movements of the body.

In our area there are two species of lugworms. *Abarenicola pacifica,* the one regularly found along the inner margins of bays, where the sand is decidedly muddy, is the more common. *A. claparedii* tends to be restricted to rather clean sand and is thus generally found near the mouths of bays and in sandy coves. The situation is further complicated by the fact that specimens of *A. claparedii* in bays and those in coves where there is at least a little wave action belong to slightly different subspecies; these are called, respectively, *A. claparedii vagabunda* and *A. claparedii oceanica.*

There are so many burrowing polychaetes in muddy sand that it would be best to concentrate on those that are relatively large or at least long enough to be easily noticed. Almost always present in muddy sand and mud are *Lumbrineris, Notomastus,* and *Hemipodus.* The several species of *Lumbrineris* (family Lumbrineridae) (fig. 194) in our region superficially resemble very slender earthworms, not only because of their general size (length up to about

194. *Lumbrineris*

15 cm) but also because the head region is unadorned by tentacles. The parapodia—the flaps of tissue on either side of each segment, on which the bristles are borne—are small compared to those of most polychaetes, but the bristles themselves are fairly large. The jaws are specialized for tearing algae. The beauty of a *Lumbrineris* will probably not become apparent unless the worm is examined in bright light and with the help of a magnifier: the iridescence of its surface, rich in luminous blue and green tones, changes constantly as the worm crawls and bends.

The most common obvious worm in many muddy situations is *Notomastus tenuis,* a member of the family Capitellidae. When it is really abundant, as is evident from the presence of numerous fine,

195. *Hemipodus borealis*

blackish fecal castings at the surface, a shovelful of mud may contain a hundred. Most of them will be broken, for *Notomastus* is so slender (about 20 cm long and only about 1 mm wide when extended) that it does not stand the strain of being stretched. *Notomastus* is much like *Lumbrineris* in having rather small parapodia and no tentacles of any kind on the head. Its prostomium (the first segment), however, has two patches of little blackish eyespots. It feeds by ingesting sediment.

Hemipodus borealis (fig. 195) measures up to about 8 cm long. Its color is usually a slightly purplish red. The prostomium is long and pointed, with four tiny tentacles at its tip. Periodically, *Hemipodus* will evert its large, club-shaped proboscis, which has four hooklike black jaws. Polychaetes with this general type of prostomium and proboscis belong to the family Glyceridae, of which we have a number of species, all apparently carnivores. Most of our glycerids that are larger than *Hemipodus* are in the genus *Glycera*. Some of them may be expected along with *Hemipodus* in mudflats, or in sandy or gravelly habitats.

The Surface Sediment on Muddy Sand and Mud

In areas where a substrate of muddy sand or mud has an ooze-like superficial layer and is covered by patches of *Ulva* (pls. XXIV, XXVII), *Monostroma,* and *Enteromorpha* (fig. 54) (these algae tend to die back in winter), there is usually a characteristic assemblage of organisms. Crawling on the surface, unless forced by bright sunlight to retreat, is the nemertean *Paranemertes peregrina* (fig. 196). A large specimen, fully extended, may be more than 15 cm long.

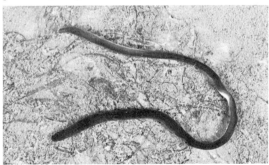

196. *Paranemertes peregrina*

The upper surface is uniformly dark brownish purple, relieved only by a narrow white border around the anterior part of the head region; the underside is pale yellow. The body of *Paranemertes* is soft, but it is at the same time highly muscularized, so the worm is capable of lengthening and shortening itself to an amazing extent. Its locomotion is accomplished in part by muscular activity, and in part by the beating of cilia which cover the body. *Paranemertes* feeds on several species of small and medium-sized polychaetes, but its favorite food seems to be *Platynereis bicanaliculata,* which is only about 2 cm long. *Platynereis* builds little tubes on *Ulva,* using bits of the alga in construction of the tubes; it also feeds on the *Ulva.*

As *Paranemertes* glides along on its track of slime, it evidently cannot recognize prey from any distance. However, when it bumps into *Platynereis* or another suitable prey organism, it recoils for a moment, then everts its large, whitish proboscis, which is provided with a sharp stylet backed up by venom glands. The prey soon becomes quiet, and *Paranemertes* then proceeds to swallow it whole. *Paranemertes* can find its way back to its burrow by following its own slime trail. The burrow is probably not permanent, and it cannot be dug out intact.

In this habitat there will almost always be a polychaete, alternately swimming or scurrying by undulating movements, then resting. This is *Ophiodromus pugettensis (Podarke pugettensis)* (fig. 197), the only member of the family Hesionidae likely to be

197. *Ophiodromus pugettensis*

seen in our area. The tip of its tail generally bears a white mark of some sort, but its color is otherwise a rich dark brown. Although *Ophiodromus* is free-living in our area, it is elsewhere found as a commensal on the bat star, *Patiria miniata.* This sea star is abundant on rocky shores in central and northern California, and in some places on the open outer coast of Vancouver Island, but it is either absent or exceedingly rare on the coasts of Washington and Oregon.

In the same general habitat, especially if the pebbles are rather numerous, one of the more common polychaete annelids is *Eupolymnia heterobranchia*. It is similar in size and appearance to *Thelepus crispus* (fig. 122), but its color is a dark brown or greenish brown. Like other members of the family Terebellidae, it is characterized by numerous extensile tentacles originating from the anterior end. *Eupolymnia* resides in a parchmentlike tube and extends its tentacles through and over the surface of the substrate. Each tentacle has a ciliated groove, along which food enmeshed in mucus is passed toward the mouth. The diet of *Eupolymnia* probably consists largely of detritus (including living diatoms), but this worm has been observed to grab with its tentacles at polychaetes of other species, and it sometimes scavenges on decaying polychaetes and crustacea. So it is probably partly a detritus feeder, partly a scavenger, and perhaps partly a predator. The little hesionid polychaete *Ophiodromus* is sometimes commensal in the tube of *Eupolymnia*.

During the spring and summer, a mollusc that looks like a flattened blackish slug may become abundant on soft mud and very muddy sand. Although it has no external shell, *Aglaja diomedea* (fig. 198), which reaches a length of about 2 cm, does not belong in the same group as "true" sea slugs, or nudibranchs. Its closest intertidal relative is the bubble shell, *Haminoea* (see "Beds of Eel-

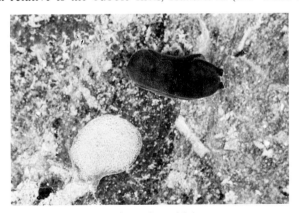

198. *Aglaja diomedea,* with its egg mass

grass" section). *Aglaja,* like *Haminoea,* has the anterior part of the dorsal surface set apart as a head shield; it also has a shell, but this is much reduced and strictly internal. The posterior end of the mantle is drawn out into a siphonlike structure. *Aglaja* moves through the surface sediment by ciliary activity; mucus secreted at the anterior end of the body helps to consolidate the otherwise loose particles of the substrate and thus facilitates progression. *Aglaja* has neither a radula nor jaws, but it is equipped with a large, muscular pharynx that produces suction strong enough to seize prey organisms and swallow them whole. It feeds on various small animals in the sediment. The gelatinous, ovoid egg masses of *Aglaja* (fig. 198), attached to the substrate by a slender, short stalk, are usually more abundant than the slugs themselves.

Under algae, and especially among small pebbles impressed into the substrate, there may be numerous individuals of a small brittle star, *Amphipholis squamata* (fig. 199). This species reaches a di-

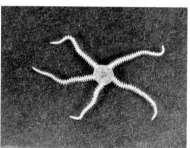

199. *Amphipholis squamata*

ameter of only about 3 cm and its color is uninteresting—gray above, whitish below. However, it does have the unusual and engaging feature of brooding its young and releasing them when they are just a couple of millimeters in diameter. Most brittle stars release their eggs and sperm into the water, where the fertilized eggs develop into free-swimming larvae quite different from the adults. *Amphipholis,* however, holds its eggs in little pockets that open to the outside near the bases of the arms, and there they develop directly into little brittle stars. The food of *Amphipholis* consists largely of diatoms.

The surface sediment covering the habitat of the animals discussed in this section contains many kinds of small organisms that cannot be appreciated without the aid of a microscope. There is almost always a nice assortment of diatoms, numerous protozoa (especially ciliates and foraminiferans), and a splendid variety of turbellarian flatworms. Some of the turbellarians are primarily herbivores that feed on diatoms; others are carnivores whose food consists mostly of small crustacea. The crustacea represented in the sediment include harpacticoid copepods, cumaceans, tanaids, small isopods, and amphipods. There are also tiny annelids, clams, and snails, as well as other animals that will not be dealt with here. All of them are interesting—some are astonishing—but the scope of this guide includes only the more conspicuous elements of the fauna and flora. Anyone who wants to study the sediment will find it teeming with many kinds of organisms, some of which are restricted to this type of habitat.

In pools in sandy and muddy bays where seaweed and other detritus accumulate and decay, there is almost always an unusual little crustacean, *Nebalia pugettensis* (fig. 200). It belongs to an

200. *Nebalia pugettensis*

order called the Leptostraca, which has only a few species. Leptostracans are in the same general group as isopods, amphipods, shrimps, and crabs, but have the odd feature of an inflated carapace which, although it covers the thoracic segments, is not fused directly with them, being attached by an adductor muscle. The head is partially covered by a little rostrum which is hinged to the carapace. The appendages of the thorax are leaflike and used for creating currents of water from which small food particles are strained out; there is a ventral groove up which the food is moved to the mouth parts.

N. pugettensis, at most about 1 cm long, is silvery, sometimes with a tinge of orange. The situations where it is plentiful generally show signs of being quite foul when they are stirred up. The easiest way to collect these interesting crustaceans is to agitate violently the accumulated detritus with a view to getting some of the *Nebalia* to the surface, where they become trapped and can be skimmed off. *Nebalia* is usually accompanied by a variety of scavenging amphipods of the same general size.

In Deeper Water

Almost altogether subtidal, but occasionally just visible in shallow water when the tide is very low, is the sea pen, *Ptilosarcus gurneyi* (pl. II). It is so frequently displayed in public aquaria that mention of it cannot be avoided. It is decidedly one of our most beautiful marine animals, and a nicely established group of fully expanded sea pens seen in nature or in a large aquarium tank is not easily forgotten. The color of *Ptilosarcus* ranges from a pale to a rather rich orange. Large specimens are about 50 cm long when extended. The lower half is almost completely buried in muddy sand; the upper half is elaborated into a series of leaflike branches, each bearing numerous little feeding polyps which capture small animals. Opening onto the surface of the main stem are less conspicuous polyps whose function is to conduct water into and out of the system of canals that ventilates the colony. When a sea pen is stimulated to contract, water is forced out of the colony, and it may be some time before it becomes inflated again. Sea pens belong to the same general group of Cnidaria as the sea anemones, but the fact that their polyps are small and organized into a featherlike colony obscures the kinship to some extent. *Ptilosarcus,* like most sea pens, is beautifully luminescent, yielding a rather strong greenish light when stimulated mechanically by stroking.

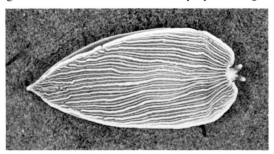

201. *Armina californica*

One of the predators on *Ptilosarcus* is a very unusual nudibranch, *Armina californica* (fig. 201). It is a large species, sometimes about 7 cm long, and is strikingly marked with alternating longitudinal white and brown stripes which converge anteriorly. *Armina* differs from all other nudibranchs of our area in several respects. It has neither the branched gills characteristic of dorids nor the fleshy dorsal processes characteristic of eolids. Instead, it has a series of flaplike gills on either side of the body, in a groove between the foot and an overhanging fold of skin. The two rhinophores of *Armina* seem to come from a common base and to be directed forward, instead of arising separately and pointing almost straight upward as they do in most nudibranchs. *Armina* only occasionally wanders into shallow waters of quiet bays.

Beds of Eelgrass

Eelgrass, *Zostera marina* (fig. 202), is found at lower levels of the intertidal region, as well as subtidally, growing on substrates that range from rather clean sand to mud. Wherever it is success-

202. *Zostera marina,* or eelgrass

ful, its spreading rhizomes and abundant roots form tangled mats that have a binding effect on the substrate and thus help to provide a stable habitat for many kinds of small animals. The leaves support a wide variety of organisms, many of which go unnoticed because they are microscopic or nearly so. A heavy growth of eelgrass also provides an excellent cover for some larger, mobile animals, such as crabs and fishes. Although it is a perennial plant, its abundance in a particular place varies considerably according to season. Colonies of eelgrass tend to build up in spring and summer, and then to regress during the fall and winter.

Eelgrass is a flowering plant and belongs to the same family (Zosteraceae) as *Phyllospadix* (fig. 101), the surfgrass found on rocky shores. The flowers, borne in spikelike clusters, are relatively inconspicuous. The leaves are thin, from about 3 to about 10 mm wide, and may be a meter or more in length.

The fauna and flora on leaves of eelgrass vary from place to place and from season to season; in general, they are richer and more interesting in late spring and summer. In a particular situation, the fauna and flora on eelgrass tend to follow the same pattern each year. A number of the more common and more distinctive animals and plants found on eelgrass leaves will be discussed here, but the user of this book will have to find the situations where they actually occur.

In certain places, especially during the summer months, the leaves of eelgrass become colonized by a variety of essentially microscopic plant organisms. Most obvious among these are the diatoms, which, if present in large numbers, constitute a furry, olive brown coating. If some of the diatoms present are of the chain-forming type, a good deal of the coating will seem to consist of fine filaments. Bacteria will also be plentiful, and once the biological ball starts to roll, detritus tends to become incorporated into the film.

The diatoms, bacteria, and detritus, as well as the decaying tissue of eelgrass leaves themselves, feed the mouths of many pro-

203. *Smithora naiadum,* a red alga attached to eelgrass

tozoa, microscopic worms (especially certain turbellarians), and small crustacea. These in turn are eaten by other protozoa, other turbellarians, nemerteans, hydroids, and jellyfishes.

Several small algae other than diatoms are here or there associated with leaves of eelgrass. However, *Smithora naiadum* (fig. 203) stands out in particular because it is almost invariably present during the spring and summer, and is conspicuous in color as well as size. It is closely related to species of *Porphyra* common on rocky shores. The very thin blades of *Smithora*—they are a single cell-layer thick—are purplish red, and when fully developed are several centimeters long. They are usually joined to the eelgrass leaf by a narrowed, stalklike portion. *Smithora* also grows on *Phyllospadix* on rocky shores.

The small animal organisms that live in the coating of diatoms and bacteria colonizing eelgrass leaves fall into several distinct zoological groups. The herbivores are represented by certain ciliated protozoa, by relatively few of the turbellarian flatworms, and by the crustacea. The carnivores include some of the ciliates, most of the turbellarians, and the nemerteans. Nemerteans are neither especially abundant nor diversified in this habitat, but a tiny *Tetrastemma,* with the four eyespots characteristic of this genus, is quite often present. The carnivorous turbellarians and nemerteans prey largely upon small copepods; but other crustacea, as the caprellid amphipods (fig. 204) and their more conventional relatives, also help out with the economy. The hydroids and the two jellyfishes associated with eelgrass also feed to a large extent on the crustaceans, but not necessarily just on those crawling on the

204. A caprellid amphipod on eelgrass

leaves. The sessile jellyfish, *Haliclystus,* specializes in caprellids, which sometimes can be found by the millions.

Hydroids, Jellyfishes, and Sea Anemones

Hydroids are routinely common on eelgrass. Some of them, as *Obelia longissima* (figs. 6 and 7), form conspicuous growths, but most of the others are small and creeping.

During the summer, two very different types of jellyfishes may be found clinging to eelgrass, especially in deeper pools that are not emptied at low tide. One of them, *Gonionemus vertens,* has a distinctly orange or light brown cast and pulsates actively when detached, so it is rather easily seen. The other, *Haliclystus auricula,* is of such a deep olive green color and so tightly attached that it is apt to be overlooked. It is, however, one of the real delights of the eelgrass fauna.

Gonionemus (fig. 205) is a hydrozoan jellyfish that usually has a diameter of about 1.5 cm and a height slightly less than this, so it is a bit broader than tall when relaxed. The manubrium, on which the mouth is situated, and the extensively crinkled gonads on the four radial canals are rather opaque and impart most of the color that the jellyfish shows. In males this color tends to be buff or light brown; in females it is more nearly pale orange. The tentacles are numerous, fairly long—some are longer than others—and have a ringed appearance because of the way the stinging capsules (nematocysts) are arranged. A particularly distinctive feature is their adhesive pads, located nearer the tips of the tentacles than their

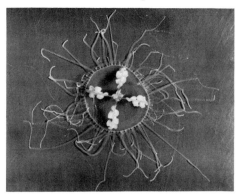

205. *Gonionemus vertens*

bases; the tentacles are sharply angled at the points where the pads are inserted. With the aid of its sticky pads, *Gonionemus* can cling very tightly to the leaves of eelgrass, and also to seaweeds on rocky shores. If it becomes detached by vigorous mechanical stirring of the eelgrass, it swims much like any other jellyfish of the same general type until it manages to get a foothold again. *Gonionemus* feeds largely on small crustacea and larvae of fishes.

Haliclystus (fig. 206) is a scyphozoan medusa, more closely allied with *Cyanea, Aurelia,* and the other large jellyfishes of our

206. *Haliclystus auricula,* a sessile scyphozoan

area, characterized by lack of a velum. Its kinship to medusae of this type is not at all obvious, however, for it is fixed to eelgrass (and sometimes to seaweeds) by a stalk on its aboral surface. It seems not to move around and it cannot swim if detached. *Haliclystus* has eight marginal lobes, each tipped with a cluster of knobbed tentacles; the little knobs are batteries of stinging cells for subduing prey, which consists almost exclusively of the caprellid amphipods abounding on eelgrass leaves. Large specimens are about 2.5 cm in diameter and in height.

A sea anemone regularly found on the leaves of eelgrass is *Epiactis prolifera* (fig. 207; pl. III). In color, it is usually brown to greenish brown, more rarely almost green, blue, or purple. (Red or pinkish red specimens are sometimes found on rocky shores, but are rare on eelgrass.) The oral disk is typically marked with radiating white lines, and there are generally white lines on the pedal disk and column also. It is an unusual anemone because of its habit of brooding young on its pedal disk. To one not acquainted with the life history of *Epiactis,* it might appear that the young are in the process of differentiating from buds formed at the base of

207. *Epiactis prolifera,* the brooding sea anemone

the column. However, the true story is far more interesting than that. These young are derived from eggs liberated into the digestive cavity and fertilized there. The embryos develop into motile planula larvae, which escape through the mouth, glide down the column, and become embedded in the pedal disk, to remain there until they are fully formed little anemones ready to migrate away and to begin life on their own. Usually they leave the parent by the time they are about 5 mm high, but there seems to be no particular deadline.

Snails, Sea Slugs, and Smaller Clams

Almost invariably, eelgrass leaves support large numbers of a small snail, *Lacuna variegata* (fig. 208), called the chink shell. Its shell rarely exceeds a height of about 5 mm, and is usually pale brown, with lighter or darker bands. It might be confused with *Littorina scutulata,* but it is more plump. It also has a very distin-

208. *Lacuna variegata,* the chink shell

guishing feature: a deep slit between the aperture and the first whorl above the aperture. The habitats of *Lacuna* and *Littorina* are, moreover, very different, for *Lacuna* is never found in the upper reaches of the intertidal region, and littorines do not inhabit eelgrass. Wherever *Lacuna* occurs, its eggs (fig. 208), which look like little yellow life preservers about 5 mm in diameter, will perhaps be noted before the snails themselves. *Lacuna* is by no means restricted to eelgrass, for it is found on a variety of seaweeds, both in bays and on rocky shores. On eelgrass, however, it is especially conspicuous and numerous.

A nudibranch gastropod sometimes found in beds of eelgrass, as well as in kelp beds offshore, is the remarkable *Melibe leonina* (fig. 209; pl. XII). It must be among the "top ten" of curiosities brought

209. *Melibe leonina* (a small specimen)

to marine biologists, or described over the telephone, for identification. For a sea slug, *Melibe* is fairly large—up to about 10 cm long—and almost colorless and transparent. It has just a few cerata on the dorsal surface, but these are large and flat and have dark branches of the digestive gland ramifying through them. Single cerata that have been detached and found out of context have brought grief to many a student who has tried to fit them into the phylum Platyhelminthes. But the most astonishing feature of *Melibe* is its oral hood, fringed with numerous slender tentacles. The hood and tentacles work together to trap small crustacea, especially amphipods. If *Melibe* is separated from eelgrass or whatever it is crawling on, it usually begins to swim by thrashing movements. It can also trap air in its oral hood, thus becoming buoyant and drifting for some time.

A number of nudibranchs other than *Melibe* are found on eelgrass; there are many uncommon species, but two are rather abundant: the almost ubiquitous *Hermissenda crassicornis* (pl. VIII) and *Aeolidia papillosa* (fig. 39). For detailed descriptions of these nudibranchs see Chapter 3. In eelgrass beds *Hermissenda* seems to subsist mostly on hydroids, and *Aeolidia* preys on sea anemones.

A sea slug that is restricted to eelgrass is *Phyllaplysia taylori* (fig. 210). Mature specimens, when extended, are about 4 cm long

210. *Phyllaplysia taylori*

and just a little wider than the leaves of eelgrass. When closely examined, the color pattern of *Phyllaplysia* does not seem to match that of the leaves very closely, for the yellow-green color is rather bright and the blackish-brown longitudinal streaks are distinct. However, *Phyllaplysia* has a translucent look about it, and in a bed of eelgrass it certainly does not stand out. This sea slug is not a nudibranch; it is more closely related to the sea hares of the California coast.

The bubble shell, *Haminoea virescens* (fig. 211), is sometimes abundant during the summer months in places where eelgrass grows on mud. The sluglike body of this relative of *Aglaja* (discussed earlier in this chapter) reaches a length of about 3.5 cm. The shell is proportionately large, but only a little of it can be seen at the top of the hump just behind the middle of the body. The prevailing coloration is usually greenish gray or yellowish, with some scattered light and dark flecks, as well as a pair of conspicuous eyespots on the head.

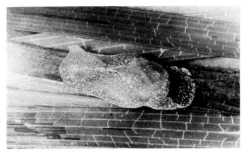

211. *Haminoea virescens*

Transenella tantilla is a tiny clam—usually less than 4 mm long —found scarcely buried in rather clean sand, especially where roots and rhizomes of eelgrass or deposits of shells help to stabilize the substrate. However, it is not at all restricted to eelgrass beds and will be found widely distributed in sandy areas of quiet bays. The umbo of *Transenella* is midway between the anterior and posterior margins; and the valves of the shell, as viewed from the side, have the outline of a rounded isosceles triangle. Of the seashore clams in our region, this one is unusual because it broods its young in the mantle cavity. The females seem to carry their young— sometimes thirty or forty—throughout the year, but release of the little clams evidently takes place only during the summer months.

The bent-nosed clam, *Macoma nasuta* (figs. 172 and 173), and its close relative, *M. irus* (fig. 174), are usually present in eelgrass beds. Both of these species have been discussed in connection with muddy sand, where they are among the numerically dominant animals.

Sea Stars and Sea Cucumbers

The little six-rayed sea star, *Leptasterias hexactis* (fig. 124), so abundant in rocky habitats, also turns up in beds of eelgrass. During daytime low tides, it may go unnoticed unless one pokes around the tight mass of rhizomes. However, in the fall and winter, when the best low tides come at night, *Leptasterias* becomes a very conspicuous feature of the eelgrass fauna, moving with some agility among the leaves, even at the surface. Its food here consists to a large extent of the little snail *Lacuna* (fig. 208), which is a good choice, for it seems to be a nearly inexhaustible resource for a carnivore to feed upon.

If the substrate is decidedly sandy, the little burrowing sea cucumber, *Leptosynapta,* will probably be just as common as it is in sandy situations where there is no eelgrass.

Isopods and Crabs

An isopod that blends in beautifully with eelgrass is *Idotea resecata* (fig. 212). A distinguishing characteristic of this species is the way in which the tip of its telson—the terminal piece of its abdomen—is cut off concavely. Large specimens are about 4 cm long, about the width of an eelgrass blade, and of a translucent green color. It is easiest to find *I. resecata* by pulling the leaves of eelgrass through one's fingers, since the animal clings very tightly to the leaves by means of its seven pairs of clawed legs. However, once detached, it swims with grace, using its flattened abdominal appendages as paddles.

212. *Idotea resecata*

Idotea aculeata is a smaller isopod, rarely exceeding a length of about 2 cm. Its telson is more like that of *I. wosnesenskii* (fig. 85), being rounded posteriorly and having a little terminal projection. However, its eyes are more or less oval, rather than kidney-shaped as in *I. wosnesenskii.* The latter species is also commonly found on eelgrass, to which it can cling very effectively, but it seems to be more typical of under-rock situations.

Cancer magister (fig. 213), the Dungeness crab of our markets, is taken commercially with traps set on a sandy bottom in rather deep water. However, it is sometimes found at low tide in sandy and muddy bays where there is a good growth of eelgrass. It can burrow backward into the substrate so that little more than its antennae and eyes protrude. The Dungeness crab feeds largely on

213. *Cancer magister,* the Dungeness crab

small clams, which it can open by chipping away at the shell with its heavy pincers. Large specimens may have a carapace 20 cm (8 inches) wide. (The minimum size for crabs of this species taken for food is 6½ inches, and only males can be kept.) The color of the dorsal side of the carapace is grayish brown, sometimes with a purplish tinge.

The red crab, *Cancer productus* (fig. 214), is not exploited commercially because it is not as large as the Dungeness crab and because its shell is so heavy in proportion to the body. It is much

214. *Cancer productus,* the red crab

more abundant intertidally than the Dungeness crab, occurring in most sandy, muddy, and gravelly bays, especially where there is eelgrass; it even occurs in rocky situations. Its carapace rarely attains a width of 15 cm, and the general coloration of the upper side of the body is a dark brownish red. The pincers have black tips, and the spines on the anterior part of the carapace are less sharp than those on this part of the carapace of the Dungeness crab.

Aside from the two species of *Cancer* just mentioned, three other crabs are regularly associated with eelgrass. These have already been considered in connection with rocky shores, where they are typically found hiding in or under kelp. In beds of eelgrass, they are not so inclined as the *Cancer* crabs to stay on the bottom, and are commonly seen clinging to the stems and leaves.

The most common of these three crabs, and also the one most likely to bask right at the surface, is *Pugettia gracilis* (fig. 215). It

215. *Pugettia gracilis*

is one of the so-called spider crabs and, like some of its relatives, it habitually promotes the growth of small seaweeds and other foreign organisms on its carapace. The basic coloration of the animal as a whole is a dark reddish brown. The carapace has a number of sharp spines on its dorsal side, as well as a characteristic pattern of large teeth on its lateral margins. A carapace length of about 3 cm is maximum.

A very similar spider crab, although much larger than *P. gracilis* and disinclined to be encumbered by seaweeds, hydroids, and the like, is the kelp crab, *Pugettia producta* (fig. 149). The carapace of this species, which may attain a length of about 10 cm, is perfectly smooth above. The color of the dorsal side is generally olive green, but it may have some reddish or orange tones, and there is typically considerable red on the underside.

More closely related to the *Cancer* crabs than to spider crabs is the helmet crab, *Telmessus cheiragonus* (pl. XXI). Its carapace, characterized by six large, jagged teeth on either side, attains a maximum length of about 5 cm, which is slightly less than its width. Both the carapace and the legs are intensely hairy. The basic coloration is greenish or yellowish green, but there may be considerable red, orange, or brown worked into this.

UNDER AND ON ROCKS

Many quiet bays have loose rocks scattered around, especially near their margins (pl. XXIV). There may also be massive boulders, and even rock islands to which one can wade only at low tide. The fauna and flora associated with rocks in sandy and muddy bays will vary according to the position of the rocks with respect to tide levels, as well as with respect to the nature of the substrates on which they lie or in which they are embedded.

Both of our periwinkles, *Littorina sitkana* (fig. 63) and *L. scutulata* (figs. 64 and 71; pl. XXVI), are common, especially at higher levels. The barnacles *Balanus glandula* (fig. 67) and *B. cariosus* (fig. 76) are also more or less routinely present, along with their predators, *Thais emarginata* (fig. 80) and *T. lamellosa* (fig. 82); *T. canaliculata,* however, is rare in bays. *Mytilus edulis* (fig. 90) sometimes forms masses that occupy much of the available space.

Two limpets are likely to be found on scattered rocks that are uncovered by the tide much of the time. *Collisella digitalis* (fig. 65) will be on the upper sides, whereas *Notoacmea persona* (fig. 69) will tend to be stuck under the edges, close to where the rocks meet the sand or mud. *C. pelta* and *N. scutum* are not especially common in bays, but sometimes they do occur, generally at tide levels at least slightly lower than those where *C. digitalis* and *N. persona* are prevalent.

The scavenging snail *Searlesia dira* (fig. 83) may be abundant at the edges of rocks, but the shells that move too jerkily and too quickly to be snails will be found to have been appropriated by hermit crabs, mostly *Pagurus granosimanus*. *P. hirsutiusculus* (fig. 84) may also be common, but is more likely to be in shells of littorines or of *Thais emarginata* than in those of *Searlesia* or *T. lamellosa*.

Nereis vexillosa (fig. 216) is the most nearly ubiquitous of our larger nereid polychaetes. It is often found in mussel beds and is

216. *Nereis vexillosa*

generally abundant under rocks and pieces of wood in quiet bays. It also burrows, but is usually close to the surface. The coloration is variable, but almost always consists largely of bluish, greenish, and grayish tones. As is the case with many other nereid polychaetes, the sexually mature phase of this species is rather unlike the phase typical of mussel beds and bay habitats. The fleshy parapodia become expanded into paddlelike structures for swimming, and periodically during the summer the ripe males and females swarm at night near the surface. The swarming behavior can be seen from floating docks if the area is illuminated. The posterior part of the body of the female is characteristically redder than that of the male. The worms do not survive long after their nocturnal orgy, during which they simply spew out their eggs or sperm through openings that develop in the body wall. *N. vexillosa,* like most other nereids, uses the heavy jaws on its eversible pharynx for tearing the algae it consumes.

Occasionally, worm watchers get a special treat when the huge *N. brandti* swarms. This species is regularly 30 or 40 cm long, and really gigantic specimens are 80 or 90 cm long; so when a few dozen of these start to thrash around near the surface it is a pretty exciting spectacle. The nonswarming stage of *N. brandti* is fairly common in mudflats, especially where the mud is stiff; but it burrows deeply and is not encountered as frequently as *N. vexillosa.*

If the substrate on which loose rocks are lying is gravelly, the crab *Hemigrapsus oregonensis* (fig. 93) and the isopods *Idotea wosnesenskii* (fig. 85) and *Gnorimosphaeroma oregonensis* (fig. 86) are usually plentiful. *G. oregonensis* is especially abundant if there is considerable seepage of fresh water from the shore.

The larger algae on scattered rocks are not particularly varied. The sea lettuce, *Ulva* (pl. XXVII), predominates on some, and the rockweed, *Fucus distichus* (fig. 70), may almost completely cover others.

Islands of rock that are well out from the shore in muddy and sandy bays generally have diversified faunas and floras of the sort one associates with rocky habitats. There will be sponges, anemones (probably at least *Metridium senile* and *Anthopleura elegantissima*), some ascidians, and representatives of other groups not likely to be found on or under rocks just scattered around near the margins of the bay. Chapter 4 should cover such situations adequately, although there are bound to be some distinctive elements in the fauna and flora, because the water will be relatively quiet and the rocks will tend to collect more silt than they would if they were exposed to considerable wave action or to strong currents running parallel to the shore.

217. *Phoronis ijimai*

One animal in particular should be looked for at rather low tide levels (about 0.0 and lower) on rocks that accumulate mud. This is *Phoronis ijimai (Phoronis vancouverensis)* (fig. 217), which is one of only three species of the small phylum Phoronida known to occur in our area. Phoronids secrete tubes of a parchmentlike material, often with foreign material embedded in it, and the animals superficially resemble sabellid or serpulid polychaetes. However, the tentacles are unbranched and are arranged in a double row, in the pattern of a horseshoe whose free ends are spirally coiled. Collectively, the tentacles constitute what is called the lophophore. They function in a type of ciliary-mucus feeding similar to that practiced by sabellids and serpulids. Small food particles trapped in a film of mucus on the tentacles are moved by the action of cilia down to a groove between the two rows and then toward the mouth. The digestive tract of a phoronid is U-shaped, so that the anus is at the same end as the mouth, though it is situated on a little papilla outside the lophophore.

A large colony of *P. ijimai,* which may be 5 cm or more across, is a beautiful sight when the lophophores are expanded. These are practically transparent and colorless, and about 5 or 6 mm in diameter. The individual tubes, often twisted around one another, are about 2 or 3 cm long. Attached to a firm substrate (usually a slab of sandstone, a pebble, or a shell), they then come up through the accumulation of silt. This phoronid is not limited to such a habitat, however. It turns up unexpectedly in a variety of situations: wooden floats and pilings, trees that have fallen into muddy lagoons, and occasionally on somewhat exposed rocky shores, providing there is at least a small accumulation of silt. Our only other intertidal phoronid, *Phoronopsis harmeri,* tends to be somewhat solitary and to prefer sand that is only slightly muddy, or a mixture of coarse sand and gravel. Its tubes are generally at least 6 or 7 cm long, and the expanded lophophore is about 1 cm in diameter.

SALT MARSHES

Some of the larger bays of our area are bordered by extensive salt marshes. Such marshes, inundated only by the highest tides, are typically rather flat, except for shallow pools and tidal channels. They are characterized principally by a very distinctive flowering plant, *Salicornia* (fig. 218). Actually, there are two species of

218. *Salicornia virginica,* or pickleweed

Salicornia in our coastal marshes: *S. virginica,* a perennial that forms spreading mats; and *S. europaea,* an annual that tends to be more compact. These odd plants, known by a number of common names such as pickleweed and saltwort, belong to the goosefoot-saltbrush-tumbleweed family, many members of which are associated with saline situations inland. *Salicornia* has jointed stems, and its leaves are reduced to tiny scales. The flowers are borne in clublike spikes at the tips of the branches. Smaller bays, especially those with a fairly steep profile near shore, may lack *Salicornia,* or have just a narrow strip of it in the zone of transition between the marine and terrestrial environments.

Parasitizing *Salicornia* almost everywhere is another flowering plant, a dodder *(Cuscuta salina)* (fig. 219), which is an aberrant member of the family to which morning-glories and sweet potatoes

219. *Cuscuta salina,* or saltmarsh dodder

belong. It grows in the form of orange or yellow wirelike stems, which entwine the stems of the host plant and are attached by connections that penetrate the tissue. The leaves of dodder are so reduced as to be nearly nonexistent, and the plant has no roots and no chlorophyll of its own. Its life as an independent plant is limited to a very short period after the seed germinates. Its small flowers do not look much like those of morning-glories, but have basically the same structure.

In addition to *Salicornia* and *Cuscuta,* there are a number of other flowering plants in salt marshes. The most prevalent of the

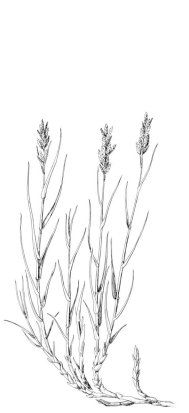 

220. *Distichlis spicata,* or salt-grass

221. *Triglochin maritimum,* or arrow grass

true grasses is saltgrass, *Distichlis spicata* (fig. 220). Arrow grass, *Triglochin maritimum* (fig. 221), belongs to a separate family. Its distinctive flowering stems, frequently more than 50 cm tall, tower above the other vegetation. The slender, fleshy leaves are concentrated in a basal rosette.

On the substrate beneath growths of *Salicornia* and its associates, dark patches of algae usually become prominent in late spring and summer. These generally consist of a variety of microscopic forms, including diatoms, and blue-green and green algae. When the growths are feltlike mats, one can be fairly certain that *Vaucheria* is present. Under the microscope, the filaments of *Vaucheria,* which are not divided up into cells, look much like those of certain green algae. However, analysis of the pigments, food storage products, and some details of structure and reproduction make *Vaucheria* fit better into a group called the yellow-green algae.

The animals of the salt marsh have to be hunted, as they remain hidden most of the time. Nevertheless, some species are restricted to this habitat. Under driftwood and other debris, and also on the soil under *Salicornia,* are found two species of small snails. One of them, *Phytia myosotis* (fig. 222), has a chestnut-brown shell up to about 8 mm long; it is a lung-breather, apparently more closely related to lung-breathing pond snails than to land snails and slugs. The other species, *Assiminea californica* (fig. 222), is tiny—only about 2 mm long—and is a gill-breather; like most of its relatives, it can close its aperture with an operculum.

222. *Phytia myosotis* (the larger snail) and *Assiminea californica*

Littorina sitkana (fig. 63), characteristic of the upper reaches of the rocky intertidal zone, and also found on rocks scattered near the high-tide mark in muddy and sandy bays, is sometimes abundant in salt marshes. *L. scutulata* (figs. 64 and 71; pl. XXVI) is less common.

Hemigrapsus nudus (fig. 92; pl. XX), a crab typically associated with rocky shores, is often surprisingly common in salt marshes. The substrate is sometimes riddled by its burrows, which it evidently has to make for itself; it also hides under driftwood. It probably ventures out to scavenge at night or when the marsh is flooded, but little is known of its habits in this situation. One might predict that *H. oregonensis* (fig. 93), regularly found in bays and estuaries where the salinity is sometimes fairly low, would be more at home than *H. nudus* in a salt marsh, but this does not appear to be the case. When *H. oregonensis* is present, it seems disinclined to burrow.

Orchestia traskiana (fig. 164), the amphipod that forms dense populations under masses of decaying seaweed high on protected beaches, is almost invariably abundant in salt marshes. It is concentrated under debris and in cracks in driftwood. Its wanderings are probably almost completely nocturnal.

223. *Orthocarpus castillejoides,* or yellow owl's clover

The meadowlike areas that are often found on the landward side of salt marshes typically support a variety of grasses, sedges, and rushes, as well as other flowering plants. One of the more interesting annuals in this situation is *Orthocarpus castillejoides,* the yellow owl's clover (fig. 223). Those who know the plants called Indian paintbrushes will recognize owl's clover as a close relative; it is a member of the snapdragon-foxglove family. The tips of the upper leaves, especially those mixed in with the flowers, are colored pale yellow. In general, members of the tribe of paintbrushes and owl's clovers are cursed by a bad habit—parasitism on other flowering plants. Our salt marsh species is probably no exception, and careful excavation of its root system should show which other plants are providing it with part of its food. As it has chlorophyll and can synthesize much of what it needs after the fashion of most green plants, it is probably only partially dependent on its hosts.

GLOSSARY

ABDOMEN. The posterior part of the body, if the body is divided into distinct regions

ABORAL. Opposite the end or side on which the mouth is located

ACTINULA. A young cnidarian polyp, already provided with tentacles

ADDUCTOR MUSCLE. In bivalve molluscs, a large muscle that pulls the valves of the shell together

ALTERNATION OF GENERATIONS. In the life cycle, alternation of a phase that reproduces sexually with one that reproduces asexually

ANTENNA (pl. ANTENNAE). In arthropods, one of a pair of jointed sensory appendages on the head

ANTENNULE. In arthropods, one of a pair of jointed sensory appendages on the head, anterior to the antenna (when both pairs are present)

ANTERIOR. At or near the front end of the body

ANUS. The posterior opening of the digestive tract

ARISTOTLE'S LANTERN. A group of five teeth and some accessory structures associated with the mouths of sea urchins and sand dollars, used for breaking up food

ARTICLE. A unit of an appendage on an arthropod

AVICULARIUM (pl. AVICULARIA). In bryozoans, a type of individual that has two jaws and resembles the beak of a bird

AXIAL. Along the midline of the body or of some other structure

BILATERAL SYMMETRY. A type of symmetry in which the body can be divided, down the midline, into two equal halves

BULLATIONS. Blisterlike areas on the blades of some brown algae

BYSSUS. In bivalve molluscs, organic material, generally in the form of threads, secreted by gland at the base of the foot and used for attachment

CALCAREOUS. Composed of calcium carbonate; limy

CARAPACE. In crustaceans, a hard portion of the exoskeleton that covers the head and thorax

CARNIVOROUS. Eating other animals or the flesh of animals

CERATA. In sea slugs, fleshy projections of the upper surface, usually with a branch of the digestive tract going up into each

CILIA (sing. CILIUM). Vibratile microscopic projections of cells, important in locomotion, creating water currents, and so forth (structurally the same as flagella)

CILIATED. Provided with cilia

CIRRUS (pl. CIRRI). A soft appendage, usually fingerlike or tentaclelike

COELOM. A body cavity lined by an epithelial layer of cells, the peritoneum

COLLOBLASTS. Sticky cells ("glue cells") on the tentacles (and sometimes other parts of the body) of ctenophores, used in the capture of food

COMMENSALISM. A type of association between two species in which one (the commensal) lives on, in, or with the other, obtaining some benefit from the relationship, but neither harming nor benefiting its host to any appreciable extent

CORBULA (pl. CORBULAE). In certain hydroids, a basketlike structure, composed of extensions of the perisarc, within which the reproductive polyps develop

CTENE. In a ctenophore, one of the paddlelike aggregations ("combs") of large cilia serving to propel the animal

CTENIDIUM. In molluscs, a "true" gill, usually resembling a comb or feather (often lacking, or replaced by other structures having a respiratory function)

CYPRIS. In barnacles, the larval stage that succeeds the nauplius and metamorphoses into the adult, characterized by six pairs of thoracic appendages and a bivalved shell

DETRITUS. Finely divided organic matter derived from the disintegration of animals and plants

DIATOMS. A group of one-celled plants characterized by cell walls that contain silica

DORSAL. Referring to the back or upper surface of the body

ECTO-. A prefix referring to something that is external (an ectoparasite, for instance)

ENDO-. A prefix referring to something that is internal

EXOSKELETON. An external skeleton, as in crustacea and other arthropods

FLAGELLA (sing. FLAGELLUM). Vibratile, microscopic projections of cells, important in locomotion, creating water currents, and so forth (structurally the same as cilia, but the term flagellum is applied when there is only one or a few)

FOOT. In molluscs, the organ used for crawling, digging, and some other functions

GONOPHORE. In some cnidarians (especially hydroids), a reproductive polyp in which the medusa stage (or an abortive counterpart of the medusa) is produced

HOST. An organism that provides a home—in its burrow, or on or within itself—for another species

INTROVERT. In sipunculans, a portion of the body that can be retracted by being pulled back into itself

LATERAL. At the side; to one side of the midline

LOPHOPHORE. In phoronids, bryozoans, and brachiopods, a circular or horseshoe-shaped ridge that bears ciliated tentacles used in feeding and respiration

MADREPORITE. A perforated calcareous plate ("sieve plate") on the aboral surface of sea stars and sea urchins that permits water to enter the water-vascular system

MANTLE. In molluscs, an outer sheet of tissue that secretes the shell and also encloses the cavity within which the true gills (if present) are located

MANUBRIUM. In jellyfishes, a stalk on which the mouth is located

MEDIAN. Referring to the midline of the body or of some structure

MEDUSA. A jellyfish

MESOGLOEA. In cnidarians and ctenophores, the "middle jelly," a largely noncellular layer between the cellular layers that line the digestive cavity and the outer surface of the body

MUTUALISM. A type of association between two species that is of mutual benefit to both

NAUPLIUS. The first larval stage of many aquatic crustaceans, characterized by three pairs of appendages corresponding to the antennules, antennae, and mandibles of the adult

NEMATOCYST. In cnidarians, a stinging capsule

NOTOCHORD. In the vertebrates and other chordates, a firm, elastic rod, composed of cells and lying between the digestive tract and the dorsal nerve cord (it may not persist to the adult stage of the animal)

OPERCULUM. A trap door, as used for closing the shell of a snail after the animal withdraws

ORAL. Referring to the mouth, or to the end or side of the body on which the mouth is located

OSCULUM. In sponges, an opening through which water passes out of the body

OSSICLE. In echinoderms, a small calcareous plate or spine

PALLETS. Calcareous, featherlike structures secreted by the mantle of shipworms (bivalve molluscs burrowing in wood), used for closing the opening of the burrow

PAPILLA. A small, fleshy projection of the body wall

PARAPODIUM (pl. PARAPODIA). In polychaete annelids, a fleshy flap of tissue on each side of most segments (the bristles are set into the parapodia); in some sea slugs, a winglike flap on each side of the body

PARASITE. An organism that lives on or in another organism, obtaining its nourishment from it

PEDICELLARIA (pl. PEDICELLARIAE). In sea stars and sea urchins, a small, pincerlike structure on the body surface

PELAGIC. Living in the open sea

PERISARC. In some hydroids, a protective covering

PERIOSTRACUM. In molluscs, the organic material, often fibrous, on the outside of the shell

PERITONEUM. The layer of cells lining a coelom, or body cavity

PINNATE. Branched in a featherlike pattern

PLANKTON. The organisms, mostly small in size, that are suspended in the water and either drift with the currents or swim only weakly

PLANULA. In cnidarians, a ciliated larva developing from the fertilized egg

PLEOPOD. In crustaceans, an abdominal appendage, used for swimming, respiration, holding egg clusters, and other functions

PODIUM (pl. PODIA). In echinoderms, a "tube foot," used for locomotion and feeding

POLYP. In cnidarians, an individual (in colonial types, it may serve only for feeding or be specialized for reproduction or some other function)

POLYPIDE. In bryozoans, an individual member of a colony (a polypide and the zooecium it secretes together constitute a zooid)

POSTERIOR. At or near the hind end of the body

PROBOSCIS. An extensile organ used in feeding

PROSTOMIUM. In annelids, the anteriormost segment of the body, in front of the mouth

PSEUDOPODIUM (pl. PSEUDOPODIA). A lobe or strand of protoplasm extended by amoebae, foraminiferans, and some other protozoa, which functions in locomotion and feeding

RADIAL SYMMETRY. A type of symmetry in which the structures of the body are arranged around a central point, so that the animal can be divided into several equal parts (as in jellyfishes, sea stars, and sea urchins)

RADULA. In chitons and gastropods, a ribbonlike band of teeth that can be protruded through the mouth and used for scraping; sometimes modified into a venom-injecting apparatus

RHINOPHORES. In sea slugs, a pair of tentacles, often elaborate, on the upper surface of the head

RHOPALIUM. In scyphozoan jellyfishes, a structure concerned with equilibrium, consisting of a fleshy outgrowth of the margin, weighted by a mass of crystals, that contacts a sensory lobe

ROSTRUM. In crustaceans, a forward prolongation of the carapace

SCYPHISTOMA. The sessile polyp stage of scyphozoan jellyfishes

SESSILE. Fixed tightly to the substrate and ordinarily not capable of moving

SILICEOUS. Composed of, or containing, silica

SPICULES. Small calcareous or siliceous structures that stiffen the body or certain parts of the body of some animals (as sponges)

STATOCYST. An organ of balance, in which a small crystalline mass makes contact directly or indirectly with sensory cells

STOLON. A "runner," creeping over or through the substrate, from which new individuals (as in some hydroids, hydrozoans, and ascidians) are budded

STYLET. In nemerteans, a needlelike structure associated with a venom gland, located on the eversible proboscis

SYMBIOSIS. A constant association between two species of organisms (includes parasitism, mutualism, commensalism)

TELSON. The terminal segment ("tail") of the abdomen of a crustacean

TEST. In sea urchins and sand dollars, the hard shell against which the spines articulate and through which the tube feet are extended

THORAX. In crustaceans and other arthropods, the middle portion of the body, between the head and the abdomen

TRANSVERSE. At right angles to the long axis of the body

TROCHOPHORE. The first larval stage of some molluscs, annelids, and certain related groups, generally more or less ovoid in shape, and characterized by an apical tuft of cilia at the anterior end and by bands of cilia encircling the body

TUBE FEET. In echinoderms, extensile projections, sometimes with cuplike tips, used for locomotion and feeding

TUNIC. The outer covering, often rather thick, of a solitary or social ascidian, and the matrix in which the several to many zooids of a compound ascidian are embedded; composed to a large extent of a material chemically related to plant cellulose

UMBONE (or UMBO). In bivalve molluscs, the oldest part of each valve, near the hinge, often elevated or somewhat beaklike

UMBILICUS. In gastropod molluscs, a pit at the base of the shell, leading into the pillar around which the whorls are spiraled

VELIGER. A larval stage of molluscs, succeeding the trochophore and eventually metamorphosing into the adult, characterized by ciliated lobes for swimming and usually provided with a shell

VELUM. In certain jellyfishes, a circular membrane extending inward from the margin of the bell

VENTRAL. Referring to the underside of the body

VIBRACULUM. In bryozoans, an individual modified into a slender, vibratile projection

ZOOECIUM. In bryozoans, the boxlike or tubelike "house" secreted by a polypide

ZOOID. In bryozoans and compound ascidians, an individual member of a colony

SUGGESTIONS FOR FURTHER READING

GENERAL REFERENCES

The books chosen for inclusion in this list provide good introductions to marine biology and natural history. One of them, *Between Pacific Tides,* is moderately helpful in dealing with the fauna and flora of this region, and also provides a valuable bibliography of general and specialized works.

Defant, A. *Ebb and Flow: The Tides of Earth, Air, and Water.* Ann Arbor: University of Michigan Press, 1958. A rather easy-to-understand discussion of tides.

MacGinitie, G. E. and N. *Natural History of Marine Animals.* 2nd ed. New York: McGraw-Hill Book Co., 1968. A compendium of observations, many of them original, on marine animals, especially those of the California coast; not intended to be a guide for identification.

Ricketts, E. W., and J. Calvin. *Between Pacific Tides.* 4th ed., revised by J. W. Hedgpeth. Stanford, Calif.: Stanford University Press, 1968. More useful on the California coast than in our region, but contains much of general interest on natural history, ecology, tides, and intertidal zonation; has an extensive bibliography.

Southward, A. J. *Life on the Seashore.* Cambridge, Mass.: Harvard University Press, 1965. Just a small book, but one that provides a good coverage of marine environments and the ways in which animals and plants are adapted to them; the examples are drawn mainly from British shores.

Stephenson, T. A. and A. *Life between Tidemarks on Rocky Shores* San Francisco, Calif.: W. H. Freeman & Co., 1972. A nearly cosmopolitan review of the subject of intertidal zonation, based largely on the authors' own observations; the chapter on the Pacific coast of North America has a few pages on zonation in our region.

IDENTIFICATION GUIDES

Invertebrates

Burghardt, G. E. and L. E. *A Collector's Guide to West Coast Chitons.* Special Publication 4, San Francisco Aquarium Society, 1969.

Cornwall, I. E. *The Barnacles of British Columbia.* 2nd ed. Handbook 7, British Columbia Provincial Museum, Victoria, 1969.

Griffith, L. M. *The Intertidal Univalves of British Columbia.* Handbook 26, British Columbia Provincial Museum, Victoria, 1967.

Kozloff, E. N. *Keys to the Marine Invertebrates of Puget Sound, the San Juan Archipelago, and Adjacent Regions.* Seattle and London: University of Washington Press, in press.

Quayle, D. B. *The Intertidal Bivalves of British Columbia.* Handbook 17, British Columbia Provincial Museum, Victoria, 1960.

Rice, T. *Marine Shells of the Pacific Northwest.* Edmonds, Wash.: Ellison Industries, 1971.

Smith, R. I., and J. T. Carlton, eds. *Light's Manual: Intertidal Invertebrates of the Central California Coast.* 3rd ed. Berkeley and Los Angeles: University of California Press, 1974. Consists mostly of technical keys for identification, and indispensable in the region for which it has been written; valuable all along the Pacific coast for its detailed bibliographies.

Fishes

Carl, G. C. *Guide to Common Marine Fishes of British Columbia.* Handbook 23, British Columbia Provincial Museum, Victoria, 1971.

Hart, J. L. *Pacific Fishes of Canada.* Bulletin 180, Fisheries Research Board of Canada, 1973. The definitive work on fishes of our region.

Seaweeds

Scagel, R. F. *Guide to Common Seaweeds of British Columbia.* Handbook 27, British Columbia Provincial Museum, Victoria, 1971. The most useful book on seaweeds of our region; covers more than ninety genera likely to be encountered intertidally.

INDEX

Boldface numerals refer to pages on which text figures are located. Roman numerals refer to color plates. As a rule, illustrations are cited only if they represent a particular genus or species.

A red sponge, *Ophlitaspongia pennata*, with *Rostanga pulchra*, a sea slug that feeds on it. The coiled egg masses of *Rostanga* are also shown.

Cliona celata, a yellow sponge that bores into calcareous shells (in this case, the shell of the rock scallop, *Hinnites*)

PLATE I

Aglaophenia, a featherlike hydroid

Abietinaria

Ptilosarcus gurneyi, the sea pen

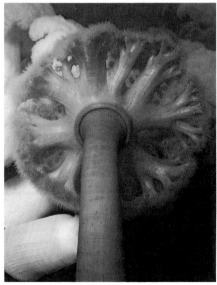

Metridium senile

PLATE II

Tealia crassicornis

Tealia coriacea

Epiactis prolifera, the brooding anemone

Epizoanthus scotinus, a zooanthid

PLATE III

Anthopleura xanthogrammica, the green sea anemone

Anthopleura elegantissima

PLATE IV

Balanophyllia elegans, the cup coral, and *Didemnum,* a compound ascidian

Tubulanus polymorphus, a nemertean

PLATE V

Schizobranchia insignis, the
feather-duster worm

Pseudopotamilla ocellata

Eudistylia vancouveri

Serpula vermicularis, with *Lithothamnion*,
an encrusting, coralline red alga

PLATE VI

Cryptochiton stelleri

Tonicella lineata, the lined chiton

PLATE VII

Hermissenda crassicornis, on an egg mass laid by a dorid nudibranch

Dendronotus frondosus

PLATE VIII

Archidoris montereyensis, the sea lemon

Archidoris odhneri

PLATE IX

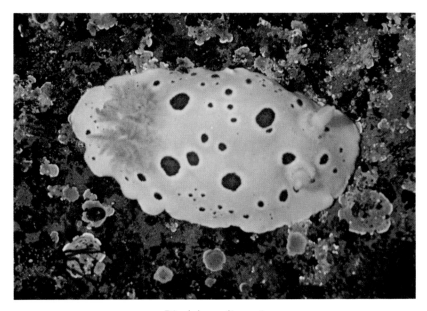

Diaulula sandiegensis

Cadlina luteomarginata. The red animals attached to the rock are *Metandrocarpa taylori,* a social ascidian.

PLATE X

Triopha carpenteri

Laila cockerelli

PLATE XI

Melibe leonina

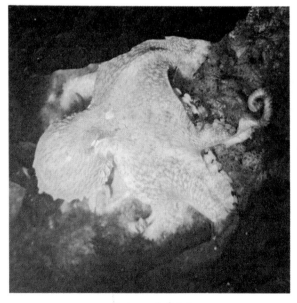

Octopus dofleini

PLATE XII

Pisaster ochraceus

Evasterias troschelii

PLATE XIII

Pycnopodia helianthoides, the sunflower star

Solaster stimpsoni

PLATE XIV

Dermasterias imbricata, the leather star

Henricia leviuscula, the blood star

PLATE XV

Ophiopholis aculeata

Strongylocentrotus franciscanus, the red
sea urchin

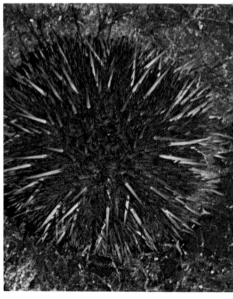

Strongylocentrotus droebachiensis, the
green sea urchin

Strongylocentrotus purpuratus, the purple
sea urchin

PLATE XVI

Parastichopus californicus

Cucumaria miniata

PLATE XVII

Extended oral tentacles of several specimens of *Cucumaria miniata*

Psolus chitonoides

PLATE XVIII

Distaplia occidentalis, a compound ascidian

Aplidium californicum, a compound ascidian

PLATE XIX

Hemigrapsus nudus

Lophopanopeus bellus, the black-clawed crab

PLATE XX

Telmessus cheiragonus, the helmet crab

Cancer oregonensis

PLATE XXI

Cryptolithodes sitchensis

Hapalogaster mertensii

PLATE XXII

Anoplarchus purpurescens, the cockscomb prickleback

Lepas fascicularis, a pelagic goose barnacle

PLATE XXIII

A luxuriant growth of *Ulva* on a tidal flat of muddy sand

A quiet bay with numerous scattered rocks near its inner margins

PLATE XXIV

Verrucaria, a blackish lichen of the spray zone

Caloplaca, one of the lichens found just above the spray zone

Prasiola meridionalis, a green alga forming extensive growths in the spray zone

Prasiola meridionalis

PLATE XXV

Endocladia muricata, with two specimens
of *Littorina scutulata*

Antithamnion (photomicrograph)

Petrocelis, an encrusting red alga that
resembles a coating of tar

Bossiella, a coralline red alga

PLATE XXVI

Enteromorpha intestinalis in a cliffside seepage area

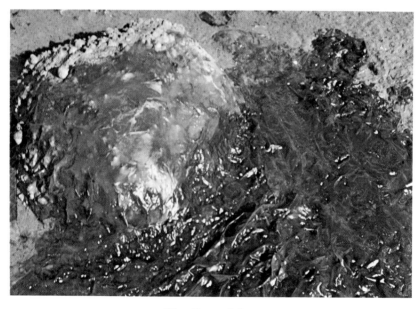

Ulva, the sea lettuce

PLATE XXVII

Spongomorpha coalita

Codium fragile

PLATE XXVIII